PRAISE FOR NEUROSCIENCE FOR LEARNING AND DEVELOPMENT SECOND EDITION

'Too much time and focus is placed on the teaching rather than on the learner. Understanding the neuroscience and psychology of the learner is the key to successful learning and training; as I often write, "It is not what you teach but what they learn that counts". This book falls within this approach, whereby one must attempt to take neuroscientific and psychological insights and apply them in order to innovate and break new ground in the area of training and learning.'
Dr Itiel Dror, Consultant and Researcher in Cognitive Neuroscience, University College London and Cognitive Consultants International

'A timely book for all learning and development professionals. Stella Collins writes clearly and gets to the point rapidly with a good balance of theory and practical application. This book is an excellent guide to using the latest findings of neuroscience in our daily practice to great effect.'
Donald H Taylor, Chairman, Learning and Performance Institute

'If you want to transform learning in your organization, this is a must-read.'
Amy Brann, author of *Make Your Brain Work, Neuroscience for Coaches* and *Engaged*

'Dispelling some of the myths and hype around the topic, Stella Collins proves you don't have to be a neuroscientist to apply key brain principles to practical learning solutions. Starting with an understandable tour of the brain this accessible book explores how factors such as attention, curiosity, personal meaning, the senses, spacing, pacing, relaxation and reflection are vital aspects of creating

New Westminster, BC

9/5

effective, engaging learning. If you haven't got time to become a neuroscientist but want to apply neuroscience's principles to learning, this is book is a great place to start!'

Andy Lancaster, Head of Learning and Development, CIPD

'If you work in L&D make this the next book you read. You will learn a lot, whether you want to or not!'

Astrid Keogh, OD Manager, London Borough of Hackney

'In our information-rich world full of distractions, Stella Collins' elegant way of describing our cognitive processes will give you an advantage in the game of learning. And who knew how sea slugs learn? Synapses created, thank you Stella for some real sticky, brain-friendly learning about the brain.'

Perry Timms, Founder and Chief Energy Officer, PTHR

'A practical and well-researched read that you will refer back to time and time again. Stella Collins has not only captured how neuroscience can inform the way we work as learning professionals but has made it easy to understand. This is a page turner which you can enjoy and apply – and both you and your learners will reap the rewards.'

Emma Weber, CEO and Founder, Lever – Transfer of Learning

'In the fast-moving field of neuroscience, a second edition of such a great book is welcome. Even if you have the first edition, this is well worth the upgrade. There are new insights, new chapters on sleep and digital learning, and a more piercing look into what the future may bring.'

Paul Matthews, author of three books on L&D, and CEO, People Alchemy

'Stella Collins has written an engaging book in which she links neuroscience, education and life. In it you will find lots of important empirical evidence and practical educational applications that will be useful to anybody in the educational field or who is interested in the improvement of education. If you are passionate about everything related to the brain and how to improve teaching and learning processes, this is the book for you! It will awaken your curiosity and allow you to learn with all your potential.'

Jesús C Guillen, author of *Neuroscience in the Classroom: From theory to practice*

$53.58

Second Edition

Neuroscience for Learning and Development

How to apply neuroscience and psychology for improved learning and training

Stella Collins

KoganPage

First published in Great Britain and the United States in 2016 by Kogan Page Limited
Second edition published in 2019

2nd Floor, 45 Gee Street   122 W 27th St, 10th Floor   4737/23 Ansari Road
London   New York, NY 10001   Daryaganj
EC1V 3RS   USA   New Delhi 110002
United Kingdom   India
www.koganpage.com

© Stella Collins, 2016, 2019

The right of Stella Collins to be identified as the author of this work has been asserted by her in accordance with the Copyright, Designs and Patents Act 1988.

Hardback   978 1 78966 009 8
Paperback   978 0 7494 9326 4
eBook   978 0 7494 9327 1

British Library Cataloguing-in-Publication Data

A CIP record for this book is available from the British Library.

Library of Congress Cataloging-in-Publication Data

Names: Collins, Stella, author.
Title: Neuroscience for learning and development : how to apply neuroscience and psychology for improved learning and training / Stella Collins.
Description: Second edition. | London ; New York : Kogan Page Limited, 2019. | Includes bibliographical references and index.
Identifiers: LCCN 2019022212 (print) | LCCN 2019018811 (ebook) | ISBN 9781789660098 (hardback) | ISBN 9780749493264 (pbk.) | ISBN 9780749493271 (Ebook)
Subjects: LCSH: Learning, Psychology of. | Training. | Cognitive neuroscience. | Educational psychology.
Classification: LCC BF318 .C656 2019 (ebook) | LCC BF318 (print) | DDC 153.1/5–dc23
LC record available at https://lccn.loc.gov/2019022212

Typeset by Hong Kong FIVE Workshop, Hong Kong
Print production managed by Jellyfish
Printed and bound by CPI Group (UK) Ltd, Croydon CR0 4YY

CONTENTS

PREFACE

What a lot has happened in the three years since the first edition of this book. The speed of change appears to have accelerated again and whilst there's inevitably some neuroscience to explain why my perception of time is probably somewhat inaccurate, you may well experience a similar distortion and feel that three years have flown past. The worlds of Learning and Development (L&D) and neuroscience are no exception and there have been discoveries, changes in practice and technology that you faced too.

Digital technology is even more commonplace and seems set to continue to be impacted by virtual reality, artificial intelligence and an ever greater array of new and accessible technologies. With this in mind there's a new chapter exploring some of the differences in how we may learn using digital technology. The important question to me was: what's different in our heads when we use digital technology as opposed to any other learning method?

Whilst researching the first edition I was fascinated by the value of sleep to learning but since then there has been a wealth of new information and attention paid to the value of sleep for health, well-being, work and learning. So in this edition sleep has its own chapter looking at what's going on in our brains to support learning when we're least aware.

Whilst I have no scientifically measurable evidence to back this up, my experience in the past three years has been that more people have an interest in evidence-based research and appreciate the value of neuroscience and psychology to support effective learning design and delivery. Gratifyingly, more people are beginning to ask, challenge and question long-accepted models or outmoded theories. Before writing the first edition I was often the first person in the room to question various myths such as 'learning styles' or 'left-/right-brain people', but now there's a positive hiss in the room if these are mentioned. Inevitably, some people still feel uncomfortable when their favourite learning models are unpicked but more often than not practitioners are keen to find out what is evidence-based and what isn't.

As L&D professionals we'll never be able to keep up with all the latest discoveries in the growing field of neuroscience but if we do no more than ask good questions and keep ourselves open to new ideas we'll be better equipped to help our colleagues, clients and ourselves learn and perform better at work.

ACKNOWLEDGEMENTS

The Oscar speeches always make people laugh because there are so many people to thank and now I know how those actors and directors feel... 'Thank you' to my mum and dad for setting me on a journey of exploration and I'm sorry for all the times I asked 'why?'

Lots of people contributed directly or indirectly to the book, starting with the many friends and colleagues who ask questions, challenge, share their ideas and make training and learning a great area to work. Special thanks to Ann Grindrod who gave me my first real training role and taught me a huge amount about the practical side of training. Thank you also to Kayleigh Clarke, Tina Harris and my team of associates who helped free up my time to write.

Thank you to the 'Other Voices' who enthusiastically wrote up their own research and ideas and continue to be great advocates of learning that is results-focused and enjoyable, as well as rigorous. I think they give the book another dimension.

During the actual writing, I was very grateful to Dr Julian Staddon who read the manuscript to check the neuroscience and pointed me in the way of more research and validation when it needed it. Ben Ashton helped enormously by doggedly tracking down all the references; sometimes with no more than a vague description of something I remembered reading. All the people at Kogan Page have been really helpful and particularly Lucy Carter who provided encouraging feedback when I needed it.

I'd like to thank all those neurosceptics out there who kept me on my toes and challenged me to check my facts. I apologize to you where I've missed something or caused any mistakes or misconceptions, but at least it will give you something to tweet and blog and shout about.

Special thanks to my supportive husband Nick who never seems to doubt I can do what I set my mind to and to our daughters Alice and Genevieve who are always willing to listen and join in my experiments; you're both the best experiment we've ever worked on.

Why neuroscience and learning are good companions

Do you know...?

Do you know that when you're curious it's as much of a buzz as a bar of chocolate, a game of tennis or a flutter on the horses? Why do we find curiosity so pleasurable? When we are curious our brains are stimulated by dopamine, a neurotransmitter that works on our internal reward systems; rats find it so addictive they will press a bar to stimulate dopamine receptors in their brains rather than eat, drink or sleep. Dopamine is our own internal reward neurotransmitter, and it's just as addictive for us as it is for rats.

This is wonderful news if you're involved in helping people learn because so long as you can make them curious you're making learning enjoyable and they'll want to come back for more, again and again and again.

Your invitation to come on a journey

I invite you to come with me on a journey of exploration of the inner workings of your brain and body when you're learning. By understanding some of the mechanisms of your brain whilst you process information, learn, remember and experiment you will grow and develop as a learning professional. By understanding some of the neuroscience about the changes that happen in our brains when people learn, you can design and deliver far more effective training sessions, learning environments, lectures, coaching

Figure 1.1 Introduction

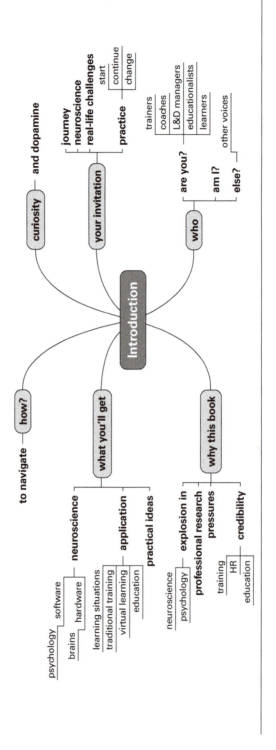

conversations or presentations. And you might even learn to learn more effectively yourself.

We all learn – it's in our human nature – because if we didn't learn, we wouldn't survive. Even the simplest organisms learn in order to avoid being eaten or hurt by predators in a dangerous environment. As we've progressed from living in caves to our current digital age, have we got into some habits in education and training that might be stopping people from learning in the most natural way? With the growing interest and research in neuroscience, the body of evidence to help us devise the most effective learning environments has grown, and it's up to us, as professionals, to take advantage of all that knowledge and new information.

What you'll get by reading this book are practical ideas to implement, in the face-to-face or virtual world of learning, from some of the neuroscience available to us. You'll find research to back up what you're already doing, to inspire you to try new things and maybe even some things that you might decide to stop doing. With this new knowledge at your fingertips you'll increase your credibility with peers and also with your managers, clients or sponsors because you'll have objective evidence to support what you do in terms of changing behaviours, increasing knowledge and improving skills. You'll also be able to influence your learners by explaining exactly why you're asking them to participate in particular activities.

You'll get answers to real-life challenges, like how to get managers to be more involved when people come back from training programmes, how to persuade clients that you can't train an entire new system just with a two-hour presentation and how to motivate and persuade sceptical people that compliance training can be cost-effective and enjoyable at the same time.

Throughout the book I'll start with an outline of each chapter and finish with a summary. Figure 1.1 provides a visual outline, in mindmap form, to tell you about the main elements of this chapter so you can prime your brain to be ready for what you're going to read.

Who you are as the reader

This book has been written for people like you who are learning professionals in a variety of roles and environments. You might be a learning and development manager, human resources director, a trainer in a team, a digital or e-learning designer, an independent trainer, an independent development consultant, working in organizational development, a coach, a teacher, a university lecturer or someone who develops technical knowledge or skills with colleagues as part of another role. You may be someone who's learning for yourself, either through a formal education route, for work or perhaps even for pleasure, and you want some ideas to keep you motivated, to help you take in information and to make it stick so you can apply it when you need to.

You may train communication skills like confidence, persuasion or negotiation or you may train business skills, presentation skills, leadership skills, supervisory skills or it could be skills related to particular roles like customer service or sales. You might be working with information transfer so you're teaching product knowledge or operational training like health and safety, compliance, or finance updates. You may be creating digital, online experiences or designing virtual reality environments. Perhaps you spend time working in virtual classrooms using webinar or conference technology. You may spend your time working on attitude change and shifts in belief, whether that's at a senior level or more widely in a change programme. Perhaps you're a coach and are encouraging other people to come up with ideas, options and possibilities. You might be working on the shop floor with apprentices all the way through from PhD students to chief executives and you're sure to be working with a wide range of ages, nationalities and cultures. Perhaps you work digitally and design and deliver e-learning, video, virtual reality or online workshops. However you work, whoever and whatever you design for, train or teach, you have one thing in common – you're changing brains, whether that's your intention or not.

And you're probably not a fully trained neuroscientist though you may, or may not, have some knowledge of psychology, memory, learning or educational principles. Like me you are probably curious about new ideas you can pick up to develop your practice and skills; after all, that's why you are reading this book.

Most of the time I'm going to use the generic word 'trainer' to describe readers like you, who help people learn, develop or change their behaviours. It's easier to read than having to plough through trainers, learning and development professionals, human resources professionals, digital designers, learning facilitators, educators, coaches, lecturers or anything else you may call yourself. I hope this works for you; if not, then please substitute your own word every time you see 'trainer'.

I'll refer to learning, training and sometimes education but whichever word I use I'd like you to think about your role as a professional who's there to help other people learn. You can't learn for them; you can only create an environment that makes it easier for them to learn and understanding some of the results from neuroscience research can help you be more effective. I hope after reading this book you might change some of what you do, develop what you do, start something new or even drop something altogether because you'll have a framework and some evidence to back up and support what works for learners, their organizations and you.

Why this book has been written now

For a long time training, learning and education have felt a bit like the poor cousins of finance, sales and operations; often the first department or activity to be cut when there are cost reductions happening. Whilst not impossible, it is notoriously difficult to measure the return on investment in training because so many other factors contribute to improved performance and so sometimes trainers struggle to get budgets or persuade other colleagues to take their services seriously. I'm sure I'm not the first trainer to arrive at a workshop to be told that one or more of the participants has been called away to an 'urgent operational matter' or that 'I just have to pop out to a really important meeting – hope you don't mind'. It leaves you feeling powerless because clearly everyone else in the environment sees training as a 'nice to have' rather than a 'need to have'.

Some things are harder to measure than others. Everyone recognizes that airline pilots need to be taught to take off and land accurately but there's less emphasis on making sure their skills are up to scratch. Robert Cialdini (2001) in his book *Influence: Science and Practice* talks about 'captainitis': the tendency for other crew members to allow their own expertise, training and common sense to be overridden by the lead of the captain, often leading to serious errors and even crashes. If they were given more training in the so-called 'soft skills' of recognizing and challenging human behaviour it is possible they would avoid some of these accidents.

Happily now there is more evidence for the value of people skills, which includes the design, training and teaching skills that you have. A research report published in 2015 (AllThingsic) suggested that people skills are worth £88 billion to UK industry alone, so there is more evidence mounting that training in these areas is vital and training the trainers ought to be at the top of that list.

And of course we've now got the neuroscience research, data and logical analysis to show that soft skills aren't soft at all. They are grounded in neuroplasticity, priming, memory research, cognitive psychology, social psychology and the nuts and bolts of what goes on in your head when you communicate with someone. There are numerous books published now about neuroleadership, neuroeconomics, and how your brain works at work and organizations are beginning to recognize that how we learn is just as important as what we learn. The Chartered Institute of Personnel and Development (CIPD) brought out three research reports between 2012 and 2014 describing the impact that neuroscience is going to have on learning. In the third report Neuroscience in Action (2014) the final conclusions say:

> Despite the great case study examples featured in this report, we have found that there are very few organizations openly using neuroscience in practice. There are two explanations for this. Firstly, perhaps it is simply too early for widespread adoption, and there is a knowledge–application gap. Or secondly, that many of the overall principles of neuroscience are finding their way into L&D practice, without being labelled as such.
>
> (*Neuroscience in action: Applying insight to L&D practice* (2014))

Bringing you up to date in this second edition, the CIPD and other bodies now actively promote the practical application of neuroscience as one of their core topics and are working to bust many neuromyths and older, less evidence-based models of learning. So this book is here to help fill some of those gaps.

The reasons I'm interested in the neuroscience of learning

This area fascinates me because I'm curious and was brought up asking questions about learning. A long time ago my dad, who was a teacher, brought home some coloured, wooden blocks to help me with my 'number bonds' because I was struggling with multiplication. I remember the feel of them, the bright colours, the sound they made as you shuffled them around and even the smell. Using those blocks helped me get past the struggle I'd had with numbers; and I still do multiplication by working in blocks of numbers. Having a dad as a teacher meant we talked about learning a lot at home and my dad knew that children needed to be 'doing' to learn, but his methods weren't always popular and he didn't have lots of measurable evidence to back up what he said – apart from the children who flourished. So I spent years listening to my dad and unconsciously learning about how people learn, but there was no way I was going to be a teacher because most of my experience of formal learning was essentially someone talking and writing key points on a blackboard – commonly known as 'chalk and talk'.

At university I studied Psychology and Communication and became fascinated by how our brains work; both the real physical hardware and the processing or software. But despite the interest in brains I took a tangent and began my working life as a computer programmer. Like many others at the time I endured multiple two-week-long training courses, most of which we sat through just itching to get back to work so we could experiment for ourselves and really get on with learning. We didn't find being talked through screenshots any more effective as a learning tool than the chalk and talk method.

My career took me in the direction of technical support and eventually I was given the role of 'Training Manager' which I didn't really want because my experience of training so far hadn't been engaging and I didn't want to inflict similar experiences on my colleagues. I had kept up to date with the world of psychology though and was curious to see how psychology might be useful but didn't have a clear route to making training more engaging until, at a training exhibition, I came upon a pirate ship! The pirate ship was full of trainers who used accelerated learning methods to train subjects that some people considered traditionally boring, like finance and accounting. But these 'pirates' brought their subjects to life and made them a) fascinating and b) easy to learn. Suddenly I realized there was a way of bringing psychology and neuroscience into the training room and I'm still hugely grateful to them for catapulting me into the fascinating, exciting and collaborative world of learning. Since then I've worked with thousands of people and many trainers keen to introduce brain friendly learning to their working methods. I created the Brain Friendly Learning Group as a way of sharing research, good ideas and challenges and people have been asking whether there's something they can read that brings it all together.

I want to share research, stories and practical examples of how neuroscience is already being used in training and learning and to stimulate new ways for you to implement them in your practice – wherever and with whoever that may be.

This is just the start of a journey for all of us who teach others and I'm still curious as to what else we can learn, how we can apply it and what the results are for our learners, organizations, communities and perhaps even nations.

The definition of neuroscience for this book

It seems that neuroscience has changed over the years. When I talk to people who studied psychology in the 1980s at about the same time as me, the view is that it was about the actual brain and how it works. It was seen as the science of what could be observed and measured in the physical brain and nervous system; it was the electrical and chemical activity, the anatomy and structure and the neurotransmitters and hormones that had an effect on the brain. Neuroscientists might record from electrodes placed in the nerve cells of snails and other simple organisms in order to understand how neurons worked. They'd devise mathematical models for the transmission of electrical signals in neurons of the giant axon of a squid. They'd mess about with the brains of rats and see what that did to their behaviour and they'd dissect brains to identify the structures or look at brain scans to identify activity in certain areas; in short the biology of how the brain works.

However, in recent years this definition has expanded considerably. Wikipedia suggests it's now 'the scientific study of the neurosystem'; and it's become a blend of many disciplines including psychology, physiology, philosophy and even computer science, engineering and physics. It may be that it's the brain scans that have expanded this view of neuroscience. Some research suggests that people give more credence to pictures of brain scans than any number of equally useful cognitive psychology findings so other scientists interested in how brains work may have picked up the 'neuroscience' label almost to validate their own findings with the general public (Munro and Munro, 2014).

What you'll find on this journey

In this book we're going to take this wider view of neuroscience because some of the studies that help us understand learning and training are behavioural, cognitive and social rather than purely biological, and therefore you'll get a far wider and more realistic view of the information that's currently available to us. (See Chapter 2 for more about neuroscience.)

As you read through you'll come across some of the slightly messy, squidgy hardware of the brain. The hardware relates to the biology and physiology of your brain, your nervous system and the chemical interactions of neurotransmitters and hormones.

You'll also delve into some of the software of your brain as it relates to learning and what cognitive psychology, developmental psychology and behavioural psychology have to say about learning. What's the latest in memory research? How will an understanding of social psychology help you create more effective learning environments, whether face-to-face or digital? How does your conscious and unconscious awareness of the world around you affect what you perceive, how well you learn and how you behave?

The focus will be on applying this neuroscience to the practical world of learning, education and training. How will you improve people's memory for information? How will you help people develop new habits? How can they forget old ones? How can neuroscience influence such old chestnuts as how to get managers involved in training and how do you design and train technical or compliance topics without being boring or getting stuck in the detail? What can the world of digital and virtual learning pick up from the application of neuroscience (despite the advances in technology you are still working with physical, messy brains that haven't changed much over the millennia)?

I urge you to use this book as a starting point and to go and read blogs, papers and other books that expand on the subject. Talk to your colleagues; mix with neuroscientists and other academics; take part in discussion groups; attend conferences; attend un-conferences and challenge, question and experiment yourself. Do whatever you can to improve your training and to help other people learn. Learn how to exploit and apply scientific secrets for learning success.

Other Voices

You're also going to hear from some other people who work in some of the same places you work in – people who have applied ideas from psychology and neuroscience and have tested them in their environments. I've asked them to contribute in their own words so that you get the story direct and I hope you find them inspiring and enlightening and they would like you to borrow and share their ideas too. Many of them will use the term 'brain friendly learning' which I'll define more fully in Chapter 4. Some of them have applied the ideas more broadly than just in a learning environment and find they have pervaded much of what they do both at home and work.

Here's your first 'Other Voice'. Pam Welsby runs a training consultancy in Slovenia and is one of those people for whom thinking about how people learn and think has pervaded her whole business.

Other Voices

Pam Welsby, *CEO and Founder, Fast Forward International*

More than 20 years ago in the East Midlands, I was first exposed to Accelerated Learning which immediately fit with my training style of Learner Centred, Highly Participative and Interactive.

Many years later, now running my own Learning Consultancy throughout Central Europe, I was searching for some further development in this field and found Stella Collins and Brain Friendly Learning. I convinced Stella to come to Slovenia and she provided the Brain Friendly Learning for Trainers programme for my team and some of our customers. I loved it.

This fresh and updated approach inspired me not only to think about how we could upgrade our training and development style and approach, but also how we could integrate the principles of Brain Friendly Learning into our brand, and our approach throughout the total sales, marketing and learning processes. This, I could see, was a key way to differentiate us in our market whilst also inspiring our clients in every contact with them to understand and realize the importance of aligning learning and communication with how our brains work, how we learn as human beings and as unique individuals.

So, two years later, I have now developed a sales process that includes documents and offers for the client that make use of colour, pictures, images or symbols to more simply explain and show our way of working. In sales presentations to clients we never actually present, but take toys and touchy feely items to make certain points, use posters and activities to let them experience our approach and utilize more of their senses and even use music to get them in the right 'state' for our short time together.

In our first contact with our potential customers we seek to immediately share something about Brain Friendly Learning and how this is an integral part of our way of working and how and why it works. We created a marketing campaign that did not directly sell anything, but more challenged their thinking and introduced a more creative way of working. The campaign consisted of e-mails, letters, and phone calls but also included sending them a postcard, a free book about change, a pencil and brain (for when they needed some extra brainpower) and some of the communications we sent included how our brains work, the impact our beliefs can have on our actions, how we each perceive the world differently and much more.

All of this is a precursor to the experience they have when they come and learn with us, where we also work hard to incorporate more and more of the brain friendly tools and techniques, but starting to use it in our sales and marketing activities also has a positive impact on our clients and increases the chances of them choosing us as their learning partner.

A start on the 'How can I...?'

You've already discovered that dopamine is released when you are curious but how can you make people curious and is there a discernible effect on their learning? Will questions like this one help? Let's explore a piece of genuine scientific research and a much more practical piece of research in a real learning environment and see what we come up with that you can use in your environment.

When you're asked a question do you try to guess the answer? Or do you encourage others to guess when you're asking the questions? Is it good practice to guess or is there a danger that people might guess the wrong answer and then remember it?

It seems, perhaps counter-intuitively, that we learn better after guessing, even if we guess the wrong answer first. Researchers at the University of California (Yan *et al*, 2014) tested whether people learned better when they were shown two linked pieces of information or had to guess the answer to a question such as 'What is the capital of Brazil?' They had either to guess the answer for 8 seconds and were then shown the correct answer, Brasilia, for 5 seconds, or they were simply shown the linked information 'Brazil – Brasilia' for 15 seconds. Which condition do you think improved the recall of the correct answer when people were tested later? It turned out that even when people guessed the wrong answer to the question, often Rio de Janeiro, their recall was better than when they'd simply been shown the correct information. And this effect persisted for up to 61 hours afterwards (they didn't measure any further than that).

We put this theory to the test in a 'Brain Friendly Masterclass' workshop (thank you to Sue Daly of Resolution for Change for asking us to participate in her experiment) and our experience seemed to tally with the research. In our small-scale experiment we were first asked a difficult quiz question and told to guess the answer, but not to reveal it. Then we were given another guess at four options. Finally we were shown the answer to check if we were correct. We identified those questions we'd guessed correctly and those we'd guessed wrong.

Four hours later, after a significant amount of other new information, we were tested again on the same questions. Whilst ours wasn't a scientifically rigorous experiment the results were broadly similar to those of the researchers; we could remember the correct answers we'd guessed at four hours later. The current explanation for this finding seems to be what's called 'semantic activation'; whereby a mental 'web' of knowledge and facts associated with the correct answer is activated and leads to better storage of the correct information. The researchers at the University of California said 'The basic idea is that this [guessing-related] activation... affords a richer encoding of the subsequently presented target'.

A question that arises is, were people curious as they guessed as to which was the right answer and did that release a shot of dopamine which somehow made the facts more enjoyable and more memorable? We don't know because that wasn't being investigated by this set of researchers and you can't create hypotheses in hindsight, but it's an interesting thought.

So what? – takeaway ideas to experiment with

Let's start to put this into your context. Scientific research is all very well but what does this mean for you in a practical learning situation?

Try this experiment: rather than telling a colleague something at work and expecting them to remember, instead ask them a question and invite them to guess. Whether they guess right or wrong show them the correct answer. The research indicates they'll remember your information more accurately if you encourage them to guess first before revealing the correct information. And it doesn't even matter if they guess wrongly at first – so long as you present the correct information quickly after the guess there's a stronger possibility they will remember it more accurately later.

This is also an easy tactic to implement in a digital environment. Ask the question and prompt the learner to guess before they click on or reveal the answer. You don't even need to record whether they got it right or wrong because guessing itself will improve their chances of remembering.

How to navigate this book

If you've got plenty of time or this is really important to you, read the book from beginning to end. Each chapter has an overview, research nuggets relating to the topic and you'll find 'curiosities' – pieces of research that are fascinating, potentially challenging or just seem to be unexpected for our current levels of knowledge.

There are stories and case studies because the research shows that humans relate to stories which are usually more 'sticky' than facts, though there'll be plenty of facts too. There are plenty of questions to stimulate your thinking and help with memory – can you remember what neurotransmitter is released when you're curious? There are takeaways, top tips and ideas to experiment or try out – ideas you can implement with your learners. Some will be specific to particular areas of learning or training and some will be more generally applicable, whether you're working face to face, digitally or remotely.

At the end of each chapter you'll find key points to help you summarize what you've read in order to boost your memory.

Alternatively you can choose to dip in and dip out, choosing chapter headings that relate to what you do, or perhaps use the summaries or headings as another way of identifying what that chapter might hold for you, based on your role and interests.

If you choose to go through in a chronological order you'll explore some of the neuroscience basics, some of the terminology and ideas that relate to learning and we'll also question what to do if someone decides to blind you with science or 'neurohype' and tells you 'research says'. After that we'll consider some of the key areas in the process of learning and what evidence there is to show us how people pay attention, adapt to different ways of learning or create strong memories. You'll also discover the neuroscience behind some of the other areas that might affect learning like the face-to-face or digital environments or the impact people like managers can have on successful learning.

Summary

The most important things you've read about in this chapter:

- Dopamine, a brain chemical, is released when you're curious – it's addictive.
- You're on a journey to find out what neuroscience can help you with in practice.
- Neuroscience is achieving a wider recognition in training and learning fields.
- Neuroscience is a broad topic covering many aspects of how our brains work – we're going to concentrate on practical applications to learning.
- Asking people to guess an answer helps them remember better.

You can choose how you navigate through this book.

References and further reading

AllThingsic (2015) [accessed 30 June 2015] The Value of Soft Skills To The UK Economy [Online] http://www.allthingsic.com/wp-content/uploads/2015/01/The-Value-of-Soft-Skills-to-the-UK-Economy.pdf (archived at perma.cc/G484-H2HG)

Cialdini, R (2001) *Influence*, Allyn and Bacon, Boston MA

CIPD (2014) Neuroscience in Action: Applying Insight to L&D Practice 2014 [Online] http://www.cipd.co.uk/hr-resources/research/neuroscience-action.aspx (archived at perma.cc/CBA7-QF7W)

Munro, G and Munro, C (2014) 'Soft' versus 'hard' psychological science: biased evaluations of scientific evidence that threatens or supports a strongly held political identity, *Basic and Applied Social Psychology*, **36** (6), pp 533–43

Yan, V X, Yu, Y, Garcia, M A and Bjork, R A (2014) Why does guessing incorrectly enhance, rather than impair, retention?, *Memory and Cognition*, **42** (8), pp 1373–83

The science of your brain

02

When was your last eureka moment?

Do you remember what happened in the story of Archimedes when he suddenly discovered how to measure the volume of an irregular object? He leapt out of a public bath, and ran home naked shouting 'Eureka!' ('I found it!'). How about your eureka moments? Can you remember what it felt like? Hopefully you didn't feel the need to run through the streets naked but for most of us it's a very particular experience. When you have a eureka moment you are literally having a brainwave, but do you know what sort of brainwave you are having?

Your brain creates electrical patterns which vary in frequency depending on what's going on in your head. As you do different things some brainwaves are more predominant than others; some are faster and some are slower. It seems that when you have a novel thought or connect two ideas together the experience of a eureka moment can be detected as a particularly high frequency brainwave called a gamma wave. Gamma waves have a frequency of between about 25 and 100 Hz, as compared to beta waves (16–31 Hz) or delta waves emitted in deep sleep of (0.1–3 Hz). Curiously, and somewhat counter-intuitively, gamma waves have also been detected when people are in a state of deep meditation which may not immediately strike you as the same experience as a eureka moment, but people who meditate regularly report strong insights whilst meditating which may be related.

This potential contradiction will lead us into a discussion of how science works and how to assess what's good neuroscience and what's not in Chapter 3. But in the meantime let's consider some of the neuroscience building blocks that may be useful to you in thinking about learning.

Read this chapter if...

You want to understand some of the basics of the brain and how they relate to learning and be able to recognize some of the tools and terms that are used in the study of the brain itself that will come up later in the book. If you're already familiar with brain cells, basic brain anatomy, neurotransmitters and research techniques then you might want to skip over to the next chapter. Figure 2.1 is your visual guide to what will be covered:

Figure 2.1   Science of the brain

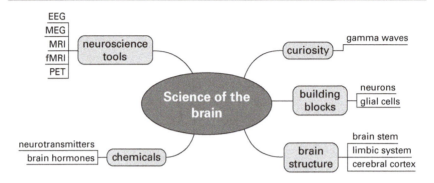

Building blocks

Neuroscience is the study of the brain and nervous system and in this book you're going to focus mainly on the brain. This is because much of what goes on in learning happens in the brain, though clearly the rest of the nervous system has a significant effect on the brain and vice versa and our bodies learn too. But the brain is where we'll start.

Brain cells

What are brains made of?

Your brain is made of different types of brain cells including several types of neurons and glial cells which actually make up most of the physical structure of your brain.

Neurons

Until recently nobody had actually counted how many neurons we have, though estimates tended to be at the nice round 100 billion mark (you'll find out in Chapter 3 why you should be wary of nice, neat numbers). In 2009, neuroscientist Suzana Herculano-Houzel and her team turned the brains of four recently deceased men into 'brain soup' (that's what she calls it) using a new technique called 'isotropic fractionation'. They measured the number of neurons in samples from the soup and then scaled up to find that 'on average the human brain has 86 billion neurons'. In a TED Talk in 2013 she explained 'Not one [of the brains] that we looked at so far has the 100 billion. Even though it may sound like a small difference, the 14 billion neurons amount to pretty much the number of neurons that a baboon brain has, or almost half the number of neurons in the gorilla brain. So that's a pretty large difference, actually.'

And even with only 86 billion neurons, each able to make multiple connections, you very quickly get trillions of possibilities as to how your brain connects up. The neuron is the basic information processing unit of a brain and, as learning is a form of information processing, this is therefore a pretty important unit to know a bit about.

Neurons were first clearly described by a Spanish researcher, Santiago Ramón y Cajal in 1888, for which he won the Nobel Prize. Before that it was thought that the nervous system might be one continuous network. Cajal built on the work of Camillo Golgi who invented a staining technique in 1873 which he called *la reazione nera* (black reaction). This technique is still used today to look at brain cells which look black against a yellow background. Golgi and Cajal had conflicting ideas about the structure of brain cells, until electron microscopy in the 1950s proved that brain cells were indeed separate cells, connected at synapses. Cajal was also a brilliant artist and it is worth seeking out his beautiful, detailed paintings of neurons.

Neurons are made up of a cell body containing a nucleus and then a number of branches radiating out (see Figure 2.2). The longest branch is called the axon, some of which are short, just a few micrometres, whilst some can be up to a metre long, travelling the length of your spine. The axons have a fatty covering called the myelin sheath which is pinched in at various points making it look a bit like a string of sausages. Axons end in branches called synaptic terminals that transmit nerve impulses from one neuron to the next one.

The shorter branches are dendrites which range from a few tens of micrometres up to several millimetres long. Dendrites collect incoming information as electrical patterns of activity from other neurons, whilst axons send information away from the cell body to other neurons.

The synapses are the junctions between different neurons where information is passed across. Information travels down the neuron as electrical energy but many neurons don't actually touch at the synapse and information passes across by the movement of chemical 'carriers' called neurotransmitters

Figure 2.2   A neuron

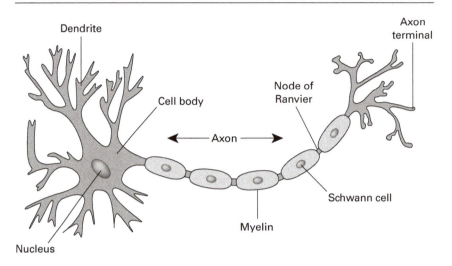

(more of them later). It's now recognized that mammals also have synapses where the neurons do touch and electrical stimuli are able to pass directly between neurons.

Glial cells

Glial cells are the support act for the neurons and the most abundant brain cells we have. You have about the same number of glial cells as neurons (despite some myths you may read about there being 10 times as many). The ratio of distribution of glial cells to neurons changes noticeably from being up to 3:1 parts of the cortex down to only about 0.01 in the cerebellum. They provide structural support, bring substances like nutrients from blood vessels to neurons and may help in amplifying electrical activity (but that's still not been proven). Unlike neurons they can divide and grow after birth and may be the structural elements in slow-growing brain tumours as well as supporting neurons that have been damaged. However, they don't form synapses and until recently it was thought they didn't transmit impulses. However, now it seems they do transmit signals but they are much harder to detect than neuronal signals. Their role in learning is like the support teams we all need to create great learning opportunities. If you're an independent trainer you may be your own support team so imagine glial cells as those other jobs you have to do yourself to run a great training programme.

Networks

Your neurons form massively complex neural networks that connect, uncon-nect and reconnect as we learn, unlearn and relearn. Your neuronal networks are incredibly important. Even though you'll come across information suggesting that one part of your brain does one thing and another does something else it's usually more accurate to talk about networks or systems that do the work.

Blood vessels

Your brain is also full of blood vessels; in fact Hercule Poirot was wrong when he referred to his 'little grey cells' – live brains aren't really grey at all but a pink colour. However, there are still parts of the brain technically called 'grey matter' which mainly consists of unmyelinated neurons, glial cells and cell bodies. There is also white matter which is mainly made of glial cells and the fatty myelin sheaths of the axons, and confusingly, in a freshly cut brain, they look slightly pink too.

What's the structure?

Brains are hungry organs and consume about 20 per cent of your body's energy resources whilst being considerably less than 20 per cent of your body weight. A human brain weighs about 1.0 to 1.5 kilograms.

Your brain is a complex structure with multiple interconnecting areas performing particular functions and much research is still going on to try to identify what's happening, where, when and how as we go about our nor-mal activities. Areas and systems significant to different activities have been identified and you'll explore particular areas relevant to your learning prac-tice as you go through this book.

There is often controversy over anything that attempts to simplify the brain's structures and functions because, of course, it's not simple. However, if you're reading this book you're probably more interested in how it applies to learning and not actually a practising neuroscientist, so you will meet some simplified models because otherwise the book will have to be much longer and you'll need to get a PhD in neuroscience.

One of the most common models for thinking about brain structure is MacLean's triune brain (1990). MacLean originally talked about this as an evolutionary model for our brain's development suggesting it had evolved in a particular way, which is indeed hotly debated. However, models can be very helpful if we see them as just that – models rather than a precise explanation of how the world works. In your role you probably use numerous models to explain concepts and ideas to people so they can grasp the general idea quickly. You and your learners know the model is only a representation of the real world that helps to make sense of it.

Initially I'm going to use the triune brain model to explain the high level structures of the brain and as you go through the book you'll be introduced to specific areas in more detail as they relate to learning; some of them you'll become very familiar with.

The triune brain model splits the brain into three basic areas (see Figure 2.3): the brain stem (MacLean called it the reptilian brain), the limbic system and the neocortex (which we'll call the cerebral cortex or more simply just the cortex).

Figure 2.3   Simple brain structure

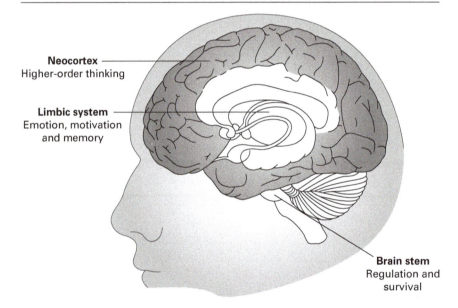

Brain stem

This is the part of the brain that helps to regulate your most basic functions and to keep you alive. Your breathing, hunger, temperature regulation, basic mobility and balance are all substantially monitored and controlled in this part of your brain and you're largely unconscious of what's happening there unless you experience problems with your normal functioning. Damage to the brain stem creates problems with mobility, motor control and central functions like breathing, sleeping, and eating.

For the purposes of learning we don't often think specifically about the brain stem but, as you'll find in later chapters, keeping these functions 'satisfied' can prevent interference that may stop you from performing at your best. Just think about how well you do or don't learn when you're hungry, tired or too hot.

Significant areas of the brain stem and their main functions are:

- Hypothalamus – regulates temperature, appetite, thirst, hormone secretions, muscle fibres.
- Thalamus – a relay area that passes messages from our senses into the rest of the brain (except smell – more of that later).
- Pineal gland – our body clock to regulate sleeping, waking and our daily rhythms.
- Midbrain – keeps us safe by coordinating our reflexes.
- Pons – a relay between the cerebellum and the cortex which is important for coordinated movement.
- Medulla – controls and monitors respiration and heart rate.
- Cerebellum – is crucial for balance and other features of movement.

Limbic system

The limbic system is central to us, sitting underneath the cortex and above the brain stem. Its primary function seems to be preservation of the individual and possibly the species – that is, it makes sure you are safe and it is also crucial in reproduction and nurturing of our young. If you're interested in learning it's an area you might want to pay active attention to because it's particularly associated, with memory and emotion which are both crucial to effective long-term learning. You'll come across the limbic system again in later chapters.

The main parts of the limbic system for learning are:

- Hippocampus – processes memories (much more later).
- A whole range of different nuclei including the amygdala – strongly linked to emotion and particularly fear, rage, aggression and sexuality.
- Corpus callosum – connects up the two sides of the cerebral cortex.
- Olfactory bulb – processes smells.

Cerebral cortex

When you watch a TV programme about brains or see pictures of brains, this is mostly what you see – that grey, or pink crinkly, wrinkly dome is your cortex. It's the part that most people imagine when you say 'brain'. The human brain is not the biggest brain in the world – that honour belongs to the sperm whale brain which weighs about 8 kilograms. But we do have the largest cerebral cortex of all mammals, relative to the size of their brains, and if you were to remove the cerebral cortex and flatten out all those wrinkles (each one is called a sulcus – plural sulci) you'd have an area about the size of a small umbrella. Our brains are wrinklier than other animals so we end up with a larger surface area of cerebral cortex to do all our complicated thinking.

Your cerebral cortex handles your higher-level processing of sensory information, communication, complex thinking like decision making and is incredibly important in learning.

It's divided up into different areas or lobes, each of which has specific, though often connected, functions (see Figure 2.4). Starting from the back of the brain, here are the main lobes and their key functions. Think about the implications for learning and you'll revisit them all as you go through this book:

- Occipital lobe – largely handles visual processing.
- Parietal lobe – seems to be very important for calculations, movement and orientation, as well as processing pain, temperature, touch and pressure.
- Temporal lobe – coordinates your senses, particularly sound and speech comprehension and it handles some aspects of memory.
- Frontal lobe – has no direct connections to the outside world and is where you do your thinking, planning, decision making and other higher-level functions.

And of course the cerebral cortex is split into two – the famous left and right hemispheres. Roger Sperry and colleagues in the 1960s researched the functions of the different hemispheres and found they do process different things, which somehow has led to multiple myths about the left and right brain and even myths about the myths (more of that later) (Gazzaniga et al, 1962).

Your brain is the most complex organ on the planet and whilst we tend to assign particular functions to particular areas for simplicity, in reality it's never as easy as that and the brain connects up in multiple ways to do even

Figure 2.4   The lobes of your brain

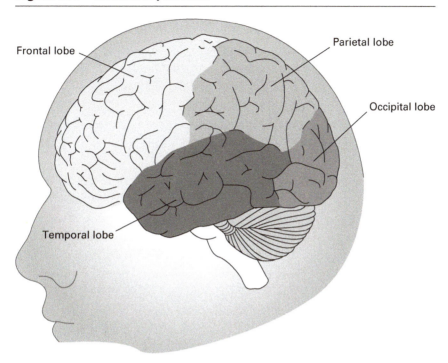

quite simple tasks. But we're not training to be neuroscientists ourselves so from necessity I'm mostly going to stick with the simplified versions, except where it becomes really important to point out a specific anomaly or piece of research. This book is about practical applications of neuroscience to learning.

Seeing pictures of brains with their different areas mapped out makes it all look relatively straightforward; however, if you want to see how very difficult it is to identify different parts of the brain in real life then the Wellcome Foundation has an amazing video dissecting the brain on YouTube: https://www.youtube.com/watch?v=OMqWRlxo1oQ (archived at perma.cc/AWH2-LZF4)

The brain's messengers – neurotransmitters and hormones

To function as humans our bodies and brains need to communicate and there's a constant chatter of messages up and down your nervous system and in and out of your brain and body. Chemical messages are carried by neurotransmitters and hormones so here are the main ones and their functions. As with the other building blocks of neuroscience, keep in mind how they may be valuable for you when you are working in a learning environment and you'll come across many of them again later.

There are many types of chemicals interacting with your nervous system. Depending how you count them, scientists say between 30 and 100 neurotransmitters have been identified and it's a very exciting, emerging new field of research. However, we'll only cover the most important and relevant to learning.

Neurotransmitters, such as acetylcholine, dopamine and noradrenaline, and hormones, such as oxytocin and adrenaline, are both chemical messengers. Generally, neurotransmitters are generated by neurons and work within the brain whereas brain hormones are released by glands in the body and distributed through the blood, though they have an effect on the brain. Neurotransmitters tend to act very quickly and more directly compared to hormones whilst the effect of hormones is longer lasting, though that length of time can vary from a few seconds to several days.

Excitatory neurotransmitters increase the chance that a neuron will fire whilst inhibitory neurotransmitters reduce that likelihood. We need both types because sometimes parts of the brain need to be 'quiet' to allow other parts to function properly. Your brain doesn't always want to be stimulated.

Dopamine activates your reward systems (remember those poor rats who preferred a dopamine fix rather than food). It controls arousal levels in the brain and is vital for physical and psychological motivation and is implicated in addiction. And as you've already found out it seems to be released when you're curious so is definitely useful for learning.

Serotonin is your 'feel good', inhibitory neurotransmitter and affects your mood. High levels are associated with optimism and it's also important for sleep. Reduced levels are implicated in depression. Apparently good-quality dark chocolate can boost your serotonin levels – we always find this is a popular fact in our 'Train the Trainer' workshops.

Acetylcholine was the first neurotransmitter to be identified as such by Otto Loewi, who initially called it Vagusstoff because it was released from the vagus nerve in the stomach. You need it to attend to the world around you, learn and remember and it may help you dream as well as controlling your muscles. People with Alzheimer's disease suffer from a lack of acetylcholine.

Glutamate, or glutamic acid is essentially what gives your Chinese takeaways their flavour. A Japanese researcher in 1906 evaporated kombu broth to find brown crystals with a distinctive taste that he named umami and then went on to produce a synthetic form, monosodium glutamate. This same chemical, glutamate, is the most abundant excitatory transmitter in your brain, is vital for linking your neurons together and is heavily implicated in both learning and memory.

Noradrenaline, also known as norepinephrine, is actually a hormone synthesized from dopamine and released from the adrenal glands above the kidneys. It has numerous functions throughout the body, including playing a role in stress and increasing blood flow to the brain. In the brain itself it helps you pay vigilant attention, a key factor in learning.

GABA (gamma-Aminobutyric acid) is usually an inhibitory neurotransmitter that helps to maintain balance and muscle tone and may have a role in physical relaxation as well as epilepsy. Whilst GABA is an inhibitory transmitter in the mature brain its actions are mainly excitatory in developing brains.

Other brain hormones are the *enkephalins* and *endorphins*, sometimes referred to as our natural opiates. This is because they modulate pain, reduce stress and can produce a feeling of calm and relaxation. Like dopamine they are somewhat addictive. Recent research suggests that endocannabinoids may play a more important part in learning than previously thought. These are some of the neurotransmitters that, like the endorphins, are associated with a runner's high. However, as you'll read later they may be vitally important for habit formation.

What else is going on in your brain?

Brainwaves

You already thought about brainwaves right at the start of this chapter. Brainwaves are the electrical activity set off when neurons are stimulated by neurotransmitters and hormones. Brainwaves can be detected as patterns of electrical activity by electroencephalography (EEG). The activity is caused by synchronized pulses of electricity from neurons communicating as you think, learn, sleep, dream and generally go about your daily business. They vary in frequency from the very slow delta waves which predominate whilst you sleep, up to the gamma waves which you've already read about as being prevalent when you have a eureka moment (see Figure 2.5). You'll explore later in the book the 'so what?' – why it might be useful to consider different sorts of brainwaves when planning learning.

Figure 2.5   The frequencies of brainwaves

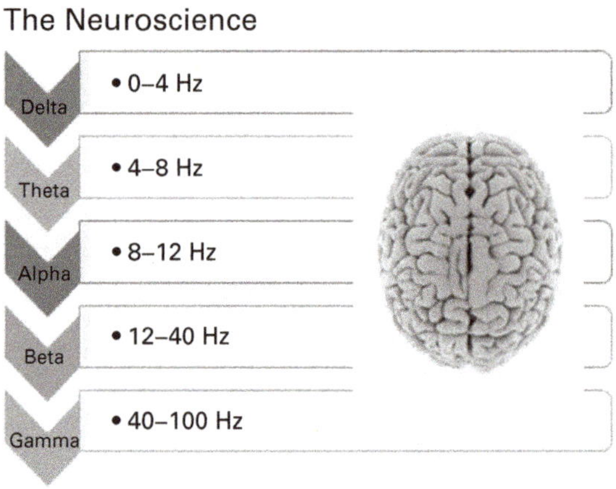

The Neuroscience

- Delta   • 0–4 Hz
- Theta   • 4–8 Hz
- Alpha   • 8–12 Hz
- Beta   • 12–40 Hz
- Gamma   • 40–100 Hz

SOURCE © Stellar Learning 2014

What are some of the tools of neuroscience?

When you consider the wider definition of neuroscience (see Chapter 1) that we're using in this book then the tools are many and varied. However, here you'll find some of the research tools that are used to peer into your brain. You'll find them referred to in many studies so it's useful to have an idea of what they are.

Electroencephalography (EEG)

You've already met EEG when you read about brainwaves. Essentially neuroscientists place small electrodes all over the skull and measure the electrical patterns happening in your brain. In modern EEG multiple readings are taken from across the brain that can be compared to build up a picture of the activity taking place. Some forms of EEG even pick up particular patterns relating to a specific stimulus like a particular touch or even a single word.

Magnetoencephalography (MEG)

MEG picks up signals from the oscillation of neurons but this time it's minute magnetic pulses that are detected rather than electrical signals. MEG has potential to be very useful because it's fast but is subject to interference and the signals are weak.

Magnetic Resonance Imaging (MRI)

MRI scanning uses huge magnets to align atoms in body tissue and then bombards them with radio waves. Different types of tissue give off radio signals in reaction to this bombardment and computer systems convert the information into three-dimensional pictures. An MRI brain scan looks a bit like a greyish X-ray that shows up different types of tissue in the brain and creates an excellent anatomic picture.

Functional MRI (fMRI)

fMRI builds on the basic MRI system by also showing levels of oxygen use as a measure of brain activity. This means you've got a combination of anatomic and metabolic information. When specific neurons are excited they need glucose and oxygen and blood flow is directed to that particular part of your brain. This blood flow can be detected by fMRI scanners and allows researchers to see how activity ebbs and flows as the brain processes information and reacts to stimuli. However, none of these systems measure in a natural environment so whilst an fMRI scan can tell you what's going on inside your head as you read a book in the scanner we can't be absolutely sure it's exactly what goes on whilst you're reading a book at home. But neuroscientists recognize it's an amazing opportunity to view our brains whilst we're actually working at real tasks.

Positron Emission Topography (PET)

PET scans use radioactive markers to see how resources are being used in your brain as you undertake specific tasks but the drawback is you need to have a radioactive marker injected into your bloodstream so the number of scans anyone can have is limited. They are not quite as detailed as fMRI scans but because the images are often very clear and attractive you'll often see them published. They are those brilliantly coloured red, blue, green and yellow images that look attractive and scientific and are being used to sell everything from 'brain games' to 'brain safe shampoo'. This causes some neuroscientists to get very cross because they feel the trappings of science are being used inappropriately to sell products which don't necessarily have any research backing them.

Thanks to computers the outputs from scanning systems can be combined together to create more and more robust pictures of the anatomy and metabolic processes in our brains and new systems will continue to be developed.

Other definitions

Here are some other phrases that are useful to define because you will come across them again in later chapters or in your other research on the application of neuroscience.

Neuroplasticity

Brain plasticity is one of the most exciting concepts in learning because it goes against the long-held belief that our brains were formed in critical periods in our childhood and couldn't really change. In fact now we know about plasticity it seems hard to imagine how we could explain learning before. Neuroplasticity is the concept that your synaptic connections and neuronal pathways change in response to the world around you; whether those changes are due to the environment, behaviours, thinking, emotions, learning or physical damage. Literally your brain has the ability to rewire itself; though don't go away with the idea of thinking it's easy. If you've ever had to break a habit you'll know that rewiring your brain can take some time and effort and you need to pay attention.

Paul Bach y Rita is regarded as one of the earliest advocates of neuroplasticity and has done groundbreaking work in the field of sensory substitution. Paul was a neuroscientist in New York, his brother George was a psychiatrist and his father Pedro was a Catalan poet. One day Pedro suffered a catastrophic stroke and, as was common in the 1950s, the family were told that he wouldn't walk, talk or function normally again. However, his sons believed that if they could only get him to rewire his brain they could help him regain his mobility. So George worked extensively with his father to get him speaking and moving again. Initially Pedro couldn't do much more than drag himself around and you can imagine the scandalized faces of the neighbours as his sons forced a sick man to crawl across the garden. However, in time Pedro regained much of his previous functionality and lived on for many more years. When he eventually died, a post-mortem showed that the original damaged tissue, largely in his brain stem, had not been replaced but he had created new pathways to enable him to relearn his previous skills.

One of the most significant concepts in neuroplasticity, particularly in associative learning, is that of Hebb's Law which in its simplest form says that 'cells that fire together wire together'. At its most basic it proposes that when two neurons connect regularly they eventually become permanently linked together – when one 'fires' so does the other. You'll come across this principle again in this book.

Ian Robertson, Professor of Psychology at Dublin University, has written a wonderfully readable book called *Mind Sculpture* (1999) looking at neuroplasticity in great detail. One of the things he talks about is research by Professor Michael Merzenich from San Francisco who has shown that in order to change or rewire our brains we need to pay active attention to the stimuli that can change them. This may seem intuitively quite obvious to you but until something can be proved by research, neuroscientists are reluctant to be firm about such statements.

Neurogenesis

Another previously common belief was that you couldn't create new brain cells which led to that slightly depressing idea that once you'd been born the rest of your life was just a process of waiting for your brain cells to be destroyed. However, researchers now know there is an ability to create some new brain cells, and the subventricular zone (research shows this might be its primary purpose) and the hippocampus (primarily involved with memory) seem to have a particular ability to generate new brain cells, which is great news for all of us. However, you can't regenerate all your brain cells so you do need to care for your brain; too many glasses of wine, lack of sleep or knocks to the head are not recommended.

So what? – takeaway

Whilst it's fascinating to spend time researching the functions and structure of the brain it's probably not really what your day-to-day job is about. So, what's the takeaway from understanding a little about how the brain fits together and some of the basic activity going on? How will you apply what you've read here to working with real people who need to learn something? How can you apply this to training programmes you'll design and deliver?

Spend a few minutes thinking about what you've read and identify if there is anything that's yet going to make a change to what you do or how you do it. Perhaps so far all it's done is clarify some terms you've heard or possibly assure you that how you teach, train or help people learn is already the right way.

And that's fine because this book is not here to necessarily change everything you do. One of its aims is to give you a framework to ground what you currently do in research, data and logic so that you have justification, evidence and data to back up your work in the same way that accountants have measures to take to the board of directors. You don't want to blind your colleagues with science but it is important that you have the confidence to talk about learning and teaching people based on what actually happens inside people's heads, rather than on vague hypotheses or latest trends. This will add to the professional standing of all of us who work in any field of learning.

Here's another voice sharing his experience. You may already be doing some of what Emmanuel is doing or you might adopt some of his ideas but what he's gained is the confidence to know why he's doing what he's doing.

Other Voices

Emmanuel Emielu, *Managing Partner/CEO, Oil and Gas Soft Skills Limited, Nigeria*

Some two years before my contact with brain friendly training, I'd struggled with a perceived flaw in my training design and delivery. More and more, I felt I could do better at connecting with my participants. Perhaps, more importantly, I worried about how to make the training stick. Happily, things came clear for me following two trainer development events I attended within one week of each other.

At one I got introduced to how the understanding of how the brain takes in, processes, and retrieves information plays a key role in learning formation and application. I found ready application of brain friendly learning principles in my soft skills courses, as well as the more technical oil and gas awareness course that I also deliver, so I share the two cases here.

Mintzberg's 10 Managerial Roles are well known in the literature. Teaching this to a class of 35 middle managers mostly in their 50s, I found that sliding through a series of PowerPoints I was provided with, would be real boring. Fortunately, I knew that to walk away feeling fulfilled I had my repertoire of brain friendly techniques to draw on. But first, I needed to 'inoculate' the participants; let them know upfront that our session would require a lot of activity and movement, and I requested their readiness to join in.

I wanted them to do a 'skit' of the roles, to reinforce what we had discussed. But it turned out that this was a new word to the whole class! So their first task was to find out what it meant, without my telling them. I think this initial activity must have added to stimulating their creative bursts when it came to coming up with their own skits. And they did come up with such an amazing performance, much talked about in the coming days! An upside was that when we came to the Creativity and Innovation module some days later, it was so natural for them to connect with the point that everybody is or can be creative.

For my oil and gas course, the challenge was how not to overwhelm participants with too much jargon, too fast. In the past, I used to spend an excessive amount of additional time beyond the allocated slot, resulting in having to rush through the later stages! But by adapting a press release of a local production company as a case study in which they have to find the meanings of new terms, jargon and abbreviations they did not understand, and with some context-testing questions added, the session became less intimidating and my time more effectively used.

In my experience over the last year, I have found distinct advantages in applying insights from neuroscience to design and deliver my brain friendly training sessions. Specifically, my sessions have witnessed: raising the level of participants' engagement; bringing seemingly boring sessions/topics to life; and becoming less of a 'sage on the stage' by consciously trying to be less 'telling' and more facilitating. It also helped with managing my large class of 35 more effectively.

Summary

As you've been reading this chapter you've learned:

- Neurons are the building blocks of the brain.
- They are supported by glial cells.
- Neurons connect together at synapses creating a complex neuronal network which processes incoming and internal information to keep you alive, communicating, thinking and learning.
- The functions of the brain are aided by particular chemicals called neurotransmitters and brain hormones which all have their own specialities.
- One of the offshoots of this stimulation is brainwaves which can be measured by EEG machines.
- Different types of scanning all help to build up a picture of the brain's anatomy and functions.
- We've got a lot of current knowledge but there is a lot more for scientists to learn about your most complex organ.

References and further reading

Gazzaniga, M S, Bogen, J E and Sperry, R W (1962) *Proceedings of the National Academy of Sciences*, **48**, 1765–69

MacLean, P (1990) The triune brain in evolution, *The Triune Brain in Evolution: Role in Paleocerebral Functions*, Springer, New York

May, K (2013) [accessed 30 June 2015] Lessons from brain soup: Suzana Herculano-Houzel at TEDGlobal 2013 [Online] http://blog.ted.com/lessons-from-brain-soup-suzana-herculano-houzel-at-tedglobal-2013/ (archived at perma.cc/R8L4-ZVVX)

Robertson, I (1999) *Mind Sculpture*, Bantam, London

What to do when someone says 'neuroscience says...'

03

Sometimes things aren't all they seem

For a long time it was commonplace to think that your memory gets worse as you get older and it seemed to be supported by multiple pieces of research. When looking at the effects of ageing on memory, researchers often measure how well older people perform on memory tests compared to younger people. Cynthia May, Lynn Hasher and Ellen Stoltzfus (1993), researchers at Duke University in North Carolina, USA, were doing a meta-analysis of the data from some of these pieces of research, and came up with an interesting observation. Not only were half of the subjects young but the researchers themselves were often undergraduates, ie young. One of the results of this observation was that they looked at the timing of the experiments. Students living typical student lives had a tendency to plan their experiments for the afternoon, once they'd had a good lie in, had woken up for the day and were feeling alert. Older people conversely tend to get up earlier and by the afternoon are ready for a nap.

So in 1993 they ran some of these experiments again but this time invited the 'subjects' to attend in the early part of the day when the students were feeling groggy but the older people were more alert. And the previously large gap in results that had been put down to memory loss due to ageing closed up. Ageing had an effect on memory but just as significant was the effect on people's sleep patterns and when they felt alert. Older people tested in the morning were better at memory tests than when they were tested in the afternoon and younger people tested in the morning did worse than when they were tested in the afternoon. So for those of you who've been worried about your memory being significantly worse as you get older, take heart – it's not going to be as bad as the research first suggested.

Overview

Is there a single piece of scientific research that 'proves' that learning is improved by spaced repetition or that we learn better when we're in the right 'mood'? Of course not. It's a bit like asking if there is a single piece of research to prove how many stars are in the sky or why small children like ice cream. There is plenty of practical evidence backing up good training practice, plenty of research that can be made to fit whatever theory you hold dear and, conversely, there may be things you do because they work, but, as yet, there is no reliable evidence to back them up.

Some of the challenges of using research are:

- Assessing which pieces of research relate to what you do and which don't.
- Reading some of the academic literature can be very daunting.
- Working out what to do with the research once you know about it.

So what's a responsible trainer to do when faced with an overwhelming amount of scientific research, not enough time to assess it and people with budgets asking you to 'prove it' when you suggest that the training room you've been allocated in the basement is too small, too dark and unlikely to be an ideal training environment? Throughout this book you'll find research and practical training tips based on that research and real-world experience but if you have different experience or an alternative view, then do what good scientists do and challenge what you discover.

What you'll cover in this chapter

As you'll see in Figure 3.1, you'll read about how science works in practice and why scientists constantly challenge, change and evolve their ideas. You'll explore some of the perils of research such as:

- What is research anyway?
- Research isn't always realistic.
- Research changes the results.

Figure 3.1 Neuroscience says...

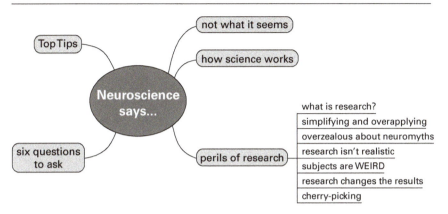

- Simplifying and overgeneralizing results often leads to neuromyths.
- Challenges of neuromyths and how you can be overzealous in seeking them out.
- Confusing models and research.

And you'll be given six useful questions to ask when someone says 'research shows' and you want to dig into their assertions a bit deeper.

Perils of research

It's useful to know how science works

If you're going to use brain-based research regularly to increase your credibility then I highly recommend you read Ben Goldacre's *Bad Science* (2009) first which will help you to assess what's good science and what's not. It's an excellent introduction to how statistics can be used and misused in the pursuit of science and it is very likely to challenge some of your assumptions or beliefs. Be prepared because Goldacre takes no prisoners and is equally dismissive of some of the claims of alternative practitioners and big pharmaceutical companies.

As a learning designer, trainer, teacher or lecturer you're often seen as the expert – the person people expect to have all the answers. After all, you're being paid to stand up there and help other people learn. So it's sometimes a bit daunting if someone asks a question you don't know the answer to or challenges you to back up what you've just said with some evidence. When you know more about how science works, even if you're not a scientist yourself, it gives you more confidence to say 'I don't know' or 'there's nothing been proven yet' or even 'it's complex and changing'.

In neuroscience, things are rarely proved with a 100 per cent certainty and then remain that way forever. It's a messy, challenging and exciting discipline that changes, shifts and moves, sometimes in tiny imperceptible steps and sometimes in huge lurches that change the way everyone thinks.

Science in general works when someone creates a hypothesis based on what they already know and a curiosity to find out more. They test their hypothesis looking for evidence to prove or disprove it. Once the evidence is there it's put to a peer review process and other people try to repeat or expand upon the experiments either to prove or disprove the theory. Eventually enough data amasses that people can begin to say that a particular hypothesis seems to be robust. Of course at any point a new piece of research might come along that throws the original ideas into question and that's OK because that's how science works – a continuous shifting and gathering of evidence, data and information to come to an agreed point before the next discovery.

In 2012 I remember hearing an excited researcher at the CERN laboratories being interviewed just before they were about to find out whether the Higgs Boson existed. The journalist suggested the scientist would be disappointed if the evidence proved them wrong and showed the Higgs Boson didn't exist. But the physicist explained he'd be just as excited if it was proved it didn't exist because that would generate a completely new way to go about thinking about physics. As far as he was concerned, pursuing good science was far more important and interesting than any one particular theory. That's not to say that scientists don't argue volubly if their particular theory is being challenged – that's human nature.

As humans we're not always comfortable with uncertainty, especially when we don't have enough knowledge to be comfortable with not knowing. So we look for simple easy solutions and models that help us explain the world. And the media makes this even worse by wanting simple newsworthy headlines. It doesn't really sell papers when you have an article hedged with 'maybes' and 'buts' and statistical probabilities. It's more likely to attract the reader's attention if you can announce, 'Neuroscientists say modern technology changes our brains!'

Perils of research – what do we mean by 'research'?

The interest in neuroscience in the world of learning should have an impact for all of us in the way we work. It will give us additional credibility with all those other measurable disciplines like finance and sales and it will help us challenge managers or other stakeholders who want us to cram vast amounts of content into a shorter space of time. With the right evidence we can explain that there's no point showing 30 slides full of data in 20 minutes if we want people to remember it. Learning is more complex and we can begin to prove it. But there is a potential overuse of the term 'neuroscience' and particularly the phrase 'research says'. Not everything that purports to be neuroscience or research is good science and even if it is good science it may not be relevant or practical to you working in a real-life learning environment. Additionally, when someone tells you 'my research shows', what do they mean by research?

Do they mean research in the sense of market research, surveys and questionnaires to find out what people think? Do they mean rigorous academic research? Or do they mean that they've had a bit of a look on Google and Wikipedia and asked their colleagues? All these forms of research are legitimate in the sense that they are all ways of finding out about the world but they are not all neuroscience and sometimes the term research can be confusing, or worse, might be used to mislead.

Another concern is that the person telling you may have had no intention to mislead you; they really did mean they riffled around in their filing cabinet and Google to find something they'd wanted an answer to but you may have misinterpreted what they meant by 'research'. You might then tell the next person about a piece of research you'd heard who then passes it on to someone else as a piece of research they heard which is then interpreted by someone on a training programme as something different altogether – and so the myths are born.

Perils of research – simplifying and overapplying results – poor Albert Mehrabian

Have you seen the silent film *The Artist* which was highly acclaimed in 2011? It surely shows us that we can communicate almost through body language alone because nobody said anything. There's even research that backs up that suggestion.

You may have heard figures suggesting we communicate 55 per cent of what we mean by our body language and that words account for only 7 per cent of what we communicate, which might explain why a silent movie can work. Now, you've probably got one of two reactions if you have heard that statistic. Either you're nodding and saying 'yes I've heard that' or you're possibly thinking 'but it's not true!' and may be about to put down the book; please stick with me.

This statistic has become mythologized, which may have come about through a process similar to the one in the previous section; we're looking for quick answers, academic papers are hard to read and interpret, so we often oversimplify or overapply the results to the wider world and then people repeat something they've picked up along the way until it comes to sound true.

The statistic is a genuine result from a scientist called Professor Albert Mehrabian who published his research in 1971 and inadvertently started the myth. Somehow it's been isolated from all the other research about communication and body language and is regularly used, inappropriately, to explain normal communication when it was a laboratory experiment under specific conditions looking at a particular hypothesis. The original research studied a limited range of communications which were about liking. People were shown black and white photos of a face with a range of emotional expressions; they also heard a recording of a single word which was in conflict with the facial expression and voice tones. For example, in the recording someone hears the word 'sad' but the tone and facial expression are 'happy'. When subjects saw and heard the clips of mixed messages, they were more inclined to believe the nonverbal communication (facial expression and tone of voice) and dismissed the verbal message – the single word.

Albert Mehrabian has spent many years explaining that he never intended this result to apply to normal human communications where, in general, people's expressions, tone and words are all conveying the same message. And it was a laboratory experiment; it really wasn't very lifelike. Albert Mehrabian himself said:

> … Inconsistent communications – the relative importance of verbal and nonverbal messages: My findings on this topic have received considerable attention in the literature and in the popular media. *Silent Messages* [Mehrabian's key book] contains a detailed discussion of my findings on inconsistent messages of feelings and attitudes (and the relative importance of words vs nonverbal cues) on pages 75 to 80.
>
> Total Liking = 7% Verbal Liking + 38% Vocal Liking + 55% Facial Liking
>
> Please note that this and other equations regarding relative importance of verbal and nonverbal messages were derived from experiments dealing with communications of feelings and attitudes (ie, like–dislike). Unless a communicator is talking about their feelings or attitudes, these equations are not applicable. Also see references 286 and 305 in *Silent Messages* – these are the original sources of my findings. …
>
> (Albert Mehrabian, source www.kaaj.com/psych/smorder.html (archived at perma.cc/6WXD-T7TJ))

If we go back to the silent film of *The Artist* all the communication is congruent – the music, the acting and the occasional words on the screen are all working to give you the same message. You can tell what people seem to be saying, up to a point, from the music and images alone but when someone says something complicated it's just not enough – we need the words too.

Being overzealous about neuromyths

You may also have heard some of the arguments about left and right brain myths and I hope you have heard enough to have dispelled the myth that people are either right-brained and creative or left-brained and logical; but sometimes a little *more* knowledge can be a dangerous thing.

On Twitter recently there was a heated debate between two colleagues over this very topic. Clare mentioned left/right brain differences and another colleague, let's call him Jack, responded very quickly and started accusing her of perpetuating the myth of left-/right-brained people. This wasn't what Clare had said at all but it was as if just seeing the words 'left brain' and 'right brain' caused an automatic response in Jack to dismiss her comments without even reading them or understanding what she was saying. It seems Jack may have labelled any information about the left and right sides of our brains as a myth and therefore dismissed anything he read without checking what he was reading. In reality there are some excellent neuroscientists working on the similarities and differences between how your two hemispheres process information but that doesn't mean they are suggesting you only use one side of your brain or the other.

Some activities are processed predominantly using left hemisphere processing and some using right hemisphere processing. For example, word puzzles tend to use the left hemisphere whilst rotational image exercises create greater activity in the right hemisphere. Psychologists and neuroscientists devise exercises to test out these principles and can see what's happening in the brain with scanners and other detection systems. But of course in the real world you rarely concentrate on one limited activity for any period of time – even if you do a right hemisphere dominant activity you may then need to access your left hemisphere (predominant for language processing) in order to tell someone what you've done. It's evident that some people find some activities easier to do than others but it doesn't mean that those people are left- or right-brained.

What do the myths and facts mean to you in your role of designing and delivering learning? Both of them should get you mixing up activities and exercises so you're stimulating brains in different ways but without access to an MRI scanner you're not really going to know whether you're doing a left-brained or right-brained activity. And even if you could tell what would be the purpose in a world where our brains normally connect left and right hemispheres?

Perils of research – research isn't always realistic

The huge amount of excellent research done on the study of learning is not all applicable to workplace learning and/or any learning in the real world. You'll find out more about the science of learning in the next chapter but be aware that lots of it will have been done in a laboratory. And learning sequences of letters or learning to do key presses in a laboratory is very different to learning about compliance or customer service at work. Learning research is also often done with children and can be confused with developmental research; ie learning that happens naturally in the developmental process, such as learning to speak your native language. It's harder to do learning research with adults in the workplace because there are many uncontrolled factors and organizations usually don't have time to carry out controlled trials.

Other Voices

Ben Ashton, *3rd year Psychology Student, University of Exeter*

As a psychology student, I have been exposed to the university side of neuroscience through lectures and coursework and never really properly engaged with the content. From the neuroscience that I have been shown through taking part in the Brain Friendly Learning programme I have realized the practical applications of basic (and more complex) neuroscience in everyday life.

Two of the more simple applications of Brain Friendly Learning I have applied are mindmaps and more physical ways to approach learning. These have opened many opportunities in terms of different ways of learning and revising which have made revising more efficient and almost enjoyable. I have also tried to incorporate the model of multiple intelligences into my learning as I learned that the more intelligences you work with the easier it is to process and remember information. I am still learning more about how I learn and think I will be for a long time but through neuroscience, I feel like I'm heading in the right direction.

I had knowledge of mindmaps and had used them before but if I'm honest only when told to by teachers. I have now begun to use mindmaps more frequently in both my university and working life. I have gone a little overboard and used them to structure my revision, my everyday life, my chores and most recently my work during a summer internship. I've learned that through a few simple pointers and tips, mindmaps can be a really useful tool for structuring thoughts and action plans in multiple walks of life and can be applied anywhere effectively both as a structuring tool and to look back on for reference.

What Stella and Brain Friendly Learning have shown me is that through a basic understanding of the processes of our brain and how it works up there, we can tailor learning to promote more efficient learning and memory and although I don't feel anywhere close to being an expert I feel I now know enough to have had a positive impact on my learning both now at university and in the future.

Perils of research – the subjects are WEIRD

Have you heard about the WEIRDest people in the world. They are Western, educated, industrialized, rich and democratic. A 2008 survey of the top psychology journals found that 96 per cent of research subjects were from Western industrialized countries which accounts for just 12 per cent of the world's population (Henrich, Heine and Norenzayan, 2010). And 70 per cent of that population came from the USA alone and a high proportion of the people included in neuroscience research are actually psychology under-graduates because they are the easiest subjects to get hold of. Applying these results to the personality, behaviour, neuroscience and psychology of people in general therefore becomes a little less realistic again. Think back to the story at the start of this chapter which was about just this sort of problem (if you're over 35 you might want to try remembering in the morning and if you're under 35 do it in the afternoon). Most neuroscience research was initially done with people who had some sort of disorder or brain damage because they had greater needs and were the ones who presented themselves to researchers.

Perils of research – research changes the results – just because it's research

Brain scans look really attractive and it's terribly tempting to think that because something shows up on a brain scan we can be confident it's true – after all we can see it. And surely if researchers have spent time analysing and collating results we can be sure they're true. They may be true, but are they realistic? As we've already discussed, a brain scan is not a normal way of going about anything and the effects of being studied may change the results.

Back in the 1920s and 1930s a series of experiments seemed to show that factory workers became more productive when the light levels were improved. However, analysis by Henry A Landsberger in 1950 showed that the productivity gains seemed to owe more to the motivational effects of being studied than the light levels; people's work improved when they had more interest paid to them. This became known as the Hawthorne effect and is one of the factors that needs to be considered when analysing data from real-life studies.

Perils of research – beware of cherry-picking

Like me, you've probably got favourite models that you've used to illustrate a point over the years and you may or may not have checked whether there's any scientific rigour behind them – which may not matter if it's simply a model that effectively helps you to tell a story. You probably also use metaphors, analogies and stories to make information easier to absorb, use and remember and they're all helpful ways of conveying information. Nobody expects a story to be necessarily true.

What's more important is that, when someone says their model or their methodologies have been researched, you need to be sure that the results weren't cherry-picked to prove their model whilst ignoring other research that may provide a different view. This cherry-picking is a form of selective attention and an example of confirmation bias; a perfectly normal tendency to search for, interpret, or recall information in a way that confirms your own beliefs or hypotheses. In scientific circles people look at a range of results to draw firm conclusions. Often you'll come across meta-analysis of scientific studies when all the research is considered, both for and against the hypothesis, and conclusions are drawn based on the weight of evidence. It helps to avoid cherry-picking individual pieces of research.

Just to be clear, models are a really helpful way to explain the world – models are different to science – they are not reality but just a possible description that may be useful to help explain something so they don't need to necessarily be proved. They are definitely better when they're tested to see whether they fit in multiple situations but so long as you make it clear it's a model then I think they're helpful. What you can question is whether any research you're being shown to back up a model is a wide analysis of available evidence or just a single result picked out to confirm the model's place in the world.

Six questions to ask when someone says 'research shows'

With good science these potential perils are countered by good practice such as statistical analysis, rigorous controls, double blind trials and peer review. Here are six questions to ask when someone says 'research shows' because not everything that's cited even as scientific research is as rigorous as it could be. Here's how you can check for yourself if you are looking at research.

These questions are commonly recognized as useful ways to challenge research, information and hypotheses and you'll find very similar questions asked regularly across the scientific community. Whilst each question on its own may not be entirely helpful, by asking all six you'll see patterns that add to or detract from the credibility of a piece of research.

1. Who did the research?

There are two elements to consider here. Who is named as the researcher and which organization has done the research?

When the research is backed by a major institution like a university or a major science business you can be fairly confident there will have been audits, checks and balances, papers published and peer reviews to demonstrate scientific rigour.

Who appears to have done the research? Has the person named as the lead researcher (theirs will be the first name on the paper if there's been one published) been cited in other papers or other research or is this their first publication?

There's nothing to say that major institutions can't get it wrong. There's a well-documented case of a renowned researcher at Harvard University, Dr Marc Hauser, who'd been getting significant recognition for his long-term studies on monkeys whilst researching cognitive evolution. He was forced to resign from Harvard University in 2011 after he'd been found guilty of scientific misconduct; he'd fabricated data in one study, manipulated results in multiple experiments, and incorrectly described how studies were conducted. Interestingly one of his projects was a 'Moral Sense Test' in which participants were presented with a series of hypothetical moral dilemmas and asked to judge each one.

Just because the research comes from a smaller company, lesser known researchers or universities you haven't heard about before is not necessarily a reason to devalue the research because everyone has to start somewhere, but it's worth asking the question.

2. What's on their agenda?

When an organization's marketing says 'research says our product is better than others' then it's relatively easy to be aware of the element of vested interest. However, if it's a piece of scientific research that shows a particular training tool improves cognitive performance then it's not readily identifiable as a piece of marketing or a public relations exercise. However, lots of research is done and funded by major corporate businesses with a product to sell and the research helps credibility and sales. This is normal and is why we have regulated industries with complex compliance and regulatory processes to check that their research is scientifically rigorous and ethical.

We all have vested interests in some way or another and we can't dismiss research just because it comes from a particular source with something to sell. However it's important to be aware and ask yourself, and them, are there vested interests in the research results?

3. Where was it published first?

Science research is usually published first in reputable science journals so that colleagues, peers and other people can look at their methodology, the results and the interpretation, and this is the process of peer review. Usually scientists will attempt to replicate the work to check that it is reliable and they'll refine and improve the methodologies. Think of it a bit like lawyers who love to pick holes in each other's contracts; scientists love to analyse and find flaws in other scientists' methodologies and results with the aim of moving the science on.

Research released first to the mass media and not peer reviewed tends to be less well regarded amongst the scientific community. Having said that there is a heated debate amongst science writers as to how to do peer review now the Internet is so all-pervasive. Should they publish first and allow the peer review to happen online or should they go through the more traditional procedure?

When something appears in the mass media it is necessarily going to be simplified because most of us won't have the time to explore the detail, but like legal documents, the detail often contains important caveats and corollaries that may mean the research is only applicable under certain conditions and can't be generalized.

4. When was it published and when else?

Have a look at when a piece of research was published. If it's 20 years old it doesn't mean it's invalid but ask yourself what's happened since? Was this the piece of groundbreaking research that everyone defers to and has been replicated many times or was it a one-off and since then research has gone on to weaken or disprove the theory? For instance, Hermann Ebbinghaus did his initial work on memory retention back at the end of the 18th century and you'll probably be familiar with the 'forgetting curve'. If you were to repeat his experiment now you'd probably get quite similar results but there's clearly far more recent work on how we remember and forget. And you might be surprised to know that Ebbinghaus wasn't memorizing interesting, connected and relevant bits of information – he was remembering random strings of words. Keep this in mind because it's helpful to remember scientific studies don't usually replicate real life; in fact they can't because being studied changes people's behaviour anyway (Hawthorne effect).

5. How was the science done?

Have the results been properly analysed? Have the researchers done double blind trials or eliminated the potential for the placebo effect or the Hawthorne effect?

Statistical analysis of results is vital to check whether they are valid and not the result of coincidence or an accidental outlying result. Have the results been tested against any base data that's required? Neuroscientists using fMRI scanning rather surprisingly have to calibrate their data against that of a dead salmon. If you're curious about this then look out for Ig Nobel Prize in Neuroscience: The dead salmon study (Jha, 2012).

Statistics help to overcome our entirely human tendency to create patterns where patterns don't exist – statistics can help you to identify a genuine pattern against a coincidence. One psychological phenomenon called salience helps to explain why often we pay attention to some things more than others because they seem more important or more familiar and it's one of the reasons we need statistics to identify the real patterns.

What's the sample size for the experiment? One of the challenges of brain scanning is that it's expensive so many experiments are only done on small numbers of people. This means that it's harder to argue that the effects or results apply to everyone. Remember, most research is done on WEIRD outliers (Westernized, educated people from industrialized, rich democracies) or people with problems. This is a bit of a challenge when we take a single piece of research and then suggest that 'humans' learn this way or that.

6. What are the results saying?

When scientists publish research they tend to hedge it with statistical probabilities and caveats because they know that it's very unlikely a single piece of research will tell them anything definitively. It's usually just another piece in a complex puzzle and that's particularly true of neuroscience because your brain is so complex. Results that show nice neat figures are usually worth questioning as to their scientific validity even if they seem to be a nice model to apply. An example of this you might be familiar with is the 70:20:10 model that suggests 70 per cent of learning should be done on the job, 20 per cent from other people and only 10 per cent from reading or 'courses'. It's a helpful model to work from and based on good practice but the research it's built on wouldn't be considered scientifically robust.

Avoid looking for 'the one true answer' – real research evolves, changes and builds on previous research, sometimes overturning it completely.

So if a piece of research suggests it's a magic bullet or a magic wand that's going to solve all your problems then go back to the previous five questions and get better answers.

Here's a bonus question: Is this research relevant to what I do and can I or should I apply it? The fact that something stimulates your 'anterior cingulate cortex' may sound impressive but is it relevant to what you're trying to do? And how on earth would you be able to tell if your carefully designed exercise did or didn't stimulate someone else's 'anterior cingulate cortex'? (In case you're wondering, your anterior cingulate cortex helps to focus attention and tune into your own thoughts; it seems to play a role in depression causing sufferers to lock onto their own sad feelings.)

The chances are, as someone whose job is in the learning world rather than research, you're more likely to encounter information second or third hand through blogs or magazines; you won't regularly come across research by reading an original research paper, and articles straight from academia can be very daunting. Brain science is really, really complicated and that's why there are thousands of scientists around the world studying tiny dislocated pieces. We, as professionals in another sphere, can't hope to understand it all so we do need people to simplify it for us, but we also need to be careful about being blinded by science and seeing 'neuroscience' as a panacea for everything in our world.

It's helpful for all of us to keep an open mind and to question the research. This helps us sort out the significant from the insignificant, the real from the hypothesized; it helps to preserve a rigour and to make sure we recognize the difference between something that's merely interesting and something that's been proven.

Top Tips for using brain-based research

Avoid looking for 'the one true answer' – real research evolves, changes and builds on previous research, sometimes overturning it completely. You need to reassess regularly, question what you find out and check against all the available data.

Keep an open mind – if the evidence seems to change then you may have to change your practice or your reasons for doing something. As professionals we need to be open to learning too.

Take a pragmatic approach – if something seems to be effective for your learners, keep doing it. Research sometimes simply confirms what you've always known intuitively.

Research articles straight from academia can be very daunting so make use of resources that have done some of the work for you. Use reliable sources like *New Scientist*, The British Psychological Society Research Digest or books that round up much of the research such as *Brain Rules* (John Medina, 2008), *Make Your Brain Work* (Amy Brann, 2013), *Mapping the Mind* (Rita Carter, 1998), *Your Brain at Work* (David Rock, 2009).

What we don't know about how the brain works is still far greater than what we do know so it's fine to say 'I don't know yet'.

Summary

Neuroscience is complicated and as learning professionals we do not have time to become neuroscientists. Instead we can become more aware of how science works, and how scientists make hypotheses in order to experiment and challenge each other's findings. Become familiar with the perils of research; be clear about what people mean by the word research and how research is regularly simplified and overapplied. Think about how neuromyths come about and how there are even myths about neuromyths. And consider how research isn't really like the real world; it's often conducted in unrealistic situations and is populated by WEIRD subjects. Research itself changes the results and people may be cherry-picking their results to sway your views.

Have a set of six questions in reserve to ask when you hear 'Neuroscience shows':

1 Who did the research?

2 What's on their agenda?

3 Where was it published first?

4 When was it published and when else?

5 How was the science done?

6 What are the results saying?

References and further reading

Brann, A (2013) *Make Your Brain Work: How to maximize your efficiency, productivity and effectiveness*, Kogan Page

Carter, R (1998) *Mapping the Mind*, University of California Press, CA

Goldacre, B (2009) *Bad Science*, Fourth Estate, London

Henrich, J, Heine, S J and Norenzayan, A (2010) The weirdest people in the world?, *Behavioral and Brain Sciences*, **33** (2–3), pp 61–83

Jha, A (2012) [accessed 30 June 2015] Ig Nobels honour dead salmon's 'brain activity' in improbable research awards [Online] http://www.theguardian.com/science/2012/sep/21/ig-nobel-awards-dead-salmon (archived at perma.cc/8UMJ-7NU7)

May, C P, Hasher, L and Stoltzfus, E R (1993) Optimal time of day and the magnitude of age differences in memory, *Psychological Science*, **4** (5), pp 326–30

Medina, J (2008) *Brain Rules: 12 principles for surviving and thriving at work, home and school*, Pear Press, Seattle, WA

Rock, D (2009) *Your Brain at Work*, Harper Business, New York

The science of learning

04

Thinking about yourself whilst learning can inhibit your performance

I'm having some squash coaching and it's ruining my game; shots I could hit before are going wrong, and the new shots I'm learning seem to be hopeless. I'm focusing on where my feet are, how I hold my racket and how to swing to the point where I miss easy shots and give away too many points. It may be a phenomenon you recognize too and I'm hoping that this unexpected effect of the coaching will wear off soon!

For a while researchers have known that focusing on body movement can impair performance. This is because we're directing unhelpful conscious attention to previously unconscious body control. However, it now seems that even reflecting on your performance, which intuitively seems like a good idea, may hinder you too because it can also interfere with your motor skills.

In a study in 2015, researchers found people who were learning to play some new ball games performed worse than a control group when they were asked to reflect on their experiences afterwards. After learning the skill, participants were asked to think or write about their personal attributes as an athlete or even their emotional experiences related to the learning. The control group were asked to think or write about something unrelated to themselves. After the reflection the groups who'd reflected were less accurate and made more errors than the control groups when they next played the game. These scientists think that focusing on what you're doing whilst learning might actually impact on your performance because of something called a 'self schema'. This sense of 'self' isn't just a psychological or philosophical construct but seems to be found in functional neural networks such as the temporoparietal junction (implicated in sensory integration) and the extrastriate body area (processing thoughts about your body). This research is new and there are many things that need to be explored in more depth but the researchers think that the self schema networks are interfering in the motor control required to perform at a higher level. This is an interesting reflection for those of us who feel that asking people how they performed is a helpful learning activity.

Overview

In this chapter you'll find out what learning is but we'll start with what it isn't. Then you'll find out about some of the brain biology of learning and explore some different types of learning that have been identified and studied. This will help you to pinpoint what types of learning you're working with and therefore how to get the best results. You'll also discover a model for the learning process that will provide a structure for the next few chapters of the book and is a practical way to help you think about designing and delivering training and creating learning environments, whether digital or face to face. Figure 4.1 provides a visual guide to the chapter.

Figure 4.1   Science of learning

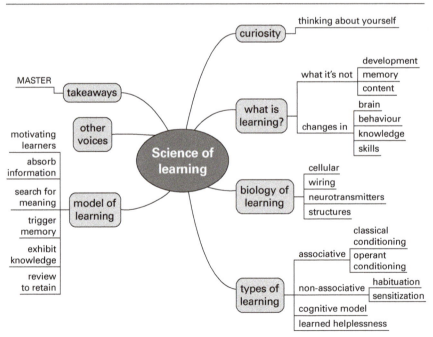

What learning isn't

It's not the same as development

Let's start with exploring what learning isn't or at least what you're not going to focus on in this book. From before birth you were exposed to different stimuli and learned to respond more or less appropriately to them. Some of what you learned is developmental; it's part of your normal maturation process and was going to happen eventually, whatever happened. Babies learn to speak a language, to walk, to develop a concept of self and to become adults, whether we want them to or not. How well they learn and how they fit into society's norms of behaviour may vary depending on the experiences that mould and shape them but this is developmental and will happen.

However, we're interested in the sort of learning that goes on alongside this developmental process and continues long after. We're interested in how we learn skills, knowledge and behaviours that don't just happen through a normal process of growing, though they are fundamentally affected by everything we experience.

It's not quite the same as memory

Memory and learning are intimately related and if you're interested particularly in memory then there is a whole chapter (9) devoted to it; plus you'll find any number of books, programmes, entire university courses and expert blogs and opinions available. We need our memories in order to learn but just having a memory isn't enough to qualify as learning. I can recall the fact that Henry I is buried at Reading Abbey but it doesn't really change anything about the way I behave or even what I believe.

As part of the learning process you need to create or encode and store memories (and you'll explore different sorts of memories later) and you will need to recall that memory later in order to demonstrate your learning, but a memory alone isn't sufficient to count as learning.

It's not information or content

As a trainer you may regularly be asked to add more content to your training because someone, somewhere thinks everyone needs to know more than they currently do. This is the lure of 'content' – you'll even hear the phrase 'content is king' but it's not. Not if you want learning to take place. Content is usually about delivering facts or ideas which can be presented to someone in multiple, complex, multisensory, multimedia and gloriously varied ways. However, facts and ideas do not become learning unless something permanent changes in people's brains. You might have to take a long hard look at what you're delivering as training and see whether in reality that's all you're doing – delivering information and creating cognitive overload rather than enabling learning.

On Valentine's Day at school, we used to tease each other about how the postman was going to need an especially huge van and the letter box would have to be widened in order to squeeze in all the beautiful and passionate Valentine's cards we'd receive. Perhaps as a designer or trainer what you've been doing up to now is being the postman with all those cards, maybe even some presents, and you've turned up at the door ready to deliver all those endearments but nobody has actually thought to widen the post box. You've got to deliver the cards because that's your job so you just have to leave them on the doorstep but you have no idea whether anyone will ever open them, read them or have a wonderful romance based on them. Only a few special cards were ever wanted anyway; in fact the one that was waited for with a yearning heart may not have been in your post van at all but delivered by someone who climbed over the mountain of dumped post, rang the doorbell and handed the card over personally. Or more likely, perhaps the important card sadly got buried in the heap and was thrown away unread, unremembered and having no impact.

Before you've finished this book I'd like you to start challenging those people who ask you to deliver more content. As a professional your job is to deliver the one true love's letter or possibly to find the key that will open the door, but it's not to keep delivering the letters just because someone posted them.

What learning is

Learning is a process by which changes in your brain allow you to behave and respond in particular ways. All animals from the simplest to the most complex learn and nowadays even machines can learn. For our purposes we're going to focus on human learning but I can't promise you that the occasional experiment with chimps, rabbits, rats and even slugs and snails won't creep in from time to time because often the same processes are taking place.

Learning happens at a cellular level (or possibly even at a sub-particle level) so the sorts of processes we can see in simple creatures like slugs who only have collections of cells called ganglion, rather than brains, can often teach us something useful about what's going on in our own brains; though the applications of this may sometimes be hard to tease out in a work or educational context.

Learning creates structural changes in your brain that help you build on what you already know and change your behaviours based on what you already do. If you're changing preferences, habits or beliefs there may even be some unlearning to do.

Over your life you're going to learn many different things. You may learn which English king had six wives or the order of the periodic table or how to cook an apple pie. You will learn culturally appropriate behaviours, like how to speak to your granny when she comes to visit or how to behave in an interview. You will learn to play sports and how to ride a bike; you may learn to paint, sing or do quadratic equations. You will learn who your friends are and who to avoid, or how you deal with conflict if you can't avoid them. You will learn how to get from one place to another and how to use a satnav. You will learn to amuse yourself perhaps by doing cross-words or Sudoku puzzles. You will learn to read and write and to doodle. You may learn things you didn't mean to learn, like silly jingles you can't get out of your head, and you'll probably learn to deal with happiness and sadness, and perhaps how to tell which charger belongs to which piece of electrical equipment.

So what's going on in your head whilst you learn all these different things?

Some of the biology that's useful

At the cellular level

For any type of learning you connect up neurons; you change the way your brain cells communicate; create new synapses and change the way your brain is organized.

What sea slugs have taught us about learning

When you learn something you're basically letting new connections happen in your brain and you may be weakening some of the older ones that are not so useful any more.

So, how do neurons connect? Scientists aren't sure about the entire process but research on sea slugs has proved helpful. Whilst you may not be very closely related to the sea slug it seems the basic cellular processes of learning are quite similar. Sea slugs can't learn to play the piano or learn numerous facts about a new manufacturing process but they can find their way around mazes and can learn to react differently to different stimuli.

They don't have brains as you would recognize them, merely collections of brain cells called ganglion, but the basic mechanisms at a cellular level seem to be the same. This was somewhat controversially discovered by Eric Kandel who eventually won the Nobel Prize in 2000 for his work on understanding the mechanism of how neurons connect. The controversy arose because applying what he'd learned from slugs to human learning was considered somewhat undignified. Now we've identified that we share significant amounts of DNA with slugs, perhaps it's easier to believe that sea slug brain cells work enough like our own to make it a reasonable comparison.

What Kandel and others (Mayford *et al*, 2012) showed is that when you learn you change the way your brain cells, your neurons, interact with each other. With a new piece of learning the ends of a neuron appear to swell, sway and then split into two, forming new projections which then connect up with other neurons. Kandel worked on the gill-withdrawal reflex of his sea slugs and found distinct short- and long-term memory storage and that the long-term storage could be seen in structural changes; cell connections were functionally reorganized depending on what they were learning.

So for you too, when you learn something, perhaps by reading this book, your neurons are swelling, swaying and creating new connections that didn't exist before.

What neurotransmitters and hormones have to do with learning

In the space between your neurons, called the synapses, numerous neurotransmitters and other chemicals are shuttling around performing different roles too.

For instance, blocking the effects of *glutamate* stops a process called *long-term potentiation* (LTP) which is the persistent improved functioning of synapses based on recent patterns of activity. It's a vital part of how you create memories. Glutamate activates chemicals in the post-synaptic cell like cyclic adenosine monophosphate (cAMP) and protein kinases which help you to synthesize new proteins as part of forming long-term memories. These new proteins are vital for forming those neuronal connections; they literally help you 'glue' your neurons together.

Serotonin is an inhibitory neurotransmitter that seems to affect mood as well as to be required for memory formation. Its role in memory is less defined and maybe more modulatory than that of glutamate but it is implicated in Alzheimer's disease. Serotonin is the one that needs *tryptophan* for its production, which you get from dark chocolate.

Cortisol, a hormone required to handle stress, can reduce learning whilst oxytocin may help you think more expansively or creatively. You can increase your *oxytocin* level by giving someone a hug, so perhaps next time you want to be a bit more creative, give someone a hug first. Be aware though, the effect doesn't last long; just long enough for the oxytocin to have an effect before it's taken up again by your neurons. Oxytocin may also be what helps you learn to trust.

Noradrenaline and *acetylcholine* help you to pay attention; you'll find out more about attention in Chapter 7 and you'll meet acetylcholine again in Chapter 9 on memory.

Wiring and the importance of Hebb's Law

Donald Hebb was a Canadian psychologist who first published a book called *The Organization of Behavior* in 1949 and he's commonly seen as the father of neuropsychology and neuronal networks (Hebb, 2002). He went to a Montessori school and was a teacher himself, at one point teaching at a school for so-called 'difficult children'. He took a slightly different approach to the strict principles of the Quebec schooling system and used to set more interesting work which he made a privilege by sending those who were misbehaving outside (presumably this was considered more of a punishment then than it may be now). After going to Yale, Harvard and Chicago Universities he started work at the Montreal Neurological Institute where he found that children's brains that had been damaged could effectively repair themselves but it was not as easy for adults. He was one of the early pioneers who proposed, what at the time was groundbreaking, that we can explain behaviour through brain function.

You may have heard of Hebb's Law (1949) which in essence states that 'cells that fire together, wire together'. This is effectively a description of neuroplasticity and a succinct description of what's called associative learning (more of that later) and the work of Eric Kandel and his sea slugs helped to explain some of the 'firing' together principle.

Hebbian theory seeks to describe how once a new connection has been established it becomes a stronger, faster and more efficient connection the more frequently that connection is 'refreshed'. So in order to learn anything vaguely 'sticky' you need to go over learning again and again – those connections need to be revisited until the cells 'wire' together.

Long-term potentiation is described as the increase in the strength and speed of nerve impulses along pathways which have been used previously. It seems that once a neural pathway has been established there are numerous mechanisms in place to make sure that nerve impulses become transmitted more effectively.

Did you know that fat is good for your brain and one of the mechanisms for long-term potentiation? Not only do the cells wire together but they also start to transmit information more efficiently thanks to fat. Our brains need fat and people who are significantly malnourished perform worse on cognitive tasks than those who are well fed. You get energy from fat but your brain also uses fatty phospholipid proteins to insulate your neurons with a *myelin* sheath so that less electrical energy is wasted – a bit like lagging your hot water pipes. As you learn something and neurons start connecting, the fatty sheath covering the long axons of your neurons allow the messages to pass along the axons from one neuron to another more quickly.

At a cellular learning level, rather than at a person-centred level, there is some new research indicating that Donald Hebb's law may have to be revisited. Hebb's Law explains learning that takes place by modifying the strength and speed of signals across the synapse (the gap between neurons). This new research suggests adaptive learning may also take place in several dendrites near to the neuron and this is a type of faster, nodal learning (Bar-Ilan University, 2018). This is related to the way learning has been modelled in machine learning. However, whilst potentially groundbreaking in the neuroscience field, this level of deep complexity is highly unlikely to impact on what we do in the world of work or education. It's a great example of how neuroscience is making new discoveries all the time and perhaps in the future might influence how we train people but it's hard to see the implications at this point.

Wiring patterns

All these neurons connecting up form wiring patterns. Nobody has the same wiring patterns as anyone else but there are similarities as to what may get wired and where. Experiments with visual illusions show that particular brain areas are specifically wired, in most people, to recognize faces versus other objects.

This famous illusion of the vase and faces lights up a particular set of neurons in your visual recognition pathway when you see the face but as soon as you see the vase an entirely different set of neurons lights up (see Figure 4.2). So almost everyone uses generally similar areas for recognizing faces but each person will have their own specific configuration for specific faces. John Medina in his book *Brain Rules* (2008) talks about a man having surgery on his brain who had a specific neuron that fired up whenever he saw a picture of Jennifer Aniston. Clearly we don't all have a neuron for Jennifer Aniston in the same place in our heads (in fact you may not even have heard of Jennifer Aniston) but most people have a generally similar area of their brain that is particular for recognizing human faces. Your own experiences and learning define which specific wiring patterns you have but you'll find the general pattern and the structures are similar to mine.

Figure 4.2   A visual illusion – what do you see?

Evidence from working with stroke patients has contributed enormously to our knowledge of how neuroplasticity enables us to create new patterns if old ones become unusable. Whilst it isn't always possible to regain a skill or function after a stroke people can 'learn' to use different neural pathways to achieve the same outcome but they need to work hard to establish those new wiring patterns.

Structures for learning

Almost all of the brain is implicated in learning in some way. However, one structure that will come up again and again is the *hippocampus*. This is because it's so important for memory and you'll explore this in more detail in Chapter 9. It's also a relatively unusual part of the adult brain because it seems capable of neurogenesis, ie creating new neurons – something that used to be thought of as impossible.

Your *frontal cortex* does all the heavy decision making and mental processing that lets you decide what you want to learn and lets you know you're learning. Of course you don't always decide what you're going to learn, or even that you will learn, but if you're making conscious decisions this is the part of the brain that's helping you.

Different parts of your *sensory cortex* and the *motor cortex* are vital whether you're learning skills or information and we'll cover them in more detail in Chapter 6 on the senses.

The *limbic system* and particularly the *amygdala* are vital to many types of learning because of the role of emotions in learning. If you do nothing else after reading this book but include emotions in your training, even for technical topics, you'll already have gone a long way to help your learners.

You also need to pay attention when you're learning so your *reticular activating system*, *superior colliculus*, *parietal cortex* and the *cingulate gyrus* will all have a part to play.

You'll come across all these areas in future chapters so, for now, take note of their names and functions so that your attentional systems will pick them up later on.

Structural changes in your brain take place as you learn partly because the number of synaptic connections are increased. Darwin himself noticed that some areas of wild animals' brains were 15–30 per cent bigger than in tame animals; presumably, wild animals have to learn more to stay alive than tame ones who can just lie back and relax. Professional violinists have a larger motor cortex in the area of fine movement control than less musically gifted people. And there's the well documented case of London taxicab drivers who have done 'The Knowledge' (a special test of all the roads in London) who have larger hippocampi than London bus drivers who follow a prescribed route and therefore don't need to learn all the roads. You'll meet the taxi drivers' brains again in this book because they are so famous.

Brainpower

Learning is a physical set of changes in your brain that includes synthesizing new proteins, releasing neurotransmitters, and changing your neurons to generate new connections. You may also have to break down previous connections and you do all this whilst you're still using some brainpower to breathe, to sit up straight and to pay attention to the person next to you. It's hard work and it needs energy.

A psychology professor, Paul E Gold, and his colleagues E McNay and T Fries (2000) measured levels of glucose in rats learning to navigate mazes and found that the energy reserves in their hippocampi alone were depleted by as much as 30 per cent. This energy drain was worse when the task became harder and when the rats were older rats rather than young rats.

Learning is hard work and we are inherently energy conscious; you don't want to use up precious resources in making changes in your brain unless you have to. So you've really got to be motivated to want to learn something new, either consciously or unconsciously, because otherwise you might waste resources that could be put to better use elsewhere.

Types of learning

Now you've considered some of the biological basis of learning you might find it helpful to also consider what types of learning you might be doing or what types of learning you're expecting of your learners. Sometimes you might come across ideas from neuroscience that can seem contradictory but if you know what sort of learning you're expecting it may help you assess which ideas will work better in your situation.

As you've seen, learning is a complex task and there have been numerous theories and masses of research about learning over the years, all of which continue to be debated and new ideas regularly supersede old ones.

Early psychological theories of behaviourism gave us some helpful models of learning that are still useful but couldn't explain everything, and then towards the end of the 20th century cognitive psychology appeared to come to help explain some anomalies that behaviourism couldn't handle, particularly around motivation. Cognitive psychology takes an approach that is more related to information processing and acknowledges the importance of mental states rather than just focusing on behaviour.

More recently the study of brain biology has added extra data about the physical changes to our brains as we learn; some of this is classed as neuroeducation. This approach, of which you've covered some principles already, focuses on how neurons link, how you create neuronal networks and pathways and create long-term changes in your brain.

As mentioned before, most biological studies on learning are done looking at animals, people with damaged brains or how children and young people learn and there is far less research done on the biology of normal adult learning. However, with the increasingly ageing population there's now a lot more work on older brains and memory which of course links back to learning. Unfortunately, there is still a significant gap as to how learning happens in the world of work, which is where our interests lie, so mainly we have to extrapolate from other research as to what might be going on for adults learning at work.

As a rule behavioural psychologists divide learning into two basic types: associative and non-associative learning.

Non-associative learning

Non-associative learning is when a stimulus becomes associated with a particular response. It's usually relatively unconscious and it's not what you would normally plan in the sorts of conscious learning we tend to do at work. But, you can be sure people will be doing some unconscious learning.

Non-associative learning is further divided into habituation and sensitization.

Habituation is when you learn to get used to something; when the stimulus fails to evoke its natural response any more. For instance, if you show a stuffed owl to a songbird it will normally go into defensive mode but if the stuffed owl is left there long enough and nothing bad happens the songbird gets used to it and goes about its normal business. You will have experienced this for yourself – if at first you found working in an open plan office very distracting because of the other phone calls or people walking past, but now you don't notice what's going on around you – you've become habituated to it. This doesn't feel like learning but it is. The question to ask yourself as a trainer is, are there things that you've habituated your learners to that are adding to or subtracting from their learning? Your reticular activating system quickly stops paying attention to anything that isn't new or novel so that amazing set of inspiring quotes that you've had painted on your training room walls soon has no more impact than the dull magnolia paint you had before.

Sensitization is just as important a type of learning because it's when the stimulus creates an amplified response. Neuronal connections are set up so that they fire again and again and start to drag in other pathways such as attentional system. It could well be something you do without even being aware of it. I remember a trainer I worked with who, in attempting not to alienate any of his audience, managed to alienate and completely distract me from the subject in hand. He almost always used the phrase 'does that make sense?' rather than 'do you see what I mean?', 'how does that sound?' or any other number of phrases. The first few times I heard him say 'does that make sense?' I thought it seemed rather clever and thought I might use it myself. However, after working with him for a few days I became sensitized to it and every time he said it I could feel myself become tense and annoyed.

'Why, oh why doesn't he change his phrase?' I'd think and of course the more annoying it became the more I listened out for it and my response was amplified. We all have our own tics, habits and pet phrases that may be causing sensitization in our learners and this could well be distracting them from the topic. Or you may have become sensitized to something learners do unwittingly and may overreact, such as the 100th time you hear 'But my boss sent me'.

Associative learning – classical and operant conditioning

The most famous example of learning through classical conditioning is that of Ivan Pavlov, a Russian physiologist, who took the natural response of dogs to a stimulus, ie to salivate when they ate, and taught them to have the same response when they heard a completely unrelated stimulus, a bell. Eventually the dogs salivated when they heard the bell as readily as when they ate. This type of learning happens all the time without us necessarily being consciously aware of it but it can be used to consciously help people learn if there's already a stimulus/response pathway in place that can be moulded.

Phobias are a good example of classical conditioning – often we fear things because there was once a stimulus paired with an unpleasant experience. If you're seriously afraid of spiders the chances are that as a child you spent time with an adult with a strong fear of spiders. As a child you came to associate that person's fear, which as a child is a scary experience in itself, with the stimulus of the spider. Phobias such as fear of public speaking (apparently significant numbers of people fear it more than death) can be cured by classical conditioning too. People are taken through a series of experiences where they learn to relax in presentation situations until they present confidently. You can teach people to create useful associations so that when they encounter a frequently occurring stimulus they automatically think of the new learning. On one of our 'Train the Trainer' programmes we teach people to associate chocolate with brain function so that every time they see chocolate they start thinking about what's going on in people's brains.

Operant conditioning is another form of associative learning, first described by B F Skinner – it's sometimes called Skinnerian conditioning. Skinner proposed that learning happens as a result of reward or punishment for particular behaviours; there is a consequence of behaving in a particular way that reinforces or decreases that behaviour. Gamification uses many of the attributes of operant conditioning such as using rewards to change your behaviour in the game.

Cognitive psychology, information processing and motivation to learn

None of this learning really helps though with learning about information which is where cognitive psychology came in and began to look at learning as information processing. It's no coincidence that it arose at a similar time to the growing interest in computers and information technology.

Cognitive psychology also looks at our motivations for learning rather than it being a pure stimulus response procedure. Much of what we learn at work in a formal sense is about information; even when we're learning about soft skills there's usually a significant theoretical component to learn, such as models of leadership. Whilst you can learn to communicate effectively by observing and practising communication skills almost all training programmes at work require us to learn some new fact, name, model or concept.

There are also other skills you learn at work that take more cognitive processing, like how to use the latest IT system, how to program a computer, how to use the coffee machine. These all require us to learn new information, transform it from short-term to long-term memory and then hang on to and use that information for as long as we need it.

Learned helplessness

Another type of learning that can explain some types of behaviour is learned helplessness. Researchers discovered that animals that felt powerless to escape from electric shocks eventually learned just to stand and receive them even when they could actually escape to a nonshock area. They had learned to be helpless.

This is a terrible thing to do to your learners but I think it happens regularly in the real world. You get sent on a course, don't know why you've gone, nobody is interested when you come back and you then get asked just to get on with the job. At first you try, you show interest and want to implement the new techniques you've learned but you don't get the chance. Then it happens again and you question whether it's the right course for you but you get sent anyway and still nobody takes any notice of your new ideas. Eventually as you go through the third change process in your organization you learn not to ask questions or show any initiative but just to do what they tell you, attend the course and come back to work. As a trainer this is your worst nightmare – the people who say 'I was sent' when you ask why they are at your workshop. This is effectively learned helplessness. Effective Learning and Development teams do their best to make sure they're not instilling learned helplessness in their participants.

Unlearning is just as important as learning

As part of your normal process of learning you also occasionally need to unlearn; we become overwhelmed if we learn and remember everything. There was a case described by A Luria in his book *The Mind of a Mnemonist: A little book about a vast memory* (1987) of a patient who couldn't forget what he'd learned which meant that he struggled with simple tasks like reading a passage because he couldn't filter out what was important. Information swamped him. It seems that the process of learning and forgetting or unlearning may be a complex balance between two proteins in the brain: adducin which stimulates the growth of synaptic connections and the musashi protein which inhibits the stabilization of connections. In our current world where the pace of change seems to accelerate constantly we need to learn and unlearn far faster than was required in the past. Possibly we need to retain less 'knowledge' but need to learn more agile learning skills so we can adapt rapidly.

New ideas on learning

More recently cognitive psychology is being challenged with concepts like embodied cognition. Cognitive psychology places the emphasis on what happens in your brain whereas embodied cognition is beginning to look at the connections between the brain and the body when you're learning and there are some fascinating studies on how our bodies might have effects on our brains we'd never considered.

But what we're really interested in is finding practical applications of all this theory to the real world of learning design, training, teaching, coaching and facilitating learning. Neuroscience has not got to the stage yet where it can say that any particular type of training/learning/coaching/facilitating is definitely the right way so it's often a case of continuing to do what works but taking into account what the research is suggesting.

Things that seem to be considered genuinely useful both from the neuroscience and the practice of learning are:

- repetition;
- spaced learning;
- smaller group learning;
- reward;
- emotional and physical state.

You'll possibly not be particularly surprised by any of them because good training has always included these ideas but at least we're now getting evidence to base our good practice on. You'll come across all of these through the rest of the book.

Other Voices

Sue Daly, *Resolution for Change, UK*

Using 3D in Brain Friendly Learning

Something that struck me entering my first Brain Friendly Learning environment was how interesting it looked from the outset. Not only were the usual paper and pens, sweets, toys and reference books on display, there was also an extensive gallery of relevant and illustrated quotes, articles and case studies – to read straight away and/or at leisure during the rest of the event. I was particularly impressed by the small potted plants – a homely touch – and some helium balloons suspended from the ceiling. The pile of jumbo Lego bricks in the corner also piqued my curiosity – this was certainly not going to be any ordinary training course!

Since that first experience of Brain Friendly Learning I have attended many events, facilitated by different trainers, and always come away with new and creative ideas to enhance the experience of my own learners. All of them fit in somehow to Colin Rose's MASTER model of accelerated learning, and magically your learning environment is transformed from the two dimensions used by flipcharts, PowerPoint and handouts to a much more engaging 3D world.

Some of my favourites include:

- Substituting pictures with small models/toys to represent key ideas.
- Availability of objects/stationery/craft materials so participants can 'construct' their ideas in a more creative way.
- Masking tape on the floor to create a framework for activities such as the customer journey in customer service sessions, or the questioning

funnel in communication modules. (In fact masking tape can be used in many ways to generate movement – horizontally or vertically – for processes and to demonstrate business models.)

- Using the environment – especially outdoors if available and weather permitting – for participants to collect (or walk you to) the items which for them signify an element of their learning.
- Use of laminated cards, each with a key piece of information, hidden in the working space to create a treasure hunt and subsequent discussion.

Which brings me back to the balloons: each balloon was carrying a laminated card with information about the model, and participants were asked to arrange the information on the cards in a logical process. This simple and creative approach embraced all elements of the MASTER model:

Motivating minds by arousing curiosity and creating a different environment.

Absorbing information through the senses of sight, touch, hearing.

Sense was made of the information through body/physical, visual/ spatial, interpersonal, linguistic, logical/mathematical intelligences.

Trigger memory – every time I see helium balloons I remember that event.

Exhibit learning – we were able to use the balloons to recreate the mnemonic later.

Review to Retain – the balloons were a constant reminder over three days of the MASTER model.

Working with a model of learning

Brain Friendly Learning – a model

Whatever theories you subscribe to about learning it's fairly clear that it's a process of changes happening in the brain that usually affects behaviour and thus performance. There are multiple models of learning and I'm going to introduce you to an extension of a tried and tested model that blends with the neuroscience and therefore gets you thinking about how you design training which makes learning easier for your learners and improves results. The extended model is called Brain Friendly Learning or sometimes Brain Friendly Training. I prefer the 'learning' version as learning is about what is going on in your brain whereas training is something that is done to you. Some people don't find the name particularly helpful which is a fair enough comment, but it's found its way into the public domain and all models have to have a name of some sort. This framework will influence some of the subsequent chapters in the book which is why I want to introduce it here as a way of navigating and providing a structure.

Imagine a bridge with two pillars. One pillar is represented by a brain and this is the neuroscience you've been reading about that underpins learning. The other pillar is represented by a light bulb and is the creativity that you as a trainer can exhibit but it also represents the creativity of learners in creating their own learning. The final part of the bridge is the overarching span of the bridge and that's the learning process (see Figure 4.3).

The learning process model is one you may already be familiar with: Colin Rose's model of Accelerated Learning (Rose, 1998). If it is then you can skip this overview and go on to the next chapters to dive in deeper. If you don't know it then read on. There are other models of learning and indeed of Accelerated Learning and they are all useful. However, in a survey we did of other models we found this to be the most popular and best known amongst training practitioners in the UK. (NB: it was a small and limited sample size so definitely wouldn't count as a scientifically accurate or valid survey.)

The model has been well researched and adapted in the light of research but like many models doesn't necessarily have a direct correlation with specific biological models. However, it's a useful framework to hang ideas from and to begin to consider different aspects of neuroscience in relation to it.

Before you start on the model I think it's useful to share my biggest criticism of the Accelerated Learning model, which is its name. It implies that learning can be faster whereas clearly learning takes time. It also gives the impression to those who are interested in the results rather than the methodology that they may be about to get more content covered in less time but they will be sadly disappointed. Learning is not usually an instant process as you've already heard and it's our role as learning professionals to begin to educate the sponsors, managers or other people who ask for 'training' about how genuine learning is totally different to information delivery (back to those Valentine's cards).

Colin Rose's MASTER model goes something like this:

Motivate minds

First of all you need to want to learn – there's got to be a reason for you to change because all that energy required for neurons to reconfigure

Figure 4.3   The bridge model of Brain Friendly Learning

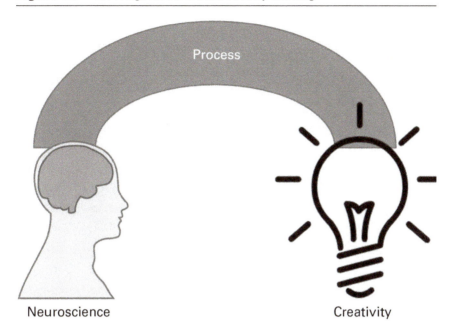

Neuroscience   Creativity

themselves is going to tire you out. You need to want to do it and be in the appropriate physical and mental state to be able to learn. You'll read more about the neuroscience of motivating learners in the Chapter 5.

Absorb information

Once you know you want to learn you can start to pay attention to the information to learn and start absorbing it. Most information about the world gets into our brains through our senses, though we clearly also build on other information that is already in our heads from previous experiences. Either way there's information that needs dealing with and in the chapters on attention and sensory information you'll uncover more about these processes.

Search for meaning

Once information is inside your head, how can you make sense of it? Rose builds on the work of Howard Gardner's 'multiple intelligences' (2011) which provides another valuable framework for designing and delivering learning interventions in the real world. There's a bit more controversy to be unearthed here but as I said right at the beginning of this book science moves forward by a process of hypothesizing, testing and critiquing. Many people, including me, find Gardner's work to be surprisingly easy to apply practically.

Trigger memory

Having processed information you're going to have to remember it when you need it so how does memory work? What makes information of any sort memorable and how do you tap into people's memories to help them? After all, it seems that 80 per cent of information is forgotten about 24 hours later if you believe what Hermann Ebbinghaus had to say way back in the 1880s and this is one piece of research that's been well replicated. You'll find out more about him and much more about memory in a later chapter.

Exhibit learning

How do people know they've learned anything and how do you as a trainer/designer know they've learned anything? You need to check they've got the right end of the stick and it helps them feel more confident to test out their new skills if they've got safe opportunities to practise and test their learning. Remember when a new neuron connects it's a weak connection – you're trying to strengthen the connection by encouraging active recall, repetition and strong positive emotional links so that people will be inclined to keep their new habit rather than revert back to the safe old one with the nice strong connection. In Chapter 11 on reviewing, you'll delve into some more neuroscience and end up with lots of practical ways to help your learners test their own learning.

Review to retain

One of the biggest challenges in organizational learning is making sure people retain and use what they learn from meetings, at training courses, through learning technologies and on the job.

It's been consistently shown that spaced repetition seems to enhance learning. Over time we need to repeat new information, behaviours, activities so that those bonds between neurons are strong, and the chapter on reviewing will provide insights as to what's happening in our heads and how you can ensure learning sticks back at work.

There are other ideas that sit around the edges of this model that also affect learning so you'll consider them and the neuroscience that fits around them as you read through the rest of the book.

Summary

What you need to remember from this chapter:

- Learning takes place at a cellular level, uses up resources, neurotransmitters, and glucose in connecting neurons and building neural networks.
- Learning is not the same as delivering content – it's a process that takes place over time in people's heads and bodies.
- There are different types of learning and when you're designing, training, teaching or getting other people to work or behave differently it pays to be aware of what sort of change you're looking for.
- Brain Friendly Learning is a framework encompassing neuroscience, a model of learning and some creativity.
- Use the MASTER model as a process to design and deliver effective training – tie it into the neuroscience for a rigorous look at learning.

References and further reading

Bar-Ilan University (2018) The brain learns completely differently than we've assumed since the 20th century, *NeuroscienceNews*, 23 March 2018, http://neurosciencenews.com/brain-learning-8677/ (archived at perma.cc/RCH7-5G2Y/)

Gardner, H (2011) *Frames of Mind: The Theory of Multiple Intelligences*, Basic Books, New York

Hebb, D (2002) *The Organization of Behavior*, L Erlbaum Associates, Mahwah, NJ

Luria, A (1987) *The Mind of a Mnemonist: A little book about a vast memory*, Basic Books, New York

McNay, E, Fries, T and Gold, P (2000) Decreases in rat extracellular hippocampal glucose concentration associated with cognitive demand during a spatial task, *Proceedings of the National Academy of Sciences*, **97** (6), pp 2881–85

Mayford, M, Siegelbaum, S and Kandel, E (2012) Synapses and memory storage, *Cold Spring Harbor Perspectives in Biology*, **4** (6), a005751

Medina, J (2008) *Brain Rules: 12 principles for surviving and thriving at work, home and school*, Pear Press, Seattle WA

Rose, C (1998) *Accelerated Learning for the 21st Century: The six-step plan to unlocking your mastermind*, Bantam Doubleday Dell, New York

Skinner, B F [Online] http://www.simplypsychology.org/operant-conditioning.html (archived at perma.cc/KZ6F-7EBY)

Motivating learners from curiosity to persistence

05

'When you're smiling...'

Did you know that smiling really changes what's going on in your brain? When I was studying psychology back in the 1980s one of my favourite hypotheses was one from William James in the 19th century that suggested that you didn't smile because you were happy but when you smiled you felt happy. He suggested it may be true of all physical manifestations of emotions; that they were the cause of the emotion as much as the result. If that was so then surely it becomes quite easy to be happy because all you have to do is smile to feel happy. Whilst clearly our emotions are complex and multifaceted, neuroscience has caught up with William James and seems to show he had a point.

You may have already heard that if you put a pen between your teeth to mimic the effect of a smile you'll rate cartoons as funnier than if you don't have a pen between your teeth.

People who are smiling see other people's frowns as less severe and when they're frowning they see other people's smiles as less happy. A recent study at City University London took EEG measurements in parts of the brain that recognize faces, like the angular gyrus, associative visual cortex and the somatosensory cortex, which are particularly active when those faces are emotional rather than neutral. They found that the EEG response was strengthened when people wearing a neutral expression looked at smiling faces. When people who were smiling looked at smiling and neutral faces their activity was increased. The scientists suggested that when you smile, your brain, at least partially, interprets someone else's neutral face as smiling as well. So perhaps this is the neurological evidence for the old song 'When you're smiling the whole world smiles with you!'

Motivated learners

What gets you out of bed in the morning? What is happening in your brain that drives enough motivation to give you the energy to overcome the inertia of lying in bed and to physically stand up, go and put the kettle on, shower, have breakfast, shave or put your makeup on, get dressed, walk the dog, walk to the end of the road, get on the bus or train, drive 40 miles, go into the office or factory and brightly say 'Good morning everyone' before spending a day doing some kind of work?

You're going to notice a theme in this book which is that learning happens in learners' heads and not in the trainer's head; though of course most great teachers say they learn as much from their pupils as their pupils learn from them. If you're truly helping others to learn it seems it's almost impossible not to learn something yourself.

People can learn things when they are demotivated but it's less likely to happen and they are more inclined to learn the stuff that you're not particularly interested in them learning, like how to disrupt a room or how to download a new app to their phone. People who are motivated to learn are going to learn faster, more effectively and for the longer term than those who have merely shown up. But, as you've already seen, learning isn't a 'once and it's done' activity and effective learning takes many different forms and needs a variety of different mind states.

This chapter will focus on what's happening in people's brains when they are in different states that help them learn; and more practically you'll think about how you can help people get into that state – what you as a designer or facilitator of learning can do to maximize the chance that people will be at maximum receptivity for the wonderful information, ideas, attitude changes or skills that you plan to share with them and that they can turn into new habits, behaviours or thoughts (see Figure 5.1 for a visual guide to the chapter).

You'll explore some more about *curiosity* in this chapter – you had a taster in Chapter 1. You'll find out how to make people *feel alert and pay attention* in a more detailed look at attention in Chapter 7. Perhaps you might find some of your ideas *challenged*, which is a useful learning state in itself. You'll uncover some ways to create that feeling of slight concern, without overwhelming people with enormous *stress* which is less helpful as a learning state.

Figure 5.1 Motivated learners

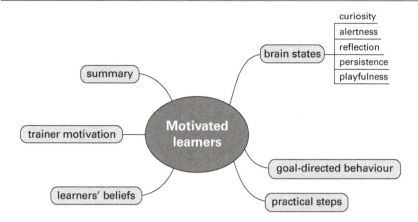

To balance all that curiosity and challenge you may have learners who need to be less on alert; they may need to decrease some of their stress responses and you'll consider what you can do to *make people feel more relaxed*.

What happens when people want to *reflect*. They need to do that to learn and you'll start the journey into reflection when you read Chapter 11. In this chapter you'll hear about some ways to create *exploratory*, *playful* and *experimental* states which will be covered in more depth in Chapter 12.

There's something about *persistence* that's vital for learning so let's see what happens in people's heads when they are being persistent and how you can help them to persist at activities to help them learn.

At no stage would you expect people to be in all these states at once but over the course of a learning session it might be useful for them to experience many of them.

This is not a chapter on motivation per se but a chapter on how to motivate people and their brains to learn; in the process you're sure to read some things you've heard before. If it's all familiar then skip on to the next chapter that is motivating for you; if it's new or there are new elements that you've not thought of before then notice what's keeping you reading.

Brain states

Let's explore some different states your brain can be in that help you learn and how to stimulate those states.

Curiosity killed the cat

Why is curiosity such a great thing for learning? Clearly if it did kill the cat then it isn't a very useful state because death tends to curb the learning process but perhaps that particular old wives' tale also goes with the one about cats having nine lives. Cats and people are curious and when you help people become curious about something they will seek out answers for themselves. Those answers are going to stick with them longer than any answer you hand them on a plate. Let's explore why.

What happens in your brain when you're curious?

Researchers at California Institute of Technology used fMRI scanning to see that curiosity seems to activate the caudate, a part of the brain associated with anticipated reward (Kang *et al*, 2009). People were prepared to spend their own experimental resources to find out answers when they were more curious about the information and were more likely to remember the answer to a question they were curious about than one they weren't.

Curiosity increases with uncertainty (up to a point), suggesting that a small amount of knowledge can pique curiosity and prime our hunger for knowledge in the same way that the smell or look of food can cause us to feel hungry even if we weren't before. The dopamine that is released as you seek the answer is of course rewarding.

So if people feel rewarded when they are curious and remember things better it seems a good idea to increase curiosity levels. So what can you do?

Agatha Christie and dopamine levels

If the number of murder mystery series and detective novels is anything to go by then people really enjoy a sense of mystery or suspense. You probably already know that stories are great for learners but sometimes it's very easy to tell a story chronologically and go from beginning to end.

Agatha Christie was a British author renowned for her mystery stories; you may be a fan of Miss Marple or Hercule Poirot on TV or film and you may have even read her books which keep you guessing right up to the end as to who did the murder and it's almost impossible to guess who it was. Have you ever thought about how she wrote them?

Instead of plotting out her story and knowing from the beginning who the murderer was she would write the story without even knowing herself. She wrote the story so that everyone could have done the murder and just like her own detectives she didn't know until the last chapter. Once she'd written everything but the last chapter she'd decide who'd done the deadly deed and then write that final chapter. Sometimes she'd have to go back and rework a few areas but on the whole she'd leave the original chapters as they were. This may be one of the reasons her books and the programmes are so addictive; that dopamine is floating around in your head as you keep wondering.

In a real-life mystery some research reported on the BBC and in *The Times* suggested a study had been done to measure neurotransmitter levels as people read Agatha Christie but no reliable published data is available to explain where these reports came from. I told you earlier on that sometimes you have to be sceptical about what you read even when it appears to prove your lovely theory. As it stands it appears nobody knows whether Agatha Christie's mysteries do actually raise neurotransmitter levels – but they clearly motivate many people to keep reading.

Robert Cialdini, one of the world's experts on influence, has also studied the power of mystery in presenting information to people. If you read his books or are lucky enough to sit in his classes he invariably tells you something curious and then asks you to think about what would make people act in that way. Once that question is in your head and you're hooked he can start to unravel the events leading up to the mystery.

What you can do to increase curiosity in your learners

Send something to engage people in the days/weeks prior to a more formal learning event whether that's a face-to-face session or a digital experience; send a themed invitation; articles/reading to review; short online questionnaires; puzzles/quizzes linked to the learning content; videos are usually a hit – the possibilities are endless!

1 Send curiosity-inducing prework – a colleague of mine once sent his participants joining information that included a £10 note and an instruction to go and buy a cushion of their choice. As you may imagine people arrived feeling very curious.

2 Send small 'taster' amounts of information to stimulate curiosity.

3 Asking questions sets off a set of neuronal connections and interconnections as your brain attempts to find answers so ask questions to stimulate thinking and get people curious about what they want to learn.

4 Remember we talked about guessing in Chapter 1 – ask people to guess the answers to your questions, even if they don't think they know.

5 Use questionnaires to motivate people to find out more about a topic or to find out more about themselves.

Raising curiosity levels through the roof – but look out for the backfire

Paul Wright, a great trainer friend who sadly died a few years ago, ran an exercise to show how you could use music when learning communication skills. He wanted us to experiment so decided not to tell us what the outcome of the exercise was but asked us to take turns communicating using simple percussion instruments. I was curious so I happily participated and trusted that it would all become clear in the end. Unfortunately for Paul his great idea to raise curiosity and experimentation backfired with Helen who partnered me. She wasn't curious and wanting to experiment but instead was stuck and frustrated because she couldn't see the point of what we were doing. She was increasing her stress hormones, adrenaline and cortisol and that interfered with her learning because she just couldn't let it go and explore. Eventually Paul had to tell her what the purpose was.

The point of this story is to illustrate how it's impossible to guess what might go on in a learner's head. All you can do is create the conditions that might work and then watch out for what does result. If you find you've created a state you hadn't anticipated then you may have to counterbalance it or think about how to change the state.

Attention and relaxation

Relaxing learners and reducing fear

When our brains are operating at high alert we are prepared for fight, flight, freeze and flock but our frontal cortices are not ready for rational thinking and information processing. There is an intricate balance between sufficient and insufficient stress which is sometimes called eustress and you'll find out more about that in Chapter 7 on attention. Here you'll focus on what you can do to reduce unhelpful stress, and in Chapter 7 you'll consider more about what keeps people at a helpful state of alertness to provoke learning.

Many people find training makes them nervous, bringing back unpleasant memories of school or other poor training experiences. Any of us can start some training feeling stressed or overwhelmed potentially because of something completely unrelated to the training. So with those people you need to reduce any high levels of cortisol and adrenaline and prevent their limbic systems, and particularly the amygdala, from dominating over the frontal cortex and preventing rational thought. Some people find technology alienating because they're not used to it.

Some of the simple things that you can do get lost in the pressure of delivering content so here are some ideas to bear in mind before you consider content.

Connect people

Social isolation has been shown to have the same effects on our brain as physical pain and can cause it to release its own opiates: endorphins. Research in mice also indicates that social isolation may reduce brain myelination which is vital to brain plasticity and therefore learning. (You'll find more about myelination in Chapter 11 about reflecting and reviewing.)

If you wouldn't hit a participant to cause physical pain, why would you let them feel socially isolated?
You can reduce social isolation by connecting with people yourself before, during and after they start learning. You can do this in really simple ways like sending personalized invitations to training events; include photos of the trainers or the other people who've participated. Take a leaf out of marketing's book and create a 'learning lifestyle' that people will want to emulate, friends they'll want to be with when they start some training, even if it's a webinar or digital learning. Make people feel this is the 'place' to be. Think how well apps include 'social' tools such as 'like' or 'forward' to increase social engagement.

Use social media as part of your strategy for connecting people and increasing their opportunities to learn. You'll probably have to work within the confines of your own organizational policies, or your clients' social media policies but, where you can use it, social media is an effective way of helping people to connect before, during and after a learning event.

In the first edition of this book in 2016 Massive Open Online Courses (MOOCs) were probably the fastest growing social way of learning, especially in the further education sector. The Open University invested hugely in this social learning phenomenon and in June 2015 became the record-holder for the biggest single run of an online course (Stansbury, 2015); more than 400,000 learners enrolled from over 150 countries on one of its English Language courses. MOOCs are online courses with unlimited participation and open access via the web and are still evolving as learning, education and business models change. A report from 2018 (Shah, 2018) suggests they will continue to be an important part of the family of digital learning. They are known for generating enormous numbers at enrolment, though completion rates are still notoriously much poorer than other educational tools. Which helps to make the point that motivation needs to be maintained throughout a learning journey – it's not good enough just at the start.

Reduce the possibility of obvious stressors

Think about what it's like when you're attending a meeting or a training course and you're lost, late and didn't really want to be there in the first place. Suddenly your sense of direction goes, you can't remember the name of the venue and you start to panic. But what if you had a picture of the venue on the piece of paper clutched in your hand or on your mobile as well as just an address? And I don't mean the sort of picture the hotel will send out looking glitzy and glamorous; I mean a photo taken from the street showing the roadworks and the dingy building next door; one that looks exactly like what people will see as they walk up to the building or drive past it.

You'll hear more about language later but for now think about the language that will help reduce stress or frustration. There's a sales technique called 'feel, felt, found' which can be useful to consider when thinking about this. For example, 'I appreciate you *feel* frustrated about attending this Health and Safety training, when you've already covered some of the content before. Other people with your level of experience have also *felt* the same way. However, what they've *found* on the day is their knowledge really helped newer people in the organization, and of course legislation (*or something*) has moved on, so they did learn new stuff too.'

Some organizations take this very seriously and train everyone involved in the learning process how to work with learners or potential learners to reduce stress and increase motivation. This is about creating a culture of learning that goes beyond trainers or learning designers and extends out to the wider team. If you've designed a fantastic piece of e-learning or a marvellous classroom session and the person sending out the information isn't part of the learning culture they can inadvertently undermine all your hard work with an inappropriate comment or lack of care. It's like having a great salesperson who encourages you to buy a product but the person at the cash till makes you wait for ages whilst they finish a conversation with a colleague. I'm sure you've occasionally walked out of shops without the desired item because of a non-attentive shop assistant; that's not what you want in a learning culture. Take the time to make the receptionist, the administration team or other people with whom your learners come into contact part of your learning team.

What else makes people feel comfortable and reduces stress and social isolation?

Here's a quick checklist of things you could check as people arrive at face-to-face training to help reduce their stress levels. I have a colleague who calls this her 'one minute check' which she does as people arrive at her workshops – she doesn't check everything with everyone but it's a great checklist.

The information is gathered by close observation, active listening, or simply asking a question:

- whether people are in the right place;
- their name and how to pronounce it;
- whether there's an immediate need for the toilet or some refreshments;
- whether their journey's been stressful, so they need time to calm down;
- whether they're hot, cold, a smoker – so you'll need to know how to change the room temperature and what the smoking arrangements are;
- non-confidential personal and workplace details – which you can refer to as appropriate;
- where they're from – where they've travelled from which might have implications for their return journey, and what section/office/organization, etc;
- technology issues or fear of technology;
- voluntary or required attendance – particularly important if there's a group (or the whole group) who've been 'sent' to the learning;
- sensory, mobility or learning disability which you haven't been made aware of;
- particular concerns about the training content, eg giving a presentation to a group;
- potential dietary, medical or diversity needs, eg to eat, take medication or pray at regular times;
- individual experience, knowledge or skills which may contribute to others' learning.

Many of these ideas can be adopted to online, virtual classrooms too. In the *Webinars Pocketbook* Andy Lancaster and I adapt numerous ideas to a virtual learning environment.

Persistence

One of the big requirements in motivation is persistence. If someone is to learn something they need to persist at it and there are all sorts of ideas about how long you need to persist at something in order to learn it. You'll come across the 10,000 hours myth in the chapter on testing and practice.

What keeps you persisting at something though? What is it that will keep 'gamers' glued to their computers for hours on end, gamblers sitting at machines, or students poring over books. It seems a common factor is dopamine which is considered vitally important for motivation. It's not the only neurotransmitter involved though and it's not as simple as a pure stimulus response mechanism. It seems we are all affected by dopamine but it can be where and how it has its effect that might determine whether you persist at a task or choose to give up at a lower level of achievement.

Dopamine is usually associated with reward but it may be it has its most important effect before you actually get a reward; it encourages you to achieve a goal or to avoid something you don't like depending on where it's acting in your brain.

One study mapped the brains of 'go-getters' and 'slackers' and found increased levels of dopamine in both types of people; but for the slackers it was in the anterior insula, a part of the brain implicated in emotion and risk perception. The go-getters had higher dopamine levels in the prefrontal cortex and striatum both involved in goal-directed motivation. It may be that dopamine helps you with the cost–benefit analysis of a task rather than providing an actual reward itself.

One way to help you persist and increase the 'go-getter' type behaviour may be to set incremental goals, according to neurologist Judy Willis. By training yourself to feel rewarded at the end of a task you rewire the brain to produce dopamine and therefore give yourself a positive feedback as you meet the challenges and complete the series of goals you've set yourself.

Goal orientation: Extrinsic or intrinsic motivation

Carol Dweck (1986), a leading researcher on the science of motivation, suggests we have two sorts of goal orientation that may be important in learning: *goal-directed motivation*, which is about performance and may be more of an extrinsic motivator, and *learning orientation*, which is intrinsic and which ties into our motivations for mastery of a skill or topic.

Should you incentivize learners or let them find their own motivation?

There is now a huge amount of evidence to show that on the whole with tasks that are cognitively interesting, and learning ought to be, people are more motivated by intrinsic than extrinsic motivation. They are more inclined to persist at a task they are self-motivated to do than at one where there are external rewards for performance or goals are externally created. If you're interested to explore this in more detail then I'd recommend Daniel Pink's book *Drive* (2011) as a good starting point.

There is some evidence that schools are now considering increasing the level of learning goal orientation in preference to performance orientation but it's not universally adopted, and is it happening within organizations and businesses? We still persist with children and adults with providing rewards for when they've learned: 'If you do your revision you can watch television', 'if you pass your exams I'll pay for a holiday', 'if you go on this course you'll get a promotion'.

Instead of looking at what people can get if they do the learning we need to look at what will encourage people to engage in the learning for its own merit. Gaming culture is taking this concept forward by studying what keeps people persisting at tasks looking at it from the different viewpoints of cognition, design, motivation and rewards and also the technology. You'll briefly explore some of the ideas from gaming in Chapter 15 on the future of learning.

One of the features of learning orientation is an increase in the require-ment to experiment, test and be open to making mistakes – the stuff of creativity.

Exploratory and playful states – creative states

What part of your brain is it that helps you to be creative? You'll perhaps not be surprised to hear that there isn't one part that's identified as 'the creative part'; it's the complex interworking of different parts that enables you to have new thoughts and to consider wonderfully impossible things. The cortex is where you do your conscious as well as unconscious thinking.

The right cortex is more associated with holistic and intuitive processing which may be linked to creativity. However, the left side of your cortex also sorts and processes information so is required in all aspects of creativity too. The idea of a right-brained, creative person is a creative generalization derived from some genuine science about the brain's tendency to process information differently in each hemisphere and you've already considered how that myth may have come about in Chapter 3.

How can you help people be more playful and creative?

Breaking patterns is a great way to do this. Neurons are linked together as networks and patterns become strengthened with regular use – the more often you have a particular train of thought the easier and more automatic it becomes. This is incredibly useful when you need to do something regularly; for instance, the neuronal pattern that links the hole in the wall and the large wooden plank on hinges and allows you to shut the door without having to work out exactly how to do it each time. This tendency to create strong patterns is less helpful when you need to be creative – when you need to break out of the patterns of thinking and create new ways of thinking.

There's no such thing as a paper jelly, but as soon as you think about one your brain creates new patterns in your neuronal networks, new links and new possibilities. Research suggests slower alpha brainwaves are particularly dominant when you're feeling creative; you may remember that the beta waves are most active when you're alert and thinking hard.

A study at The Royal College of Music using neurofeedback seemed to help music students be more creative by stimulating theta waves and teaching them to access those waves more deliberately; those are the slow waves you get in light sleep and in dreaming.

In a training environment you're going to have trouble wiring people up to machines to stimulate their brains with particular waves so instead you've got to harness people's natural abilities to do this.

One way is to induce feelings of relaxation with a guided visualization and this can be particularly effective if you do it in those parts of the day, like after lunch, where people may be already inclined to feel drowsy. Another study seemed to indicate that you can increase the benefits of taking time out like this by drinking coffee just before having a short 15-minute nap or relaxation exercise. Caffeine has been shown to enhance cognitive performance and it takes about 15 minutes for the caffeine to kick in. So you take 15 minutes to have a pleasant alpha wave break, maybe even drifting into a theta brainwave break and then when you come out of that ready to be alert the caffeine is ready to give you an extra brain boost too.

You can easily find video clips or recordings of music and visual effects that will allegedly help you get into alpha and theta brain states but you'll probably also know how to stimulate your most creative thinking. You are also likely to find most other people will tell you the same sort of things. In a workshop on creativity I ran regularly for two years we found the most common answers to what makes you creative were daydreaming, walking, showering, taking a bath, running and 'when I'm not thinking about the problem'. Later in this book there are numerous references to creative thinking where you'll come across some more practical ideas.

If we go back to thinking about creative thinking being the opportunity to create new pathways then it's important to keep the brain plastic by regularly exposing yourself to new experiences, new places, new people and new ideas. If you need learners to be more creative then expose them to new things too.

Other Voices

Nikki Ayles, *Independent Capability Development Consultant*

Of Dendrites and Positivity

The power of positive emotions to broaden perception and scope of attention has been explored by Barbara Fredrickson through her 'Broaden-and-Build theory' (2001). Barbara describes how 10 positive emotions of joy, serenity, amusement, awe, pride, gratitude, interest, inspiration, hope, and love are like tiny engines for growth. Just as a waterlily expands its petals outwards to take in more rays from the sun and grow, so positive emotions drive our brains to open, taking in a broader variety of information, moving towards new possibilities, ideas and alternative explanations. In one study supporting this theory, brain-imaging researchers found that *only* when participants were in a positive emotional state, was neural activity present in parts of the brain responsible for registering global components of a test picture (Fredrickson, 2001). Positivity had literally given participants a wider perceptual field of view.

This and similar findings hold exciting implications for the training room. The more positivity learners feel, the more open their minds and the more opportunities they should perceive for applying learnings to their own situations/jobs – a yardstick for measuring any training's 'stickiness'.

Even more thought-provoking is pairing the findings of cognitive neuroscientist Mark Beeman with those of Ronald Friedman and Jens Förster (2005) to take this idea further. Using EEG and fMRI scans, Beeman and co. found that when solving problems using insight (involving thinking broadly and openly rather than using narrow analytical strategies) there was greater activation in the right hemisphere (RH) of the brain than the left (LH). Beeman explains this phenomenon has a neural basis: pyramidal neurons (brain cells) collect information through their dendrites (branches). Dendrites in the right side of the brain are more numerous, further from the cell body and make more connections (synapses) with other neurons, than those in the left hemisphere. The left hemisphere's shorter dendrites seem incredibly adept at accessing and pulling in 'close-to-hand' information to solve problems quickly. The activation is strong, but narrow. This has evolutionary significance, since, if our ancestors were facing attack from a sabre-toothed tiger, sitting around pontificating the many ways to escape would be a sure-fire way to become the tiger's next meal! Survival was dependent on our ability to access and focus on immediate and dominant problem solutions. This strategy is less effective when addressing problems that require us to look for the non-obvious. For example, in order for learners to get to grips with application of new concepts, they often need to abandon well-learned and automatically generated assumptions. This is where activation of the right hemisphere is valuable. Beeman and co.'s research showed RH activation is weaker, but critically also broader. RH dendrites have a larger input field, 'reaching out' further into the brain to access more remotely associated information, locate alternative interpretations of stimuli and to make more novel connections.

So then, if we as trainers could stimulate activation of learners' RH neurons, this could be valuable in promoting openness to new ideas presented, broader approaches to workshop exercises and self-generation of more extensive applications for learnings. But how to do this?

We loop back to positivity. An intriguing study (the mouse maze experiment) by Ronald Friedman and Jens Förster induced one group of participants to feel negative emotions through anticipation of and focus on a negative outcome to a situation (avoidance-related motivation); another group was induced to expect and focus on a positive outcome (approach-related motivation) and a third control group was placed into a neutral state with little emotional arousal. After this 'priming', all participants undertook tests requiring either creativity (greater RH activation) or analytical problem-solving (greater LH activation). Those in the positive outcome group performed better on creativity tasks, generating more novel solutions than the negative outcome group. It seems positivity stimulated higher relative activation of RH brain regions and pathways, broadening and expanding the focus of participants' attention in two ways: broader *internal conceptual attention* – better targeting and activation of relatively remote information and mental representations, ie finding and using more of the 'stuff' you've filed away in your brain and normally can't remember!; and broader *external perceptual attention* – heightening responses to a broader range of external environmental stimuli, ie you notice more!

These findings have a plethora of applications for trainers. Most directly, I have put them into practice helping learners frame personal learning outcomes. Having individuals craft these before attending workshops is key to a brain-friendly approach. I also ask learners to bring a current project/challenge to work on throughout. When learners are able to frame desired outcomes for their challenge in positive terms (eg *I'd like to find ways to increase productivity of my team over the next six months'* rather than *'I'd like to stop my team bickering and slacking so much'*), and by visualizing 'what good will look like' when their outcome is achieved, the positive emotions generated within that individual (eg interest, pride and inspiration) tend to motivate him/her towards broader thought patterns and eventually more numerous, novel and effective solutions.

The broadening effect of positive emotions has more far-reaching applications for capability development than just outcome framing.

CHALLENGE: how many ways can you imagine in which stimulating positive emotions – hence promoting relatively higher right hemisphere activation – could be valuable for learners you work with?

More practical steps to motivation

One thing that has been shown to increase motivation to learn is an expectation that you will need to teach – and if you're a trainer I'm sure you've already experienced this. You're told you're going to have to take over a new course or subject that you've not taught before and you spend all weekend swotting up. But perhaps this isn't the best thing for you or your learners.

In a study of schoolchildren by John Nestojko (2014), pupils who learned a passage of information and thought they'd have to teach another group remembered more of the information than those who had to learn it just for themselves. This study required further investigation to see how valid it would be in all circumstances; but that's the nature of research. Once you start asking precise questions you need to drill down deeper and deeper. Suffice it to be said, most of us know that the best way to learn something is to have to teach it.

Next time you've got a new course to teach perhaps you don't need to do all the work. Find the resources that you'd use yourself, give your learners the resources and ask them to teach the next group – that will motivate them to want to learn it and is much better for everyone than you trying to stuff a lot of information into brains that aren't really interested. And you keep your weekend free to relax.

Other influences on people's beliefs about learning – negative and positive

People approach learning very differently and as a learning facilitator some of these things are under your control and some are not. Think about which of these ideas you may be able to have an impact on and what you can do.

There'll be some things out of your control but you may still be able to put things into place that counteract or enhance them:

- parents and others who were present during people's formative years;
- teachers and the education system;
- peers – what else does everyone around your learner think about learning?;
- organizational culture – particularly line managers;
- other learners or previous training experiences;
- perceived benefit of the learning to the person – the WIIFM factor (what's in it for me?);
- expectations of what they'll have to do, eg role play/make a presentation, pass a test;
- environment – external/lighting/heating/refreshments/noise/décor, etc;
- technology issues or fear of technology;
- financial implications, eg self-funding/promised pay rise/redundancy;
- why they're there, ie voluntary or mandatory;
- how they've been invited;
- trainer knowledge/skills/attitude/how they welcome learners;
- location and transport issues;
- weather – anticipated or actual;
- medical and physical conditions;
- outside issues with employer/friends/family;
- outstanding work in the office;
- how they feel that day.

Here are some things you can control to increase motivation to learn when you're working with people face to face or virtually:

- Make the initial environment as welcoming as possible – it breaks down barriers.
- Pay regular attention to the environment.
- Apologize sincerely once for problems, then move on.
- Have backup plans if equipment doesn't work.
- Use humour advisedly – let it flow naturally from the group.
- Give people WIIFMs regularly.

- Listen fully to individuals – even if you know you've heard it before, you haven't heard it from that person's perspective and they may not have been able to express it.

- Be congruent in your words and actions with the learning you are sharing.

- Value all contributions, even if you have to work with the meaning to make sense of what has been said!

- Be vigilant about body language – manage yours and watch for messages of theirs. 'Digital' body language can tell you a lot about how engaged a virtual learner is.

- Don't criticize, argue, or put people on the spot.

- The meaning of communication is the response you get – if your audience doesn't understand you or they do something 'wrong', it's usually down to you!

Motivating yourself

Before we move off the chapter of motivating learners it might just be worth thinking about how you motivate yourself and the impact that has on you and your audience.

At the beginning of this chapter you read a story about how we see other people as smiling more when we're smiling ourselves. This is another of those findings that shows your motivation matters when you're training. There's also the slightly vexed question of mirror neurons. When they were first discovered in the 1990s at Parma University in Italy there was a lot of excitement that they might be the neurons that allowed us to show empathy, amongst other things. When a monkey saw someone else pick up food particular neurons appeared to respond as if the viewer had also picked up the food. fMRI scanning studies went on to suggest that humans have significant networks of mirror neurons, particularly in the sensory and motor cortex, that might enable us to feel what it's like to move like someone else. The leap to imply that we can empathize with others on an emotional level due to these mirror neurons is one that's been hotly disputed and is probably too much to conclude from the research.

However, most of us recognize that we are affected by other people's moods and if you as the trainer start by sounding grumpy or bored by what you're teaching you're not going to be the greatest example to your learners.

Many performers have a routine they develop before going on stage that helps them get into the 'zone' and this can be useful to you as a trainer too. You might choose to do breathing exercises, anchor a particular movement or piece of music to your best mental state for working with people. Once it's fully 'anchored' you will find it easier to attain that state. And if all else fails put a pencil between your teeth and 'grin and bear it'. You'll soon convince yourself that you feel on top of the world.

Summary

You've covered a number of ideas in this chapter:

- Motivation is the first stage in the process of learning.
- There are different states, both emotional and cognitive, that help us learn more easily.
- Curiosity releases dopamine and this may act as a reward itself but is also implicated in goal-directed behaviour and in assessing risk and avoidance of unwanted behaviours.
- The right level of attention is needed to learn effectively and you can reduce stress in learners by meeting their physical and emotional needs, including connecting people socially.
- Exploration and playfulness increase creativity and brain plasticity and help people become open to new ideas as well as creating their own.
- Persistence is a required state for most learning – we need to practise, repeat, and practise so helping people persist is valuable.
- As a trainer you can help to foster and create these states.
- There are lots of practical things you can do to make people feel more inclined to learn, reduce their fear, and increase their motivation.
- Remember to stay motivated yourself.

References and further reading

Bowden, E M and Jung-Beeman, M (2003) Aha! Insight experience correlates with solution activation in the right hemisphere, *Psychonomic Bulletin and Review*, **10** (3), pp 730–37

Bowden, E M, Jung-Beeman, M, Fleck, J and Kounios, J (2005) New approaches to demystifying insight, *Trends in Cognitive Sciences*, **9** (7), pp 322–28

Collins, S and Lancaster, A (2015) *Webinars Pocketbook*, Management Pocketbooks Ltd, Alresford

Dweck, C (1986) Motivational processes affecting learning, *American Psychologist*, **41** (10), pp 1040–48

Edutopia (2015) [accessed 30 June 2015] How to Rewire Your Burned-Out Brain: Tips from a neurologist [Online] http://www.edutopia.org/blog/teacher-burnout-neurology-judy-willis-md (archived at perma.cc/D2FL-Z7ZD)

Egner, T, and Gruzelier, J H (2004) EEG biofeedback of low beta band components: frequency-specific effects on variables of attention and event-related brain potentials, *Clinical Neurophysiology*, **115** (1), pp 131–39

Fredrickson, B L (2001) The role of positive emotions in positive psychology: the broaden-and-build theory of positive emotions, *American Psychologist*, **56** (3), pp 218–26

Fredrickson, B L (2013) Positive emotions broaden and build, *Advances in Experimental Social Psychology*, **47**, pp 1–53

Friedman, R and Förster, J (2005) Effects of motivational cues on perceptual asymmetry: implications for creativity and analytical problem solving, *Journal of Personality and Social Psychology*, **88** (2), pp 263–75

Kang, M J, Hsu, M, Krajbich, I M, Loewenstein, G, McClure, S M, Wang, J T Y and Camerer, C F (2009) The wick in the candle of learning epistemic curiosity activates reward circuitry and enhances memory, *Psychological Science*, **20** (8), pp 963–73

Kounios, J and Beeman, M (2014) The cognitive neuroscience of insight, *Annual Review of Psychology*, **65**, pp 71–93

Liberman, M (2005) [accessed 30 June 2015] Language Log: The Agatha Christie Code: Stylometry, serotonin and the oscillation overthruster [Online] http://itre.cis.upenn.edu/~myl/languagelog/archives/002728.html (archived at perma.cc/LG4D-4X76)

Nestojko, J, Bui, D, Kornell, N and Bjork, E (2014) Expecting to teach enhances learning and organization of knowledge in free recall of text passages, *Memory and Cognition*, **42** (7), pp 1038–48

Pink, D (2011) *Drive: The surprising truth about what motivates us*, Canongate Books, Edinburgh

Schmitz, T W, De Rosa, E and Anderson, A K (2009) Opposing influences of affective state valence on visual cortical encoding, *Journal of Neuroscience*, **29** (22), pp 7199–7207

Sel, A, Calvo-Merino, B, Tuettenberg, S and Forster, B (2015) [accessed 1 September 2015] When you smile, the world smiles at you: ERP evidence for self-expression effects on face processing, *Social Cognitive and Affective Neuroscience* [Online] http://scan.oxfordjournals.org/content/early/2015/03/22/scan.nsv009.abstract (archived at perma.cc/GA7D-75C6)

Shah, D (2018) By the Numbers: MOOCs in 2017, https://www.class-central.com/report/mooc-stats-2017/ (archived at perma.cc/3RYZ-AB5P)

Stansbury, M (2015) Is there more to a MOOC than its completion rate? *eCampusNews*, retrieved from http://www.ecampusnews.com/top-news/mooc-course-completion-973/ (archived at perma.cc/GHM2-X5C8), November

Treadway, M, Buckholtz, J, Cowan, R, Woodward, N, Li, R, Ansari, M, Baldwin, R, Schwartzman, A, Kessler, R and Zald, D (2012) Dopaminergic mechanisms of individual differences in human effort-based decision-making, *Journal of Neuroscience*, **32** (18), pp 6170–76

Willis, J (2012) How to Rewire Your Burned-Out Brain: Tips from a neurologist [Online] http://www.edutopia.org/blog/teacher-burnout-neurology-judy-willis-md (archived at perma.cc/3GU6-HXBX)

Use your sense   06

Getting information from the outside world and into your head

What do you notice if you read or hear the name Derek? Possibly it will bring back a memory of someone you know called Derek, you might think of other words that sound like Derek, or names like Eric. But unless you are very unusual you probably don't get a taste of ear wax. However, James Wannerton, who runs a pub, has this very unusual sensation quite often because one of his regulars is called Derek and whenever he hears the name he experiences this odd, unrelated taste.

He is one of an unusual group of people who experience something called synaesthesia when some of the senses appear to be blended. Other people with the condition may experience colours when they think of specific letters or numbers, others hear music in particular colours. Brain imaging studies show that when some synaesthetes listen to words their visual cortex as well as their auditory cortex lights up; for most people only the auditory cortex is activated.

Dismissed initially as fanciful, synaesthesia is now recognized as a specific condition and may be more widespread amongst the population than was originally thought; after all not everyone is going to confess to their friend Derek that he tastes of ear wax. It may even be developmental: as babies we may all experience the world in multiple sensory ways but our brains start to categorize sensory information in a more rigid way as we develop. And perhaps there is a little bit of the synaesthete in all of us – can you identify with the 'sharp' taste of a lemon, the 'loud' colour of a cotton shirt or how you might 'smell a rat' when you hear something that seems incorrect?

Learning through your senses

Your senses are effectively the only way for the information in the outside world to get inside your head, so if you're to learn anything about what's going on in the world, whether it's a new fact, a physical activity or improving a soft skill like developing your negotiation skills the chances are you're going to have to pay attention to what's going on in that outside world. However, you'll also have to pay attention to your internal world too, especially if you're learning a new skill.

Whilst most of us are familiar with the Big Five senses of sight, sound, touch, taste and smell it seems this may owe as much to the Greek philosopher Aristotle and his book *De Anima* (*On the Soul*) which had a separate chapter for each of what we call our main senses. There are still rigorous debates in the scientific community as to what constitutes a sense but broadly it's seen as a group of receptors or organs that receive information either from outside the body (exteroceptive) or from inside (interoceptive). This information then enables you to know what's going on in and outside your body so that you can make choices as to how to respond; sometimes consciously and sometimes unconsciously.

Currently there are up to 21 different senses suggested. We'll cover the main five in more detail and then there's a short section on the additional senses you may not have known you have and how they impact on learning (see Figure 6.1).

Figure 6.1   Learning through your senses

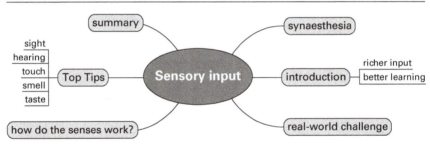

Having no sensory input, a lack of sensory information, leads to hallucinations, depression and other unusual perceptual anomalies. Sensory deprivation has been used as a method of torture. Our brains are designed to work with rich sensory input; they don't function well without our senses feeding them. Rich sensory input is the normal way for our brains to learn about the world outside our heads. We're incredibly good at taking in sensory information, but how much attention do we pay to the quality of what is around us and how can we improve our ability to learn, and those of our learners, by using richer more sensory inputs?

Try this exercise

Think back to your last holiday and identify the first memory that comes to mind. You may be:

- seeing the world from a different perspective at the top of a high mountain;
- listening to children shrieking with pleasure as they shout excitedly to their friends;
- lazing on a warm beach feeling fine granules of sand running through your fingers;
- smelling the perfumes of clear night air, unclouded by the fumes of the city;
- savouring the different and fresh tastes of food sizzling above open fires.

Did you see, hear, feel, smell or taste your memory? Go back to that memory… and now experience it through the rest of your senses. If you were seeing a new world, what can you bring to mind of what you could hear? What do you feel when you are there? What can you touch? What scents are around you? What can you taste? Try to capture all those sensations that weren't your first memory but are probably still in there as a deeply encoded experience. When we run this activity at training events, the typical feedback we get is how much more people remember when they access all the sensations they experienced at the time, rather than just their first memory.

This ability to recall sensory information that you may not have consciously been paying much attention to at the time can help you and your learners to recall and use information later. That elaborate sensory experience is still there to build on and as a trainer, lecturer, teacher or coach you can develop people's ability to learn.

In this chapter you'll look at some of the real-world challenges of training and information delivery. Then you'll hear about the different senses and how they're processed in your brain. You'll think about why and how you can enhance training and learning by increasing the sensory inputs available and learn about how your sensory perceptions of the world help to make learning resonant, stronger and more vivid. You'll explore some practical suggestions as to how you can create lush, multisensory environments and some new ideas from technology that can help us learn more effectively by building on our increasing knowledge about how our senses work and tie into the processes of learning.

Real-world challenges

1. Some topics are conceptual and not multisensory

Many of the things we have to learn at work don't intuitively lend themselves to multisensory presentations. If you have to train someone or design some e-learning for the latest Health and Safety regulations, or how to do zero-based budgeting or perhaps using macros in Excel, it's not immediately obvious how you can make these topics multisensory, but I hope as you go through this book you will begin to see how you can make these themes come to life for your learners.

2. An overemphasis on PowerPoint and textual learning

Sometimes in training departments people get distanced from the learning process and even very practical types of learning can get caught up in a style of training that actually strips out the sensory information. For example, I came across someone a few years ago who was asked to train people on cleaning techniques by talking them through PowerPoint slides! The cleaners and this poor trainer were sitting in a darkened room learning a structured cleaning process complete with labels, complicated words and pictures of mops instead of getting out into the real world and doing it for real.

3. Labelling people as particular types of learners – don't!

The senses have been used as a way of describing how some people prefer to learn but there is no evidence to support these or any other 'Learning Styles'. Whilst some people may find they prefer to read the booklet first and others prefer to hear someone explain what to do first, there is no evidence to support the concept of multisensory or any other sort of learning styles. Imagine you are learning to ride a bike. How useful is it to watch a video or look at pictures and how quickly do you think you'll learn to ride a bike? The only way successfully to learn to ride a bike is to get on one and make lots of mistakes, experience the feedback of scraped knees and knuckles and get your balance, correct your errors, practise and practise until finally you're speeding along.

If so far you have had a belief in learning styles but are reading this book because you're interested in evidence-based learning you need to know that in science you can't prove a negative. There's no proof that learning styles don't exist but there is a lack of evidence that they do. This doesn't usually feel as satisfying as being able to prove something and it leaves proponents of particular theories such as learning styles arguing that the research hasn't been done well enough yet and that we're just waiting for it. However, assigning learning styles to students is neither useful nor predictive. A study of anatomy students in 2015–16 assessed their learning styles and then asked them to study using that style both in and out of the classroom (Willingham *et al*, 2015). They found most students didn't use their so-called 'style' and whether they did or not made no difference to the end results; it simply didn't create better learning. There are some people who argue that learning styles can be damaging because it can stereotype people and prevent them from exploring all possible ways of learning.

What is more useful for learners is to fit the learning strategies to the material or skills that need to be learned. To ride a bike or learn to use a new tool at work uses a strategy based around physically practising, experimenting and improving your skills over time. If you're learning information and it's presented as text it might really work to map out the ideas graphically.

People are not visual, auditory or kinaesthetic learners but we all benefit from learning through rich multisensory environments. As you go through this chapter you'll read about visual, auditory, kinaesthetic, olfactory and gustatory senses because they will be terms that many people are familiar with, but I'm not talking about Learning Styles.

How the senses work

Let's take the processing of your five main senses step by step. Then we'll examine each sense in more detail and how you can use the senses to enhance learning, and then we'll dive a bit deeper to look into the rest and see how they have an impact on learning. Let's start with what happens when you see, hear, feel, smell or taste something.

A sensation is registered in the relevant, specially adapted sensory organ, your eyes, ears, nose, skin or tongue. Those organs translate their own particular stimulus, light or sound waves or physical vibrations into electrical pulses that pass along your nerves, through your spinal cord, until they reach your brain. These different messages are all converted into electrical form inside your brain. Once they get there they are destined to go to specific sensory areas which can then process them in greater detail. However, the information is effectively split into different streams which are also processed by other parts of your brain in parallel. There's another complication because in most cases, information from the left side of the body goes to the right side of the brain, eg information coming in from the left eye goes to the right side of the brain first. And information from the right side of your body goes to the left side of your brain.

The sensory cortices themselves are split further into distinct areas that deal with particular stimuli; your visual cortex, for instance, has areas to deal with colour, movement, shapes and even very specific stimuli like faces.

Once the information has been registered in your sensory cortex it moves to something called the association area where different information is assembled together from other parts of your cortex to give you your own personal perception of that sensory stimulus. So, for instance, when you see a particular pen your brain adds in the concepts of writing, drawing, other types of pens, and memories of the last time you saw that particular pen.

One of the parallel streams of information passes to your limbic system so you may well experience an emotional sensation associated with that particular pen – perhaps it was one you picked up at a particularly useful training course or you used to write a love letter. The emotional data is sent to your cerebral cortex so that you become consciously aware of seeing that pen and the feeling you associate with it.

So in fact when you see something it is actually a complex set of activations in different parts of your brain that gives you the sensation of seeing. Your perceptions are not the real world but what your brain tells you about the real world. Consequently your senses are fallible; sometimes you miss information, sometimes you see things that aren't there, sometimes you interpret it differently which makes learning all the trickier because you're really using your slightly less than perfect sensory perceptions to inform you of what's going on. So there's a lot that can go wrong but, time and time again, research demonstrates that learning is enhanced through sensory information.

Whilst most of the evidence shows that multisensory learning is valuable, are there any learning experiences where we might want to turn our senses off? In a 2008 study students learned the mathematical relations that linked three items in a group. Some students learned using metaphorical water jugs and pizza slices whilst others learned the rules using abstract symbols and these students were better able to transfer the rules to real-life situations. The team of scientists at Ohio State University, led by Jennifer Kaminski, thought that the concrete examples may have made it harder for the children to transfer the knowledge across to different situations despite them being more engaging. However, in this study the water jugs and pizza slices were only metaphorical. What would have happened if they'd been real and could have been touched?

Let's examine each sense in a bit more detail and how you can enrich sensory experiences to make learning stick.

Sight

The *visual cortex* sits in your occipital lobe at the back of your brain and more brainpower is devoted to processing visual information than any of the other senses. The visual cortex is split into distinct areas for processing different elements of vision, eg colour, shape, size, etc and there are specific neurons that look out for very particular elements of vision such as neurons that detect corners or straight lines; even vertical as opposed to horizontal lines.

There is no direct map of what you see in your brain – the 'map' is distorted as it is processed. The central area of your visual field has more neurons and greater cortical area than the peripheral area so your peripheral vision isn't as strong as your centrally focused vision. What you actually see is inverted on the back of the retina so the 'map' in the brain is upside down but you are used to processing it that way, so it seems entirely normal to you.

So how does vision enhance your experience of learning? Do pictures help you to learn better? It seems they do and that most people find pictures and video improve their ease of learning and the retention of information.

Drawing something yourself can improve your learning or uptake of information. Children were asked to learn some biology facts (Schmeck *et al*, 2014): some were encouraged to use pictures and draw whilst others worked with text alone. The group who used drawings were about a third more successful than their peers when they were tested afterwards on a multiple choice (scoring 61 per cent correct on average vs 44 per cent) and a drawing test (scoring 52 per cent on average vs 28 per cent). The researchers believe that drawing has this benefit for learning because it 'encourages learners to engage in generative cognitive processing during learning such as organizing the relevant information into a coherent structure, and integrating it with relevant prior knowledge from long-term memory'.

Whilst this particular study was conducted with schoolchildren there's enough evidence to suggest it's worth asking people at work to draw the information they need to learn. These researchers acknowledged they didn't test whether drawing works for all types of information but it seemed to be effective for causal chains of events – so if you're learning a process, drawing should make it easier.

Pictures may not always be the answer

If pictures are often easier to understand and more memorable than text alone is it true in all cases? Sometimes people even worry that they'll dumb something down by including pictures because it will seem too easy, though why some people believe learning must be hard isn't clear to me. However, are pictures always the answer?

Researchers writing in the *British Journal of Educational Psychology* (Prangsma *et al*, 2009) showed that academic achievement may not always be improved by the use of diagrams. History students showed no real difference in their learning when tested, regardless of whether they'd learned using illustrations or text or both. So perhaps using pictures doesn't always help to make the point or make information more memorable. However, one interesting finding was that students *felt* the information was easier to understand and they had learned better when they had pictures as well as text. So what's the implication of people thinking the information is easier to understand?

Feeling better about information can't be underestimated. The researchers said 'The goal of educational motivation is not only to make learning more efficient... or effective... but also to make learning more pleasant such that the affective learning experience is more satisfying and learners will want to learn more'. You've already covered the importance of motivation in learning which is particularly relevant when you need people to learn on their own or to encourage them to come back for more training. When people enjoy the experience of receiving the information they are more inclined to engage with it and make the effort to process and understand it. So whilst pictures may not *always* make a difference as to how well something is remembered they do make a difference to the motivation levels. And, importantly pictures don't seem to make learning any worse.

The impact of colour on learning

As a highly visual signal, does colour make a difference to people's learning? Colours affect how we pay attention and our levels of arousal; higher attention and arousal levels increase our ability to learn. We pay more attention to warm colours such as yellow, red and orange compared to the cool colours like brown and grey. People show faster response times when identifying the differences in colours compared to differences in the shapes of objects indicating that colours have a better and greater ability to capture attention than other variables. Colour helps with remembering information but it needs to be consistent. If the information appears in red as people are learning, it needs to appear in red again when they are retrieving the information later.

What else can colour do for you, the trainer?

Surprisingly, as a trainer, teacher or learning facilitator the colour you wear may have an impact on the learning. As one of the most significant motivators to learning you need to feel on top of your game and wearing red can help you feel more confident. The colour red has been shown to increase testosterone levels in sports players and improve their chances of victory. So if you wake up feeling less confident than usual then grab that red cardigan or red tie and make sure you wear it to let yourself and your learners know that you're confident they will learn well today.

You'll explore some more about the psychology of colour in Chapter 12 when we consider the environment because colour can induce different emotional and motivational states in people.

Top Tips for using visuals

When you're teaching a new procedure, experiment with handouts that have text labels and ask people to draw the procedure or the sequence of events. Or you could encourage them to draw the process from scratch once it's been explained to them. Not everyone is initially comfortable with their drawing skills so reassure people they don't need to be Leonardo Da Vinci; a few stick men and blobs will be better than text alone.

Ask people to mindmap information rather than take notes; mindmaps are more visual then text. Increase their visual impact with pictures, colour, highlighting, arrows and differing text sizes.

When using images of people, pay attention to where the attention of those people is focused. If their gaze extends to some point of observation beyond the border of the graphic, we tend to be drawn to follow their focus so don't look at the slide. Therefore, face images of people into the graphic when you want your images to take centre stage.

If you're running webinars you'll need to use more slides rather than fewer. People are wired to pay attention to 'change' so keep visual change happening with plenty of highly visual slides – pictures rather than text – or short video segments. You will appeal to parts of the brain that notice change and you'll be telling people 'If you look away, you'll miss something'. This is intense for you and your learners though so don't keep it up for a whole day; 10 minutes is probably more than enough and only include one point per slide – or you might even make one point across two slides. Hand control of the whiteboard over to your users and let them create graphics, sketches or doodles to illustrate their thoughts.

Create really visual slides and build them into a concert review to play at the end of a learning programme. See Chapter 11, 'Review and reflect', for details of how to do this.

Use the same colours, pictures and symbols on all your graphics, slides, in notes, on wall posters, etc relating to the same piece of learning. This helps with encoding and retrieval of information by associating the same images with the same ideas.

Encourage people to make huge wall murals with coloured craft or flip-chart paper because then people feel ownership as well as having strong visual reminders of what they are learning. Some organizations take those murals back into the workplace to share learning with others or to continue to remind them once they are back at work.

Or work with graphic recorders – people who help you create graphics and images about the learning as it happens.

Rather than always using slide presentations create visual flash cards instead and use them for inputting information and reviews. The beauty of using flash cards is they are not serial like slides. You can show them and then stick them on a wall and they remain there for the rest of your training session. People don't have to hold information in their working memory in the same way as they do with slides.

Highlight different materials with different colours or better still ask the learners to do it though it's a learning myth that simply highlighting text is a useful way to learn. People need to recall rather than recognize (as you'll find out in the chapter on memory).

If you're regularly using pictures on a flipchart or webinar whiteboard then a short course on drawing graphics will increase your confidence enor-mously. When you use something regularly then create a poster – permanent marker on 'magic whiteboard' can be brilliant.

Use a variety of visual media: diagrams, charts, timelines, cartoons, ani-mations, film clips, video, DVD in a blended approach. Just make sure you've got permission to use them if you didn't create them yourself.

Digital learning is often very good graphically and the use of good visual animations can really enhance a piece of e-learning. But what can you build in that enables the learner to contribute to the visual elements? Most e-learn-ing software lets users add text but how often can learners draw?

Sound

When sound is transmitted it goes from each ear to both left and right hemispheres of your brain but most of the sound from the left ear goes to the right hemisphere and vice versa. Both hemispheres have different roles in processing sound information, so sounds will be experienced differently depending on the ear they enter. For example, a person who is deaf in the right ear may find words more difficult to distinguish than music because words are processed mainly in the left hemisphere whereas music is processed mainly in the right.

We are very used to the idea of sound in training and learning because most of us have had the experience of being talked to or lectured at. It may even be that if you're looking at slides you're actually hearing because some studies suggest that seeing text on a screen causes you, in effect, to hear that information in your head and subsequently to encode it as verbal information.

So how effective is sound and auditory information in learning? There's far less research done on auditory than on visual learning and like most of the research done in laboratories it's usually extremely specific and not always directly applicable to the real world. For instance, research focuses on whether people can learn to tell the difference between two tones or two different frequencies of sound which is great for detailed research, but unless someone is specifically having to learn to do that as part of their job it doesn't help you in the more practical world of learning soft skills or learning new information.

Sound is serial rather than parallel. Whilst you can scan a picture over and over again, once you've heard something it's gone and needs to be repeated for you to hear it again, so in some ways it's harder to listen and process sound than pictures. Fortunately we are helped by something called echoic memory. Have you ever been really immersed in something when somebody says something to you and you say 'what did you say?', but even as you say it you realize you've heard what they said? That's your echoic working memory replaying what you heard so you can hear it again. Your echoic memories are short, only holding about 3–4 seconds' worth of information. This form of sensory memory passes information to your short-term memory but it's easily disrupted. Studies show that when you're distracted whilst you encode information your initial learning is disrupted.

One of the key areas where sound may therefore be particularly important in learning is where it can distract from learning. Most parents of teenagers will recognize the experience of asking them how on earth they can concentrate on their school work whilst listening to music on their headphones. Does listening to music whilst they're learning help them or not? Oddly enough it may depend on what they are listening to and whether the music is acoustically varied, which is typical of pop music. When students were tested on a memory task they performed worst when listening to pop music they liked but their performance was better when the music was 'a cacophony of sound, in which the segmentation of each individual sound from the next is difficult to identify' (Perham and Sykora, 2012). Unsurprisingly, for most parents, their performance was improved when they had to learn in silence. Though music can be used to block out external distractions so the case is not fully made for silence.

Listening to information as you sleep

In the past a lot of research focused on the idea that people could learn whilst listening to information as they slept, but sadly the results consistently indicate that this is not going to help you become fluent in Spanish or remember the key facts for an exam. However, whilst we're on the topic of sleep there was an interesting experiment that showed that sleep may be more important to learning than auditory input.

A particular study looked at whether playing sounds and associating them with pictures of objects would increase people's ability to remember the specific location of the object. Subjects saw 50 objects in specific locations on a computer screen, and at the same time they heard a relevant noise; for instance, a kettle was paired with a whistle and a cat with a meow. They were then tested as to how well they knew the location of the object to set a baseline. As part of the experiment subjects were then allowed to nap but whilst they slept the researchers played the sounds of 25 of the objects. The subjects were then better at locating the objects for which they'd heard the sound, whilst asleep, than the 25 objects without the sound cue. However, on further study it turned out that it was actually letting subjects sleep that made a difference rather than the sound. When people were tested without sleep, but with the sound cues, there was no difference in the results of cued and uncued objects.

There's a lot more on sleep in Chapter 13, which is dedicated to sleep and learning.

Does music make you smarter?

You may well have heard that listening to Mozart makes you smarter and if you do an Internet search you'll find plenty of information to tell you that music helps you think better, study better or generally become more intelligent. Much of this data seems to stem from an original piece of research in 1993 by a psychologist called Frances Rauscher (*et al*) who reported findings of 'enhanced spatial task performance' amongst college students after exposure to Mozart's music. These findings were overinterpreted to lead to the popular 'Mozart Effect' myth.

Subsequent analysis (called meta-analysis) of multiple experiments and papers shows that the accumulated evidence does not demonstrate any enhanced abilities through listening to Mozart. There do seem to be some short-term effects on temporary arousal and positive emotions from listening to certain types of music, and learning to play music may help children develop their working memory so helping them to learn languages and to read.

One of the hardest things when you start learning a foreign language is working out where one word starts and another ends and music has been found to help here. First of all music is more emotional than spoken language but, when that was controlled for, people still learned made-up words more easily. What seemed to make a significant difference was that music gave people statistical information about which syllables tend to follow each other in words, and which don't; this helped them to segment the different parts of the words. So for language learning, music may well be a valuable tool, certainly as you start to learn the language. There's also some evidence from Cambridge University that suggests that training specific rhythm and sound differentiation may help children with dyslexia learn to read more easily (Bhide, Power and Goswami, 2013).

Music to change the emotional context for learning

We've already discussed how being motivated is vital for learning and we'll go on to consider the use of emotions in learning, so perhaps music can be used to change people's emotional states and therefore readiness to learn even if it doesn't actually make you smarter. You may be aware that major and minor keys can sound happy or sad respectively and it's thought this might be linked to our speech patterns. An experiment in 2010 (Muir, 2010) found that the frequency relationships in excited speech closely matched those of music in major keys, whilst those of 'forlorn' speech matched minor music. The team also found the same association for Mandarin Chinese speakers, suggesting the link is common to different cultures, if not universal. So you may potentially induce different emotional states in your learners through your own tonality. And of course you can play music in major or minor keys to change the mood too. My favourite virtual classroom presenter, Jo Cook of Lightbulb Moment, almost always has some upbeat music playing as people enter the webinar which serves to create the mood Jo intends.

Top Tips for using sound more

We pay attention to change so, as a trainer, vary the voices that people hear. Instead of you speaking or reading, encourage your audience to take turns reading out loud from books, handouts and documents.

Pre-record some material and play it in the background, whilst other less cognitive tasks are being performed. This is a form of priming and whilst not everyone will consciously be aware of the information it will have been processed at one level or another.

Instead of always presenting information as prose, how about creating a poem, song, rap or jingle or, better still, ask your learners to create their own. There's some interesting research that suggests we believe information that rhymes more than the same information written as prose, even if we don't think we'll be hoodwinked by such a simple suggestion.

Another way to use music in a training environment is to condition particular pieces of music to particular activities. So, for instance, at the start of a training programme play a particular tune to signal the end of break, play it consistently and eventually learners recognize that the end of break has arrived and you'll find they come back to the learning space without you having to shepherd them back.

Touch, movement and the kinaesthetic sense

You'll often hear the phrase 'kinaesthetic sense' when people talk about touch and movement and they may also consider the kinaesthetic sense to include feelings but, as you're now aware, feelings come from an entirely different part of your brain so I'll not include them here.

You've got lots of information feeding into your body that gives different physical sensations. *Touch* is a perception resulting from activation of neural receptors, generally in the skin, but also in the tongue, throat, and mucous membranes. A variety of pressure receptors respond to differences in pressure. You also have temperature receptors in your skin.

The motor cortex runs over the top of your head like a hairband – ear to ear – and tells you where your body is amongst other things. Proprioception, sometimes called a 'sixth sense' of body awareness, is the equivalent of an internal touch; one example is you know where your limbs are in relation to the world.

Whilst information comes into your brain through the senses your control of movement happens in the cerebellum in the brain stem. It passes information backwards and forwards from the sensory systems to other parts of your brain and is highly connected to all parts of the brain associated with learning. In this section you'll also consider the inputs that movement give us when learning and you'll revisit the importance of moving again in other chapters.

Does touch and movement help with learning? Clearly if you're learning a physical skill actually doing the task is vital to perfecting the skill; if you're learning to do something simple like thread a needle you can feel the thread and the needle and your brain puts all the sensory information together to tell you where the two objects are in relation to each other so you can bring them together. But do touch and movement help in other ways when you're learning something conceptual?

There are many reasons for moving whilst learning, not the least of which is that your brain requires oxygen, and one way to get oxygen to the brain is to move. Even standing can raise heart rate (hence, blood flow) by as much as 5 to 8 per cent in just seconds (Krock and Hartung, 1992). So possibly you'd be able to read this book much better if you were standing up – which if you're reading it on public transport you may be.

There's more and more evidence that our brains need movement in order to function well and that our cognitive skills are enhanced for the short and long term by being active. John Medina's excellent book *Brain Rules* (2008) has a whole chapter devoted to the importance of movement.

Top Tips for stimulating a sense of touch

- Stimulate the sense of touch by providing information as cards that people have to hold, organize, move around.
- Give out black and white handouts to colour in – you've got the double impact of visual stimulation and movement.
- Physically pace out concepts, walk them through.
- Develop physical mindmaps – lay them out on the floor.
- Put information into puzzles – a jigsaw puzzle can be visual and tactile at the same time.

Figure 6.2 The MASTER model

- Build models of concepts and let people walk around them or hold them.
- You can have key facts put onto physical objects like magic cubes (a bit like Rubik's cubes) or banner pens.
- Use the real world of concrete objects as much as you can – explain concepts using real physical metaphors. I saw one client explain the complex technology of the crystals behind e-reader screens using a small electric candle and an origami cube.
- Even in the digital learning world you can encourage touch; invite people to write or draw in learning logs, send materials to construct, set tasks in the real world and report back and use sensory language.

With some energetic learners you might ask them to create human sculptures of models, as shown in Figure 6.2.

Smell and learning

Smell or *'olfaction'* is one of the chemical senses and, unlike the other senses, odours are processed on the same side of the brain as the detector, your nostril. The olfactory cortex is nearer the front of your brain, so it's very close to your nose! Smell is your most primitive sense and, unlike other senses, your olfactory perceptions go directly to the limbic system. This fast route to your emotional centre gives smell the power to elicit strong memories – consider how the smell of cabbage or changing rooms can take you straight back to learning at school!

Smell can influence your emotional responses, heart rate, blood pressure, and respiration and we know that the neuronal substrates of olfaction (the parts of the brain that underlie our experience of smell) are especially geared for associative learning and emotional processing. The olfactory bulbs are part of the limbic system and directly connect with limbic structures that process emotion (the amygdala) and associative learning (the hippocampus). No other sensory system has this type of intimate link with the emotional areas of your brain creating a strong neurological basis for why odours trigger emotional connections.

A number of studies have shown that the odours people like make them feel good, whereas odours people dislike make them feel bad. These mood responses have also been reported physiologically. For example, skin conductance, heart-rate and eye-blink rates in response to various liked or disliked scents coincide with the mood the person is experiencing; and of course how we feel can affect how we learn. Pleasant smells mainly light up your frontal lobe's olfactory area whilst unpleasant smells activate both the amygdala (associated with negative emotion) and the cortex in the temporal lobe (processes sound, speech comprehension and memory).

It seems that people in a positive mood can be more creative and that odours can have the same effect; when people smelled something they liked their creative problem solving improved compared to smelling something unpleasant. Pleasant smells may also increase attention during tedious tasks, though this is not an excuse to create a boring learning event and improve it with the smell of roasting coffee. And if there is an unpleasant smell around it may lower people's tolerance for frustration, so there's another reason to pay attention to the environment people are in when they learn.

Unfortunately you can't just decide to use a particular scent to evoke a particular emotion. It seems the pleasantness or not of scents is personally and culturally conditioned and is due to associative learning. In an experiment by the US Army to create a universal stink bomb they couldn't find any universally disliked smell (*New Scientist*, 2001).

A sense of taste

Taste or *'gustation'* is the other chemical sense. This sense may not be as readily applied to learning in a formal sense in quite the same way as the other four – unless the learning is specifically food-related where taste is going to be vitally important like being on a wine-tasting course or learning to be a tea taster. However, it is still possible to appeal to this sense whilst learning. Facilitators will recognize the well-known 'happy sheet' scenario where the most positive mention is about lunch!

A strong taste can bring back amazing memories or cause us to behave quite out of character in that we might spit it out, even in public. What's the neuroscience of taste?

Taste activates the amygdala and the dopaminergic system so is closely connected to reward and aversion. Therefore you might use pleasant-tasting food as a reward for learning. Whilst your mouth can taste sweet, salt, sour and umami, it seems there are 'hot spots' in your gustatory cortex for the main tastes of sweet, salt and umami but not one for sour tastes.

Most of the neuroscience research on taste is on taste aversion and how we learn that and there's almost none on whether taste can help us learn other things better. However, tastes linked to learning can be used as anchors rather than them being a specific way of absorbing information.

For instance, we run a session explaining the main brain structures to our participants and the stimulus for the brain to be 'distracted' from the learning is a bar of chocolate. Throughout the session we use chocolate as a link to the brain – they see it, smell it and taste it – and ask people to think about what they learned about the brain whenever they see or taste chocolate in the future. When we see people many months and even years later, if we ask them about chocolate they are always able to recall some of what they learned about the brain. They have associated chocolate with thinking about brain structures.

Top Tips for using olfactory and gustatory senses

- Use images and props with food content – most people will get a taste for this theme.
- Choose spaces with natural air – and open the windows regularly.
- Spray scents around the room to stimulate different reactions.
- Food and drink metaphors and stories are easy to swallow!
- Use scented pens.
- Handouts can be impregnated by placing them in a warm, scented place.
- Make eating/drinking/celebrating part of the learning – a multicultural feast, barbecue, picnic, tapas, etc.
- Flowers and plants add colour and scent.
- Be subtle and aware that people may react strongly to some scents for personal or health-based reasons.
- Learn specific topics with a specific scent on a tissue and then take the same scent back into a test or exams.

Additional senses

Some of the additional senses have already been mentioned within the 'kinaesthetic' section but we're going to classify them a bit more clearly here.

First they are separated into exteroceptive senses which perceive the body's position, motion and state and then interoceptive senses that tell you what is happening inside your body.

Your **exteroceptive** senses include:

- the proprioceptive senses;
- balance (equilibrioception);
- where the parts of your body are in space (proprioception);

- being able to detect temperature differences (thermoception);
- sensing pain (nociception).

These are important for learning physical skills of any sort as are some of the interoceptive receptors.

Interoceptive senses tell you what's happening as a response to changes within your body and internal organs and some, such as cutaneous receptors in the skin that measure touch, pressure, vibration, are also valuable for learning motor skills.

Interoceptive senses also include a wide range of what we often refer to as feelings but are non-emotional feelings, for example hunger, thirst, needing to go to the toilet.

When you feel 'unwell' it's your interoceptive senses registering that you feel nauseous or want to gag, for instance. Most of them are relevant to learning at work only in that they are potentially very distracting but they do make learning 'sticky'. If something makes you vomit you usually don't want to eat it again or if something causes pain you learn to avoid it a second time. But they're unlikely to be the sort of learning we want to design at work.

Some scientists suggest we have another type of senses that are usually detected by a complex network of brain, and body, regions rather than a specific sensor. Experiences such as a sense of:

- Time which is measured by a diverse group of brain areas including the suprachiasmatic nucleus (see Chapter 13 on sleep).
- Personal 'agency' or control which is sometimes disrupted in people who have schizophrenia and who then believe they are being controlled by external forces. It could be argued this sense may be important for a motivation to learn as it makes us feel autonomous and in control.
- Familiarity which we already discussed in terms of recall and recognition. Research shows it's easier to learn new information if you are already familiar with the chunks that make up that information probably because it places less strain on working memory. Researcher Lynne M Reder (Reder *et al*, 2015) says, 'Learning requires bricks not sand'. Previously unknown parts of the brain have also been identified as able to distinguish between familiar or unfamiliar faces (Rockefeller University, 2017). One area is associated with declarative memory and the other in a region that processes social knowledge. Researchers were able to record the 'aha' moment in these areas when rhesus monkeys, who have similar facial recognition systems to ours, recognized the familiar faces.

Multisensory learning – an experiment

One of our colleagues, Nicki Davey from Saltbox Training, ran a session where we became her experimental guinea pigs. Her premise was that learning through a more multisensory experience would be more effective. In true scientific style she set up three experimental groups to generate ideas about 'oranges' in five minutes:

- Group 1 – had a blank piece of paper to receive their multiple ideas.
- Group 2 – had a picture of a lovely juicy orange, and a blank piece of paper.
- Group 3 – had an orange on an orange board with an orange knife, and a blank piece of paper.

Group 1 identified many fascinating and interesting ideas about oranges including links to orange-related literature and films: *Oranges Are Not the Only Fruit* and *A Clockwork Orange*.

Group 2 waxed lyrical about the 'community of orange' – how within the skin of an orange are segments, which contain little sacs of juice and how they all work together to be an orange. And they came up with lots of ideas about orange-coloured items, including jumpsuits from Guantanamo Bay.

In Group 3 we cut up our orange, smelled it, tasted it, looked at it and discussed ideas and memories about oranges themselves: how warm and sunny it is where they grow, the way they get stuck in your teeth, how to make false teeth out of the skin, how sticky they are on your hands...

There was definitely a difference in the types of ideas we all had which got us talking about creativity as well as multisensory learning.

But Nicki wasn't satisfied with just generating ideas – she wanted to test our memories. So she distracted us with another task where we produced *72 ways to make learning multisensory*. Then Nicki asked us to recall what we'd had on our lists about oranges. The groups which didn't have the multisensory orange experience *recalled 17 of their ideas each* (pretty impressive), but Group 3, who had had all their senses stimulated, *recalled 33 ideas in the time available*. In fact we were remembering the ideas so quickly that all of us wrote at once in order to keep up and we were frustrated by being stopped because we knew we hadn't captured them all.

There are many serious scientific experiments showing the value of multisensory stimuli in learning but this was an easy and practical way to demonstrate how much more powerful memory is when you stimulate the sensory cortices rather than just enlist the frontal cortex. I can still remember the feeling of how sticky my hands were!

Summary

What you've covered in this chapter:

- We process information from our multiple senses both internal and external.
- Each of the five main external senses has its own dedicated sensory area in your cortex.
- Apart from smell, the other four external senses are routed through the thalamus before being sent off for parallel processing throughout your brain creating rich emotional memories associated with the senses.
- Making learning more multisensory makes it more 'sticky'.
- Vision is usually the strongest sense; providing visual information helps more people learn more easily.

References and further reading

Aristotle, *De Anima*, 350BC, Penguin 1987, available from https://www. penguinrandomhouse.com/books/260882/de-anima-on-the-soul-by-aristotle/9780140444711/ (archived at perma.cc/4REL-AUNG)

Bhide, A, Power, A and Goswami, U (2013) A rhythmic musical intervention for poor readers: A comparison of efficacy with a letter-based intervention, *Mind, Brain, and Education*, 7 (2), pp 113–23

Cisco (2015) [accessed 2 July 2015] Multimodal Learning Through Media: What the Research Says [Online] http://www.cisco.com/web/strategy/docs/education/Multimodal-Learning-Through-Media.pdf (archived at perma.cc/T84E-K6AV)

Goldstein, N, Martin, S and Cialdini, R (2007) *Yes!* Profile, London

Jensen, E (2005) *Teaching with the Brain in Mind*, ASCD, Alexandria VA

Kaminski, J, Sloutsky, V and Heckler, A (2008) Learning theory: The advantage of abstract examples in learning math, *Science*, 320 (5875), pp 454–55

Krock, L P and Hartung, G H (1992) Influence of post-exercise activity on plasma catecholamines, blood pressure and heart rate in normal subjects, *Clinical Autonomic Research*, 2 (2), pp 89–97 [Online] https://www.ncbi.nlm.nih.gov/pubmed/1638110 (archived at perma.cc/F8H9-A6QV)

Medina, J (2008) *Brain Rules: 12 principles for surviving and thriving at work, home and school*, Pear Press, Seattle WA

Muir, H (2010) Songs in the key of life: What makes music emotional? [Online] http://www.newscientist.com/article/dn18367-songs-in-the-key-of-life-what-makes-music-emotional.html (archived at perma.cc/WZ2J-TQMF)

New Scientist (2001) Stench warfare, https://www.newscientist.com/article/
mg17122984-600-stench-warfare/ (archived at perma.cc/Q9W7-NZVR)

Perham, N and Sykora, M (2012) Disliked music can be better for performance
than liked music, *Applied Cognitive Psychology*, **26** (4), pp 550–55

Prangsma, M, Boxtel, C, Kanselaar, G and Kirschner, P (2009) Concrete and
abstract visualizations in history learning tasks, *British Journal of Educational
Psychology*, **79** (2), pp 371–87

Rauscher, F H, Shaw, G L and Ky, K N (1993) Listening to Mozart enhances
spatial-temporal reasoning: towards a neurophysiological basis, *Neuroscience
Letters*, **185** (1), pp 44–47

Reder, L M, Liu, X L, Keinath, A and Popov, V (2015) Building knowledge
requires bricks, not sand: The critical role of familiar constituents in learning,
in *Psychonomic Bulletin Review*, published online 3 July 2015, doi:10.3758/
s13423-015-0889-1

Rockefeller University (2017) How the brain recognizes familiar faces,
NeuroscienceNews, 10 August, https://neurosciencenews.com/brain-facial-
familiarity-7282/ (archived at perma.cc/8BPT-BJ8Q)

Schmeck, A, Mayer, R, Opfermann, M, Pfeiffer, V and Leutner, D (2014)
Drawing pictures during learning from scientific text: testing the generative
drawing effect and the prognostic drawing effect, *Contemporary Educational
Psychology*, **39** (4), pp 275–86

Uksynaesthesia.com (archived at perma.cc/QY5H-AFTL) (2015) [accessed 2 July
2015] UK Synaethesia Association [Online] http://www.uksynaesthesia.com/
(archived at perma.cc/8PKF-KATQ)

Willingham, D T, Hughes, E M and Dobolyi, D G (2015) The scientific status of
learning styles theories, *Teaching of Psychology*, **42** (3), pp 266–71, http://
psycnet.apa.org/doi/10.1177/0098628315589505 (archived at perma.cc/YJQ6-
PKKR), http://dx.doi.org/10.1177/0098628315589505 (archived at perma.
cc/8YYJ-A4NY)

Attention, learning and why Goldilocks deserves recognition

07

Look over there!

There you are minding your own business when you see someone looking intently at something. Do you look away or do you find yourself being irresistibly drawn to whatever they're looking at? It seems we find it almost impossible not to follow someone else's gaze and focus our attention on the same things they are looking at. Magicians and pickpockets use this distraction technique regularly to get you to look in a different direction to their sleight of hand.

A study in Italy in 2012 (Galfano *et al*) asked subjects to look at a target that appeared on the left or right of a screen, and to make it really easy, in one trial the target always appeared in the same place and in another the words 'sinistra' (left) or 'destra' (right) appeared to tell the subjects where to look. However, like all good psychology experiments it wasn't that easy and subjects, in some circumstances, also saw a cartoon face, or an arrow, that they were told to ignore. But they just couldn't. When they saw the face or the arrow pointing towards the opposite side to the target they were significantly slower at looking at the target. The scientists concluded that their attention was momentarily distracted and evidence from studies with babies shows we're practically hard-wired to follow the gaze of other people.

If you're a trainer this may be important to you – where are you gazing and therefore what are you drawing attention to? If you're designing learning then you need to ensure that you're directing attention where you need it; distraction is a significant problem in a digital world.

What attention is and why you need it in learning

Sometimes people say they aren't good learners or they have a terrible memory but perhaps it may be they aren't paying sufficient attention. But what is attention? At a basic level attention is about security – we pay attention to things because they could be a threat and we need to stay safe or because they are important to us.

In this chapter you'll read about your brain's systems of attention, your attention span and whether your attention is internal or external. Then you'll uncover some of the things that can help to focus and distract attention (see Figure 7.1).

Figure 7.1   Attention and learning

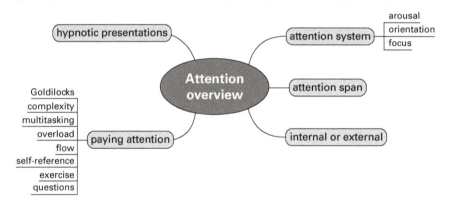

System of attention

Attention comes in three parts: arousal, orientation and focus. This means you first of all need to be alert enough to attend to something, then you direct your attention to the particular stimulus and finally you focus on it. When something captures your attention you immediately go into a state of arousal – a bus passes your window, or you hear someone shout. The external stimulus grabs your attention and your reticular activating system, just at the top of your brain stem, goes on the alert. It releases a burst of adrenaline which travels around your body to put you on alert. Activity in other parts of your brain closes down and goes quiet. If you were to do a brain scan just at that arousal point you'd see that a lot of the brain is inactive, quietened and not firing or sending messages.

Once you're alert your superior colliculus, still in your brain stem, starts to orientate towards the source of the alert looking for clues as to what's made you pay attention. Rats with damaged superior colliculi can't make meaningful directional movement to the source of a stimulus; they tend to be initially frozen and then become hyperactive (Harrison *et al*, 1984). And at the same time your parietal cortex tells your brain to disengage from what you're doing now and to pay attention to this novel stimulus that's attracted your attention.

Now you're alert and orientated towards the source of the stimulus you can focus on this new stimulus. A part of your thalamus, the lateral pulvinar, which is slightly higher up and in your midbrain, shunts information into your frontal lobes for you to start to make sense of it. Remember that one of the functions of the thalamus is to relay sensory information into your sensory cortices and it's very well connected with multiple parts of your brain.

So in the case of a bus going past your window you've heard the noise, felt the adrenaline, and turned to look at what's made the noise almost before you know what's happening. And then your frontal cortex processes the degree of threat and recognizes that it's just a noisy bus, it's nothing to do with you, it's continuing on its journey and you can go back to writing your report.

When you're learning something you need to pay attention otherwise the information doesn't really register and start being processed to get into your memory properly. But when you're learning you need to keep up that alert focus for longer than just a bus going past your window so you've got to sustain your attention. As you've just heard it's quite a complex process and you'll remember from earlier chapters that your brain uses a lot of energy in directing attention and processing information, which is one reason why staying alert for long is tiring and can become stressful.

Attention span

The amount of time you can sustain focused attention is a complex and disputed territory and is affected by numerous factors, such as whether you're being observed, which makes experiments in laboratories somewhat trickier to control for. There are many estimates of human attention span ranging from 5 to about 20 minutes, though we can choose to refocus at the end of an attention span if we're engaged enough. Of course attention span is also affected by what other distractions are happening too, so in a cinema you can pay attention to a long film because they turn off the lights, ask you to switch off your phone, increase the volume and bombard you with changing visual images. Your attention keeps getting pulled back to the action on the screen, but blockbusters spend millions of dollars on getting your attention. Particularly in a digital world attention can be easily pulled away from the task in hand because it's so easy for learners to be distracted by other easily available stimuli. How can you compete?

Attention from inside and outside

Attention can be provoked by internal or external stimuli. Imagine those times when you're sitting on the train, completely lost in a wonderful book that captures your imagination so that you don't notice the shrieking children, ringing phones or even that they've just announced your stop. Compare it to trying to pay attention to a not terribly interesting report on the train and all you are aware of is how sticky that child's hands are and how likely it is to spill its drink over your new suit.

When you pay attention to what's going on in your head it's as if your sensory input is tuned down so you don't notice all the sensory stimuli that bombard your brain constantly. Your anterior cingulate cortex seems to be active and this is the part of your brain that helps you maintain internal focus. It also registers pain and emotions; in fact your brain can't really tell the difference between external pain and emotional pain. Studies have shown that the pain of social isolation can be reduced by taking aspirin in the same way as if you actually had a headache. The anterior cingulate cortex has been implicated in certain sorts of depression because it seems to keep people fixed and focused on internal stimuli.

Conversely, when you're paying attention to the outside world your internal systems are turned down and the sensory cortices are more activated. Think about when you're really paying attention to something that's external – perhaps dancing to your favourite music or watching a brilliant film – and how you don't really notice what your thoughts are because your references are to the outside world. That's where your attention lies – you are so fascinated you don't notice the worrying, nagging feeling that you had all day or even the headache you had earlier.

So if you want people to learn, how do you encourage people to pay attention? They may need to attend to you, to the content, to their bodies, to their thoughts, to their colleagues; whatever it is that is going to provide a source of information.

There are ways you can do this and you'll uncover each in more detail as you read this chapter:

- Find the Goldilocks level of arousal – not too much and not too little.
- Make the level of processing complex enough to pay attention.
- Consider whether multitasking is helping.
- Assess multisensory input.
- Get people into flow and help time to fly.
- Increase the levels of self-reference.
- Increase levels of exercise.
- Direct attention to what's important.

Give Goldilocks the attention she deserves

For anyone who doesn't know the story of Goldilocks, it is the tale of a little girl who goes wandering in the woods and finds an empty house and, possibly foolishly, she goes inside. She tries eating the porridge that's been left on the table and finds one portion too hot, one too cold and one just right. She does a similar thing testing out the chairs and eventually the beds where she falls asleep on the 'just right' bed. She's discovered by the bears who live in the house and depending on which story you hear she either runs away, gets eaten or becomes best friends with the bears. The point is she was always comparing things and looking for the optimum level.

One way to make sure you have attention is to keep people's levels of stress at the Goldilocks level. In psychology and neuroscience stress isn't the unpleasant thing we talk about in everyday life – it is just a measure of the level of arousal someone feels.

The *Yerkes–Dodson law* shows the relationship between arousal and performance and was originally developed by psychologists Robert M Yerkes and John Dillingham Dodson in 1908. The law dictates that performance increases with your physiological or mental arousal, but only up to a point. When levels of arousal become too high, performance decreases (see Figure 7.2). Of course the type of activity has a strong part to play in this and the original Yerkes–Dodson law noted the difference between easy activities where performance keeps increasing and more novel or difficult activities.

When you are in a low level of arousal, your stress level is considered low and your performance on a particular task is low. Both can increase, moving through an optimal level of stress for the task and a maximum performance, until you do potentially reach a level of high stress, which is distress, and performance falls again.

Figure 7.2 Yerkes–Dodson law

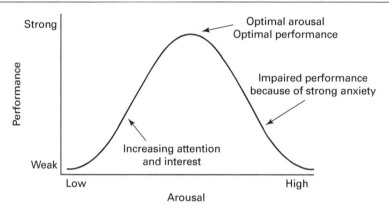

SOURCE https://en.wikipedia.org/wiki/Yerkes%E2%80%93Dodson_law
(archived at perma.cc/ET5Y-ANYL)

At low levels of psychologically defined stress, when you're practically asleep, your performance on focused cognitive activities is going to be reduced. You won't really be paying attention or able to learn much because you're just too laid back. Once you reach too high a level of stress your performance on cognitive activities is impaired again because, with high levels of adrenaline and cortisol rushing around your body, you're prepared for fight or flight rather than rational analysis of a new concept.

The optimal levels of arousal, sometimes called eustress, are where performance on cognitive tasks reaches its peak. This is the Goldilocks level of stress – not too little and not too much. As a trainer this is probably about where you want your students to be for the best chance of learning something cognitively new or challenging.

So how do you start to move people to eustress, keep people's attention from wandering, and make learning interesting enough that they are paying attention to what they need to?

Make the level of processing complex enough to pay attention

The more deeply you process information the more attention you pay to it. This also helps you to remember it. So, how can you increase the complexity of information to just the right level?

Much of the information we encounter at work, in school or academia is presented to us through language, so should you use simple language and dumb things down or should you use complex language to help people learn? We'll talk about language briefly later in Chapter 12, but what you'll consider here is the lexical complexity of the language you use.

Language can be processed at a structural, phonological or semantic level. For instance, think of the word 'House'. If you were to process it at a structural level you're asking about the structure of the word itself; for instance, 'what is the first vowel in this word?' At a phonological or lexical level the processing is a bit more complex; for instance, 'what rhymes with this word?' And finally at a semantic level you're thinking about the meaning of the word which is much more cognitively stimulating; for example, 'what do you do in this place?' What types of responses do you want from your questions?

There are plenty of psychological studies that show we pay attention and learn more easily when there is a higher level of complexity or processing challenge. Many of these studies have been conducted using TV shows to test what keeps people's attention but one study focused on looking at extracts from radio (Potter and Callison, 2000). Results show that when auditory complexity was higher people reported feeling more alert and their physiological levels of arousal were also increased; for instance, they showed an increased heart rate. Interestingly people were also more inclined to rate the messages more positively and they remembered them better than simple messages. They created these structurally complex radio messages by using multiple voice changes, sound effects, music onsets, and/or production effects whilst the structurally simple messages contained only a few of those features. The researchers concluded that 'variation in auditory complexity has greater effect on attention behaviour than variation in visual complexity in commercials'. This study, contrasted with studies on visual stimuli, suggested that sounds can draw our attention back to something because we can still hear them even when our visual attention has wandered off. For these experiments it seemed something as simple as a change from one announcer to another did the trick in recapturing attention, which probably means that having one person lecturing or talking in a webinar for up to an hour is probably not the greatest attention-grabbing tool of all – or at least you're going to have to work much harder in other ways to keep people's attention. This will be even more vital when you're working in a virtual classroom or e-learning because of the ease with which other distractions can draw attention.

Multitasking and attention

People love to say they can or they can't multitask but the research seems to consistently demonstrate that whichever side of the fence you fall on you won't perform as well on each task if you multitask rather than focus. I'm focusing on writing this book right now by being alone, turning off my e-mail, sitting out of my usual 'work space' and surrounding myself by materials related to the book. You might be reading it sitting on a train, in an office or possibly even sitting on the beach. Are you multitasking whilst you read? David Rock in *Your Brain at Work* (2009) talks about multitasking being like trying to keep multiple actors on stage at the same time, all of whom demand the limelight. Multitasking impacts on your working memory, drains your mental resources and affects how well you encode information into long-term memory.

You can switch your attention rapidly from one task to another and this change of focus may help your attention levels so perhaps there is some value in multitasking if performance is less of an issue. For example, many people now enjoy watching a sporting event on the television, talking to whoever is with them and following social media at the same time – it probably doesn't matter if your performance on all tasks isn't 100 per cent focused. And I suspect most people can manage to make a cup of tea, carry on a conversation and keep an eye on what their children are doing in the garden without any significant drop in performance. In the chapter devoted to digital learning you'll find out that games players actually improve their multitasking abilities.

When multisensory may not be the right thing

If you're reading these chapters in logical order you've probably just read the one urging you to use lots of multisensory input because it helps us to encode information more strongly which will help with recall later. But is it always crucial to use multisensory inputs?

Do you remember your brain switches activity to either the anterior cingulate cortex or your sensory cortices when you're paying attention to your own thoughts or when you're externally referenced? When you are learning it may be useful to pay attention in both ways at different points in your learning. At a practical level you may need to decide when you want multisensory material and when you may need internal thinking time to get away from colour, noise, touch, taste, smells.

I still remember the first accelerated learning 'Train the Trainer' programme I went on. I'd been totally attentive all day with my senses assailed with colours, noises, movement, emotions; even tastes and smells because we did a wonderful visualization of a lemon that had us salivating, even though there were no lemons! By the end of that day I was overwhelmed and had to go into the swimming pool and deprive myself as much as I could of sensory stimulation. I needed to focus and pay attention to what was going on internally and reduce the distraction from external stimuli. As my head sank under the water and I closed my eyes and floated I was exquisitely attentive to what was happening in my brain, and so pleased to have a rest from all the external stimuli.

This is one of the biggest challenges to trainers and designers who think they have to be providing input all the time – let people pay attention to what's going on inside their heads as well as outside.

Make things more multisensory when you want people focused on the outside world, perhaps their learning materials, a quick video or the discussions, but potentially reduce the multisensory input when you want them to reflect or process internally.

Get people into flow and help time to fly

We can't talk about attention and focus and not think about the concept of *flow*, which is a concept from positive psychology described and investigated by Mihaly Csikszentmihalyi (2008). It's the idea of being completely immersed and fully focused on something; you have an energized focus and complete involvement in an activity. Sometimes people talk about feeling joyful or energized when they are in flow but sometimes you're not consciously aware of your feelings at all because you're so focused on the activity. Time often flies by without you noticing and it's intrinsically rewarding. It's essentially a great place to be for a while, though people in flow don't always pay attention to others or to their own bodily needs like eating, drinking or sleeping.

Csikszentmihalyi's theory suggests three things need to be in place to achieve flow so it's worth thinking about how you can create these conditions for yourself and your learners.

You need a task or activity with clear goals and progress, clear and immediate feedback so you can adjust your performance to maintain the flow state and the right balance between the perceived challenges of the task and your perceived skills. You need to be confident you can complete the task but it needs to be complex enough to be challenging.

The enemy of flow is apathy or boredom. In fact I'd argue boredom is the enemy of most learning though there is some evidence that being bored can lead to creative thinking (Rhodes, 2015).

Increase levels of self-reference

It's common sense really that we pay attention to things when they refer to us but it's one common sense idea that is backed up by evidence. A meta-study of the research at the University of Connecticut in 1997 concludes that people pay more attention to and remember information more easily if they are able to relate it to themselves, potentially because it creates more elaborate processing of information (Symons and Johnson, 1997).

Our own feelings of self and conscious awareness are incredibly complex and the study of consciousness is still uncovering new ideas every day. We're not going to start unpicking that here because otherwise you'll end up in deep philosophical conversations about what is self and what is consciousness and if Anil Seth, co-director of the Sackler Centre for Consciousness Science, can't explain it quickly then I certainly can't.

If you're looking for the biological location though, the sense of self seems to cause activation in various cortical structures. This includes the medial prefrontal cortex, the prefrontal cortex and activity has also been measured in the ventromedial prefrontal cortex when subjects were asked to encode self-referential material. Other studies have shown that an area of the visual cortex, the extrastriate body area, seems to be important to us in recognizing parts of our bodies as belonging to us.

So what can you do as a trainer to create a strong self-reference for people? Some of these things are really simple and you probably include many of them in your design and delivery of them already; at least now you know it's backed up by research:

- Use people's names regularly when you're talking to them.
- Capture registered names and use in digital training too.
- Ask people what their reflections are on what they just learned.
- Ask them how they'll use the material later.
- Use people's names as you ask questions to significantly boost attention.

- Use stories that are specifically about their business, their organization, their situations, or ask them to tell their own stories.

- Adapt exercises and case studies so they fit with their own experiences.

- Use the word 'you' far more than 'I' in text and when you're talking to people. Instead of 'I need you to complete this exercise' write 'You need to complete this exercise'.

- Write instructions using direct rather than indirect speech: 'When you've finished reading the text, answer the questions'.

Even talking about people's relations has been shown to have an effect on self-reference and memory so those discussions in the coffee area where you find out about people and can refer back to friends or family are important in terms of attention.

One activity that a client of mine took to doing to increase attention through self-reference, during a computer-based presentation, was to hand the mouse to his audience instead of keeping it to himself. The 'users' became far more alert, plus could then choose when they wanted to move on and what they were focusing on.

Increase levels of exercise

John Medina in his book *Brain Rules* (2008) makes exercise his number one Brain Rule, and if you haven't read somewhere that exercise is going to keep your brain going, increase your life span or do something amazing for you, I'll be very surprised. More and more evidence shows that exercise is good for us and sitting down is bad and it doesn't all have to be about donning running shoes and taking serious exercise.

Students asked to read e-mails and text whilst walking at 2.25 km/h at a treadmill desk improved their memory for the material and also said they felt they were able to concentrate better during the 40-minute reading task (Labonté-LeMoyne *et al*, 2015). Their brainwaves were also measured using EEG and showed signs of lower theta frequency and higher alpha frequencies which the researchers interpreted as superior mental functioning. Researchers have found that students who engaged in moderate physical exercise before taking a test that measured attention spans performed better than students who didn't exercise. The researchers found that exercise primarily helps our brain's ability to ignore distractions, although they weren't exactly sure why.

So instead of asking people to sit down during any form of study, why not encourage them to move or at the very least stand up.

As anecdotal evidence I regularly have people standing up to view, discuss or share information and believe the quality and quantity of questions that people ask are far superior to when they are sitting down.

We've done this even more since an incident where I was talking to a group about the neuroscience of memory. They all seemed pretty interested and engaged; certainly everyone looked alert and as if they were paying attention. One colleague, Carole Elam, came in late and indicated she was just going to grab a coffee before she sat down and so she busied herself at the back of the room getting coffee and didn't really even seem to be concentrating particularly on what I was saying. And then she sat down and 'paid attention'. Later that day, as part of the session, we did a test as to what people had remembered. Carole came up to me afterwards and explained she'd done better in the test for the section whilst she'd been making coffee than when she'd sat down. Her experience was that as she was making coffee she'd felt alert and needed to concentrate in case she missed anything but as she sat down she felt herself slip into 'sponge mode'. Of course we can't measure what it was about the experience that actually increased her attention but we both believe a strong factor was because she was moving rather than sitting. Of course coffee helps with attention levels too, so don't forget that when you're training.

Questions as a powerful tool for directing attention

I'm sure you already use questions when you're designing or facilitating learning but I want you to think about them as additional attention grabbers:

- They increase self-reference, particularly if you use someone's name.
- People have to search in their heads for the answer to a question so they have to recall rather than just encode information.
- They tend to promote eustress; if you're being asked questions you tend to be more alert than if you're just listening or clicking.
- Asking 'why' you might use a particular technique requires more thinking than asking what it is because you increase the processing from structural to semantic.

And also questions are incredibly influential as to where we place our attention.

Here are some quick questions for you to answer. Have you got a pet? Do you know anyone with a pet? What is it about pets that you like or dislike?

Before I asked those questions I don't suppose you were particularly think-ing about animals were you? But merely by posing the question your brain goes off to find answers. A lot of digital learning tends to deliver informa-tion but it is very easy to ask a question and prompt the user to think before revealing the information. So you can direct people's attention to something really quickly just by asking a question about it, which is possibly why so many speakers and orators start with a rhetorical question to grab your attention.

Paralysis by presentation

We've already talked about exercise and some of the other things that might help attention so here's a story about a different scenario for you to consider.

Have you ever been hypnotized? You may not know it yet, but even if you think you've never been hypnotized it possibly happened whilst you were in a training course or a meeting. You may find this story of a coincidence enlightening.

I had the opportunity to participate in a group hypnosis session. I don't think I'm particularly susceptible to hypnosis but after 20 minutes we were given a suggestion that we couldn't move our arms. I wanted to prove I wasn't hypnotized; I knew I could move if I really wanted to, but, somehow just didn't drum up the energy to move – it was too comfortable lying there without moving and I was effectively paralysed. This is apparently quite a normal experience of hypnosis and I have to say quite enjoyable.

Then a few days later I found myself behaving in the same way but this time I hadn't willingly or knowingly been hypnotized – and it wasn't the intention of the 'hypnotist' either. In a seminar one morning the room was comfortably warm, the seats were soft and deep, the lights were dimmed for the slides and the presenter was familiar with his material.

After about 30 minutes he decided it was time for the 'interactive part' and asked for questions. Nobody volunteered, so the facilitator asked some questions of the 'expert panel'. One of them made an interesting point to which I wanted to respond, but I couldn't rouse myself to say or do any-thing; I recognized that I was paralysed again. I was in the same physical and mental state as when I'd been hypnotized. The conditions for this, and many face-to-face training sessions, are similar to those deliberately chosen for the hypnosis session; muted lighting for the PowerPoint, comfortable warm surroundings, lots of other people being still, and someone talking to us in a comfortable way.

On reflection, how often do you experience slowness in getting your participants to actively participate or ask questions at the end of a session – are they in a state of light hypnosis? Do you ever find that people said they were interested in your ideas before your session but then it's hard to get them to respond once you've got started? Or have you told a group that you'd really like this to be interactive and to ask questions and then felt frustrated when nobody asks any? Even more frustrating is the experience when you've asked for a decision, nobody disagrees but then you find people seem to be going against it when they are back in the office.

In a hypnotic state we absorb information quite effectively but a key feature of hypnosis is that some of your critical faculties are turned off – you stop evaluating what you see, hear or feel – you become suggestible and you're certainly not in a highly attentive state. Perhaps you may want to consider what state people are in when you present your information to them. Perhaps they are literally in no fit state to critically evaluate the information they've been given and respond. They can only do that when they've been reawakened by walking back to the office – by which time it may be too late.

So if you need people to actively absorb and learn something, particularly if you want them to consider it, challenge it or engage with it, presenting it through the power of hypnosis is not the most effective way of doing it. But if you want to let information be dripped in non-critically, then use a guided visualization to boost ideas about creativity or confidence for example.

Summary

People will learn better if they've paid attention to what they are learning. Without attention information may not start to get encoded into long-term memory (more of that in another chapter). To increase attention levels:

- Find the Goldilocks level of arousal – just the right amount of eustress.
- Increase the complexity of processing.
- Decrease the amount of multitasking you ask people to do.
- Decide whether multisensory input is helping or hindering.
- Get people into flow to help time to fly.
- Get people to feel it's personal by increasing the levels of self-reference.
- Stand up, walk around, get people moving.

- Encourage more complex digital interaction; eg sorting rather than clicking.
- Direct attention to what's important – questions are an easy way to do this.
- Don't hypnotize people.

References and further reading

Csikszentmihalyi, M (2008) *Flow*, Harper Perennial, New York

Galfano, G, Dalmaso, M, Marzoli, D, Pavan, G, Coricelli, C and Castelli, L (2012) Eye gaze cannot be ignored (but neither can arrows), *The Quarterly Journal of Experimental Psychology*, **65** (10), pp 1895–1910

Harrison, C A, Byrne, S L, Hagan, M L, Redgrave, P and Dean, P (1984) Reduced locomotor activity as an acute effect of damage to superior colliculus in rats, *Behavioural Brain Research*, **13** (3), pp 273–77

Krock, L P and Hartung, G H (1992) Influence of post-exercise activity on plasma catecholamines, blood pressure and heart rate in normal subjects, *Clinical Autonomic Research*, vol 2, pp 89–97, https://doi.org/10.1007/BF01819663 (archived at perma.cc/29UC-NW7S)

Labonté-LeMoyne, É, Santhanam, R, Léger, P, Courtemanche, F, Fredette, M and Sénécal, S (2015) The delayed effect of treadmill desk usage on recall and attention, *Computers in Human Behavior*, **46**, pp 1–5

Medina, J (2008) *Brain Rules: 12 principles for surviving and thriving at work, home and school*, Pear Press, Seattle WA

Potter, R and Callison, C (2000) Sounds exciting!!: the effects of auditory complexity on listeners' attitudes and memory for radio promotional announcements, *Journal of Radio Studies*, **7** (1), pp 29–51

Rhodes, E (2015) [accessed 2 July 2015] The exciting side of boredom [Online] https://thepsychologist.bps.org.uk/volume-28/april-2015/exciting-side-boredom (archived at perma.cc/GTU5-4W4W)

Rock, D (2009) *Your Brain at Work*, Harper Business, New York

Sciencedaily.com (archived at perma.cc/WDN8-Q2WJ) (2015) [accessed 2 July 2015] Physical activity may strengthen children's ability to pay attention [Online] http://www.sciencedaily.com/releases/2009/03/090331183800.htm (archived at perma.cc/J2LQ-ZTT4)

Symons, C and Johnson, B (1997) The self-reference effect in memory: a meta-analysis, *Psychological Bulletin*, **121** (3), pp 371–94

Yerkes, R and Dodson, J (1908) The relation of strength of stimulus to rapidity of habit-formation, *Journal of Comparative Neurology and Psychology*, **18** (5), pp 459–82

Making learning meaningful and valuing intelligence

Beautiful mathematics

$$e^{i\pi} + 1 = 0$$

How beautiful do you find this equation?

Apparently it's called Leonhard Euler's identity and mathematicians find it beautiful (Zeki *et al*, 2014). Whereas the one below is considered ugly, sadly for Srinivasa Ramanujan who derived it:

$$\frac{1}{\pi} = \frac{2\sqrt{2}}{9801} \sum_{k=0}^{\infty} \frac{(4k)!(1103 + 26390k)}{(k!)^4 396^{4k}}$$

It turns out that non-mathematicians who don't understand these equations, me included, *and* mathematicians all show similar reactions in a particular part of the medial orbitoprefrontal cortex when making judgements about beauty – even the beauty of equations. On the other hand when you're actually looking at and processing numbers a different area of your cortex, the inferior temporal gyrus, which is known to be involved in the processing of visual information, seems to be particularly and specifically active. Yet this area isn't activated when you look at numbers that are written as words, eg 'one', 'two'.

Processing numbers isn't something that is hard-wired into your brain; you're not born with a number recognition neuron (or set of neurons). It's something that you learn, and you learn to use parts of your brain that were originally designed for something else. It's as if you develop a mathematical skill on the back of some other processing you do more naturally and yet some people seem to have a real strength for maths and some of us don't. Many of us feel mathematicians are very intelligent, but if they are just hijacking part of the brain that normally does something else is there anything especially intelligent about them?

The disruptive element in the classroom

Have you ever, as a trainer, educator or learning facilitator had a disruptive element in your learning environment – someone who doesn't seem to want to pay attention, doesn't get it or just generally seems out to cause trouble? On 'Train the Trainer' workshops we're regularly asked the question 'How do I deal with difficult delegates?' And our response is usually that we don't believe there is such a thing as a difficult delegate but that some people may not yet have found the best way to process the information or skills that they're learning. Your job as a facilitator of learning is to help them explore and find their best way through the information. There may be 1,001 reasons why someone might be disruptive but perhaps they just don't quite get learning in the way that it's being offered to them.

Have you ever seen the film *The Full Monty*? There's a lovely moment in it to demonstrate a group of people being taught something that they're just not getting, until they can translate it into something meaningful for them. Gerald, the ex-foreman of this group of ex-steelworkers, is teaching them to dance like the Chippendales (a dancing group famous for taking their clothes off as part of their routine). Gerald knows some dance steps, and is used to being boss, so he explains and demonstrates the steps but none of the guys are 'getting it'. To them it makes no sense and has no meaning for them. They can hear what he's saying, they can see what he's showing them, they're even able to put one foot in front of the other when he tells them to – but they're still not able to make real sense of what they're learning and apply it; they can't dance and certainly not how Gerald wants!

Until one of them, called Horse, relates it to something else he already knows and shouts out 'It's the Arsenal offside trap isn't it. Why didn't you say that before?' and suddenly they're all dancing! They've found something meaningful to them that makes sense of the new information so they can express it and use it.

All of us need to make sense of things to help us learn. Perhaps there's another way of designing learning that will make more sense to more people, so they can understand and process it. In this chapter (see Figure 8.1) you'll explore multiple different ways of processing learning and making sense of information that's been presented to you and you'll also find some ideas to help you recognize that perhaps you haven't got difficult delegates at all – just people who may want to process information differently or a task that is better suited to another mode of delivery.

Intelligence and learning

There's a real-world challenge to learning related to the concept of intelligence. People are considered 'intelligent' if they have a high IQ (Intelligence Quotient) and children and adults are graded and assessed depending on this measure of intelligences that is now more than 100 years old. People with a high IQ often do well at school and academically, given the right circumstances; but there is an anomaly in that the people who do well academically aren't always the most successful in other areas at school, at work or in life generally. And the people who are successful in other ways aren't always recognized as being intelligent and certainly may not be academic but they seem able to learn what they need without getting good grades in school.

When you were at school you may have known children who were deemed to be 'intelligent' – they usually got top marks in academic subjects like maths, science, English or history. There were other children who excelled at sport, art, music, dancing or maybe making friends but they weren't always classified as 'intelligent' by the standard measures, despite the fact they clearly had strong abilities in certain areas and that these activities all require complex cognitive processing. You yourself may fit into one of these characterizations. IQ tests, a commonly accepted measure of 'intelligence', measure your verbal skills, mathematical and logical reasoning skills, and an element of spatial awareness, but there are many things that IQ tests don't measure adequately or at all.

Consider people like Neil Baldwin from Stoke-on-Trent, England who is registered as learning disabled and yet has had an amazing life which was documented in the film *Marvellous*. He has an honorary degree from Keele University which he was awarded because:

> He has watched, supported and kept in touch with successive cohorts of Keele students building an impressive network of alumni contacts both national and internationally. He serves the students offering advice and support to students, remaining steadfastly proud and loyal to Keele

(Wikipedia, 2015)

Figure 8.1 Making learning meaningful

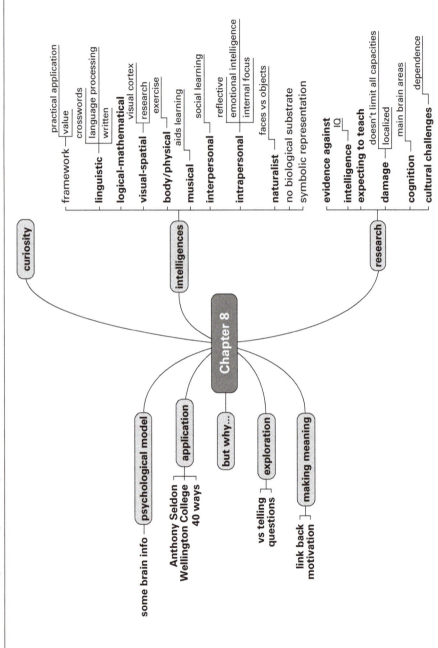

He counts an Archbishop of Canterbury amongst his friends and once even played for Stoke City Football Club as well as being their kit man for many years. Neil Baldwin has achieved success in numerous fields and has certainly learned and adapted throughout his life despite, and possibly even because of, his learning disabilities.

Learning is about far more than just taking information in and remembering it – once you've successfully absorbed information, through your senses, and it's in your head, you have to make sense of it to understand it, and ultimately remember and use it.

Expanding the scope of intelligence to make more sense of learning

Howard Gardner from Harvard University introduced the concept of Multiple Intelligences back in 1993 with the publication of a book of that name. He poses the idea that people are intelligent even if they are not academic, and has identified eight major intelligences. Daniel Goleman coined the phrase Emotional Intelligence with the publication of his book in 1996, whereby he argued that people with a high level of emotional intelligence are more successful in life than those with a high IQ. And before that came the concept of Social Intelligence in the 1930s. So what's important about all these different types of intelligence?

Success doesn't seem to be down solely to IQ – there are many successful people in the world who do not have a particularly high IQ, but still blossom in their chosen field.

Who can you think of that is an 'expert' or excels in a particular field but you wouldn't necessarily class as traditionally intelligent? What areas of expertise are you good at and enjoy and yet you don't necessarily have an academic qualification for?

Multiple Intelligence isn't Learning Styles either

Before we go any further I just want you to be clear that Multiple Intelligence Theory is not the same as Learning Styles. Learning Styles have been largely discounted as having any scientific validity and there's an excellent analysis of why they are not the same by Howard Gardner himself in the *Washington Post* 2013. Learning Styles implies that people have a particular style they favour over others and that it's applicable across a wide range of activities whereas Multiple Intelligence theory suggests that people may have strengths in certain areas and that certain activities might be more appropriate to learning different things in different ways. Gardner's suggestions are to:

- individualize or personalize where possible;
- 'teach important materials in several ways, not just one'; and
- drop the term Learning Styles.

The Multiple Intelligence Theory in learning

Howard Gardner came from an investigative, scientific background and studied neurophysiology and neuropsychology as well as working with people who had various types of brain damage. He came to recognize that all abilities require complex cognitive processes beyond those measured by IQ tests. He originally defined an intelligence as 'the ability to solve problems or create products that are valued within one or more cultural settings' and after 20 years has refined this to 'a biopsychological potential to process information that can be activated in a cultural setting to solve problems or create products that are of value in a culture'.

He has proposed eight criteria to decide whether something is an intelligence and has identified eight intelligences that he believes meet the following criteria:

1 Potential of isolation by brain damage.
2 Evolutionary history and evolutionary plausibility.
3 Identifiable core operation or set of operations.
4 Susceptibility to encoding in a symbol system.
5 Distinct developmental history with defined set of expert 'end-state' performances.
6 Existence of savants, prodigies and other exceptional people.
7 Support from experimental psychological tasks.
8 Support from psychometric findings.

Many intelligences have been suggested but dismissed. Gardner has specifically considered the concept of a 'spiritual' intelligence, but for now errs on the side of caution and does not believe it fully meets his own criteria for classification as an intelligence.

Whilst Gardner's intelligences do not have direct physiological counterparts, ie you can't exactly map them to specific regions of the brain, these criteria do provide a means of categorizing different skills and activities and are certainly useful in helping to design learning interventions that meet the needs of a wider group of people. As more is revealed about the specific neurobiology of the brain there will be some things that map well onto Gardner's theory and others that may throw doubts upon it. Gardner himself, like most good scientists, adapts his work in the light of new evidence.

So how does this matter for you, either as a learner yourself or as someone working with people and helping them to learn? How can you apply this knowledge to help people process information and make it meaningful using their own strengths and how can you use the breadth of your intelligences? You're going to see that Gardner's intelligences can be a pragmatic way to think about how you learn and how you can adapt your learning designs to meet more needs. Gardner's intelligences theory is already adopted across the world in many educational curricula and at the very prestigious Wellington College in Berkshire they think the intelligences are so important they've had them physically built into their environment.

First of all, let's find out what Gardner classifies as intelligences and some quick ideas about how you could use them. You'll read briefly about how some parts of the brain process different sorts of information but remember there is, as yet, no evidence for a full physiological description of the multiple intelligences – and certainly not a physiological test.

Multiple Intelligences in action

Linguistic

The skill with words, used by writers, advocates, story-tellers, poets. You can explore this intelligence by writing or recording all the key points. Write a letter to a friend or a fictitious newspaper article. Develop a written learning summary. Create word searches or crossword puzzles for learners to explore. Language is processed mainly in the left cortex and damage to either of the two main areas, Broca's and Wernicke's, can create unusual effects such as fluent speech with no apparent sense or comprehension or the inability to speak whilst comprehension remains intact. Reading and writing use language processing brain areas with additional visual and motor cortex activation.

Logical–mathematical

The skill of analysis and logic is used by scientists, economists, statisticians, mathematicians.

You can explore this intelligence by sharing flow charts or infographics, asking learners to list main points in a logical, numbered sequence. You can use this logical framework to discuss an idea. Prompt them with the following (AEIOU) questions – what Assumptions; what Evidence; is there a good Illustration of this; what are my Observations; what are the Unique points? The left side of the brain has long been associated with logical thinking and there is some evidence that it may also be more optimistic; better able to work things out to a logical conclusion than 'awfulize'. Neurons on the left side are more densely packed, which may be one reason why the left brain is better at processing detail.

Visual–spatial

The ability to visualize and create pictures in your mind's eye is used by architects, navigators, designers, artists, photographers. You can support learning by creating a learning map, a poster, a cartoon, a video or a visual timeline. Use colour, symbols, linkages, texture and white space.

The visual cortex has enormous processing power and is split into different areas, each responsible for a different quality of visual perception, eg scanning, motion, colour etc. Finding your way around in space calls for right-brained activity in the hippocampus and parietal cortex.

Body/Physical

Using your body skilfully is demonstrated by surgeons, athletes, dancers and craftspeople. You can explore this intelligence by writing, circling or ticking words, building something, sorting flash cards, moving around whilst talking out loud, role-playing or perhaps designing a jigsaw. Just don't sit still!

The primary motor cortex, just about in the middle of your head, sends and receives messages from your muscles to coordinate them. You're also using the cerebellum for balance and coordination and the basal ganglia may play a part in learning repeated actions and habits.

Musical

The skill of creating or identifying complex sound/rhythmic patterns is used by musicians, composers, sound engineers, piano tuners and DJs. To explore this intelligence you could redevelop a jingle, advert, song, rap, rhyme or poem, with the key points from your learning. Or even invent some verses of your own!

Musicians have been found to have, on average, 25 per cent more of the right auditory cortex given over to musical processing. This is particularly strong for people who start to play early in life.

Interpersonal

This is the ability to communicate well or be empathetic and is demonstrated by trainers, counsellors, salespeople, social workers. You can explore this by setting up learning circles or discussion groups or embracing the use of social media and digital collaboration tools. You could also get a mentor, co-coach a friend or colleague or find a study buddy. Make sure you collaborate with others rather than compete.

Working effectively with people calls on many parts of the brain: the limbic system is vital for emotion but part of the prefrontal cortex seems to be involved in understanding other people's mental states.

Intrapersonal

This is the ability to be reflective or at peace with oneself, as practised by Buddhists, diarists, philosophers and life strategists. To explore this you can ask yourself – how can I use this idea/what is its significance to me? Keep a diary or a learning log or produce a personal timeline. Think an idea through before sharing.

Self-awareness is clearly a complex activity, but one area that has been associated with focusing on internal stimuli is the anterior cingulate cortex in the fissure between the two hemispheres. Areas of the prefrontal cortex are responsible for complex cognitive activities like planning and decision making.

Naturalist

This is the ability to recognize and classify the numerous species of an environment. It is demonstrated by naturalists, gardeners, environmentalists, and perhaps even collectors of cars, ornaments, sound systems. This intelligence can be explored by sorting items into categories, creating subsets of different categories, looking for details that make things similar or dissimilar or by searching for environmental implications.

Categorizing and recognition of objects is an activity that seems to take place between the relevant sensory cortex and an 'association' area that is next to it. Memory is important for this task, as is emotion. Single brain lesions can erase all knowledge of a particular object and there are different parts of the brain for identifying man-made and natural objects and even discriminating between familiar and unfamiliar faces.

Other Voices

Nicki Davey, *Director, Saltbox Training and Events Ltd*

Using Nature to Enhance Learning

Being in nature nourishes my body, mind, heart and spirit. I know that I am part of nature and nature is part of me, and I know that my energy, creativity, insight and productivity is vastly improved when I am in and connected with nature.

My years of experience of designing and delivering training have also shown me that nature has a similar effect on learners. When they are connected with nature their willingness, capacity and ability to learn is significantly increased.

Throughout our evolution as human beings, our lives have been totally interconnected with the rest of the natural world. Only very recently in our evolutionary history has this changed. Humankind has become increasingly disconnected from nature and our physical, mental, emotional and spiritual connections with nature and our planet are breaking down.

Since 2009, more people worldwide live in urban environments than in rural environments, and in the West people spend 90 per cent of their time indoors. However, we have a deep-seated human need to affiliate with nature, known as biophilia and research shows that nature is good for us: when people are in or near nature they are more relaxed, more creative, more enthusiastic, and their focus and concentration is better – all of which lead to better learning. Some key findings include:

- Flowers and plants in a workplace increase cognitive functioning and can create a 15 per cent rise in innovative ideas and more creative, flexible problem solving (Ulrich, 2009).

- Connection with nature has a significant positive effect on autonomy, personal growth, and purpose in life (Nisbet, Zelenski and Murphy, 2011).

- When people relate to nature they experience greater feelings of vitality, regardless of levels of exercise and social activity (Ryan *et al*, 2010).

- People who spend 15 minutes each day in nature developed a more positive outlook than those in urban conditions (Mayer *et al*, 2009).

- Plants in classrooms made schoolchildren feel more comfortable, relaxed, sociable and friendly than in classrooms with no plants (Han, 2009).

- Using nature analogies and embedding experiences in a larger natural context helps people to find meaning when experiencing change (Berger and McLeod, 2006).

- People who affiliate with nature derive a greater sense of meaningful existence which in turn boosts well-being (Howell, Passmore and Buro, 2012).

- When immersed in a natural environment, people report feeling more connected to others and to the world around them (Terhaar, 2009).

- Walking in nature improves memory by up to 20 per cent (Berman *et al*, 2008).

- People are more considerate and generous when exposed to nature (Ryan and Weinstein, 2009).

- Being immersed in nature and disconnected from multimedia and technology increases creative problem-solving ability by 50 per cent (Atchley *et al*, 2012).

- Exposure to nature leads to improved cognitive functioning and mental well-being (Kaplan, 1993, 2001).

Rachel and Stephen Kaplan found that people concentrate better after spending time in nature, or even looking at scenes of nature, and they developed the concept of Attention Restoration Theory (ART) to explain why this is so. They suggest that nature is full of 'intriguing stimuli' which gently gain our attention without us having to actively process information or control our responses. Our brain is stimulated whilst still relaxed. In contrast, urban environments are filled with a different kind of stimulation that constantly pulls our attention in different directions. All this busy sensory 'noise' and constant buzz means we continually have to decide where our attention should be directed and make decisions about our actions. Our brain is therefore unable to relax and becomes tired. It requires no effort to reflect on 'soft fascinations' such as clouds moving across the sky, leaves rustling in a breeze or water bubbling over rocks in a stream, and this 'effortless attention' is enough to engage our minds, but not so much that we need to focus our attentions or our mental processes on any challenges, decisions or worries. This gives our brain a chance to rest and replenish which in turn improves cognitive processing and neural function.

So what does all this mean for us as trainers and facilitators of learning and how can we use nature to improve the learning process and outcomes? It's in our interests, and the interests of our learners, to capitalize on the effects of nature to maximize people's learning potential. I use nature to enhance learning in three different ways: Learning *in* nature; Learning *with* nature; and Learning *from* nature.

Learning in nature

We have evolved to function best in nature-rich surroundings and, since being in or near nature is good for us, it also makes us better at learning. Where possible we should use venues with access to nature and outdoor space, or use the local park if necessary. If access to nature outdoors isn't possible, then we can bring it into the training room using flowers, plants and natural materials, or put up posters of beautiful images from nature on the walls. We can open the windows so that people can hear the sounds of birdsong, rain, or the wind in the trees, and if this isn't even possible, we can use recordings of these sounds from nature.

Learning with nature

Nature is infinitely complex, diverse, subtle and inventive and therefore provides an excellent set of tools to help the learning process. For example, we can use nature as a metaphor to help people understand and remember learning points – whether it's from geology, geography, the animal and plant kingdoms, astronomy, ecological systems, meteorology. Look around and you will almost certainly find something somewhere in nature that provides the perfect metaphor for the concepts you are helping people to learn.

Nature also provides us with free training materials. Provided we don't damage the natural world, we can use leaves, branches, flowers, stones, seeds, feathers and other natural items as materials, props and models for training activities.

Nature also provides a powerful mirror which promotes self-reflection and self-awareness. When people connect with nature they connect with themselves and this can lead to deep insight and personal growth.

Learning from nature

Nature has spent millions of years successfully overcoming its problems and challenges and we can learn from nature's experience by looking directly to it for solutions. *Biomimicry* is the imitation of the models, systems, and elements of nature for the purpose of solving complex human problems, and there are many examples of products, services and solutions that developed as innovations inspired by nature, such as Velcro and dirt-proof paint. As trainers we can design activities which encourage learners to solve problems by studying nature's best ideas and replicating these. In doing so, we promote creative problem solving and innovation as well as a connection with nature.

Whatever approach we use to incorporate nature into our training, we can be confident that it will help to create lasting and powerful experiences for learners. As trainers we should also take Einstein's advice to '*Look deep into nature and you will understand everything better*'. Being in nature sharpens our senses, focuses our thinking, opens our hearts and soothes our spirits, and by making time for nature in our own lives and work we become more enlightened, inspiring facilitators of learning.

Measuring the Intelligences

Whilst IQ can be measured using paper-based or online tests it becomes much harder to assess the Multiple Intelligences. Gardner himself suggests that there isn't an easy way to assess them because the tests in themselves are usually inherently skewed towards those with a linguistic or logical–mathematical strength. He believes in observing people to see where they excel and therefore demonstrate their abilities.

And there are so many processes involved in any one skill that even that becomes problematic. So there are criticisms of Gardner's work in that it is self-referential – an intelligence cannot be classified as such unless it meets his own criteria and it cannot be tested because the tests themselves are not 'multiply intelligent'. However, like many personality profiles or other psychometrics there is value to be had in recognizing difference and diversity, and the Multiple Intelligences are a very helpful framework to design learning environments and interventions.

Whether the intelligences exist as physical entities or as psychological concepts there will be differences in the relative strengths for different people. Some will have real areas of expertise whilst being weaker in others; some will have a broad spread. Whilst it is not useful, or even possible, to categorize people as having a particular intelligence it is useful to acknowledge there are differences and to help them approach learning using different techniques.

Criticism of Multiple Intelligences

There are critics of this approach and you can read some of the criticisms and rebuttals online or in a helpful chapter in the book *Multiple Intelligences in the Classroom* by Thomas Armstrong (2009).

MI theory isn't fully mapped or correlated with precise areas of the brain, ie you don't have a 'musical intelligence' area in your brain despite having particular brain areas that process music. This is because these concepts are broadly defined and include diffuse skills and our brain processes are too complex for such a simplistic mapping.

Some of the criticisms come because of the way science unfolds and because it's not always possible to do hard science in the real world. Businesses and organizations don't have time to run double blind trials of training methods; schools need to be careful about risking children's education just to see if a particular methodology is better than another. We do need evidence to assess what does and doesn't work but sometimes we have to adopt a more realistic approach.

Speaking as a pragmatist, multiple intelligences have been adopted by many teachers, trainers and professionals across the world who find they offer a helpful framework for improving performance and there is enough useful corroboratory evidence for me to use it until something better comes along.

Takeaways

Seeing learners differently

When I saw Howard Gardner speak a few years ago he referred to an interview with Wayne Rooney who was describing how he played football. Gardner explained how Rooney needed a different type of processing to kick the ball to someone who was writing a professorial paper about football – and in the appropriate context Rooney was more intelligent. Some of what Wayne Rooney did was complex mathematical processing but he couldn't 'explain' it in a traditionally intelligent way – ie he couldn't wax lyrical and write a professorial paper on it but on the other hand most of the academically intelligent professors probably couldn't do the unconscious mathematical reasoning that Wayne Rooney does to kick a ball accurately.

Could it mean that it would be easier to help Wayne Rooney learn formal maths if you did it through the medium of football rather than talking and writing? I don't know the answer to that question but there is evidence that people can apply complex mathematics because they use it in the real world without actually being able to talk about it in an abstract way. Street children in South America are particularly good at the sort of applied mathematics that allows them to calculate change, percentage discounts and their profit and loss on the day, whilst struggling in the classroom to do formal mathematics (Saxe, 1988; Pluck, 2015). Which of those activities is going to be of more use to them in the real world?

Adopt a growth mindset

Biologically, scientists can see that different people have developed their brains differently and this affects how they process their worlds. Remember the London taxi drivers who were found to have a larger hippocampus when compared with bus drivers? It is hypothesized that their complex driving experience had developed their hippocampus, partially responsible for spatial awareness, as compared to bus drivers who followed a prescribed route. More recent research on these same drivers shows that it was only the part of their hippocampus that deals with visuospatial memory that was enlarged and other areas may actually have become relatively smaller. The author of the original research also wants to see what happens when the taxi drivers eventually retire but it appears she's being thwarted because most of them seem to be continuing to work to a ripe old age.

The great thing about the concept of multiple intelligences is that it is fluid; you can develop your intelligences by exercising them which fits much more easily into our knowledge about neuroplasticity than the concepts of a fixed IQ.

Growth and grit

Research by Carol Dweck (Dweck, 2007) at Stanford University builds on the ideas of neuroplasticity and changing brains and suggests that you can learn even better by adopting a Growth mindset. When students see intelligence as malleable and not fixed, they react to adversity by working harder and trying out new strategies. This ability to persevere is popularly being referred to as grit.

These two non-cognitive skills, more associated with emotional intelligence, may have at least equally important bearing on learning than cognitive skills traditionally associated with success and intelligence. It seems that both grit and growth mindset activate connections between prefrontal networks that are associated with behavioural control but thoughts related to growth mindset provoke activity in the error monitoring areas such as the dorsal anterior cingulate cortex. Behaviours and thoughts associated with grit act more in the ventrostriatal network that supports perseverance, and the delay and receipt of reward (Myers *et al*, 2016). Dopamine and serotonin are both important neurotransmitters linked to grit and growth mindset providing both reward and the ability to keep going.

Educators can have an effect by giving praise or feedback that avoids comments on innate ability and focuses on how people have performed and what they can do to improve. Telling children they've worked hard at something seems to improve their performance more than telling them they are clever at something because this is something they can repeat easily. If they believe they are already smart or stupid they are more inclined to either rest on their laurels or fail to try. Grit and growth mindset are easier to teach and develop than 'cleverness'.

It's well worth researching the work of Carol Dweck and particularly some of the very simple 'tools' she shares about promoting a growth mindset (Dweck, 2007). The simplest one of all is the power of 'yet'. She worked in a school where students were graded as having 'passed' or 'not passed yet' and the results in the school consistently improved. Children began to realize that learning was not a one-off event in which you succeed or fail but a journey that is made more effective when you persist at the learning process. Many organizations would do well to create this kind of learning culture where people associate learning with a continuous process rather than tickbox compliance activities, stressful exams or one-off 'magic wand' training events that will change behaviours overnight.

Teach the intelligences to your learners

As well as designing training that adopts a multiply intelligent approach you might find it useful to teach the multiple intelligences to your students and participants so they recognize there are multiple ways to tackle learning and that by trying new and different ways of learning they are developing their overall intelligence. In a 2007 study of adolescents, it was found that understanding about concepts such as neuroplasticity improved both self-concept and achievement.

I have a very good friend whose son is about to finish school and if social skills were taught, and assessed appropriately at school, he'd be top of the class. As it is he's probably not going to leave school with 'good' qualifications – does that make him less intelligent? If you met him you'd know he is intelligent, bright and smart; he's had various part-time jobs and his employers really value him because he's great with customers and when he needs to learn something that relates to people he's a fast and effective learner. Helping him see that he's intelligent despite what his exam marks are saying may well give him the confidence to continue what he's good at and to build on his strengths. (Since the first edition of this book this young man progressed quickly through an apprenticeship scheme, onto a more responsible role and now works as a very competent consultant for a business in London and is studying for a business qualification for which he's self-motivated.

His own confidence, social skills and growth mindset got him much further than any number of what he saw as irrelevant qualifications.)

As we uncover more about the neuroscience of behaviour and see that it's a complex set of cognitive processes, perhaps we'll stop talking about 'soft skills' and instead talk about valuable intelligences that could be taught at school. The challenge may be in assessing them and measuring in a way that the current education system, with an emphasis on tests that are inherently skewed towards a subset of intelligences, may not be set up to handle yet.

Use Multiple Intelligences as a framework to notice and adapt what you do

The main benefit of the theory and practice of multiple intelligences is that you can begin to move away from a more academic and sedentary method of training, teaching and learning and move into more meaningful learning experiences that people relate to more readily and that are more relevant to the actual knowledge or skills they are learning. Our experience is this significantly reduces levels of boredom, disruption and concern amongst learners as soon as they realize that they aren't going to have to sit in a formal learning environment doing the same thing all day long. Once they realize they will be given multiple different ways to encounter, manipulate and think about information or skills they become engaged and participate more fully. It rarely happens, but if someone does seem to be distracted or disruptive you've also got a useful framework to reflect on what might be happening for them and to devise alternative strategies. Perhaps they have a strong intrapersonal intelligence and haven't been given sufficient time for reflection or a strong body physical intelligence and haven't been able to move for ages and exercise their own particular skills. Think how great you feel when you've been able to do something you're good at – you feel valued and valuable. Give your learners that opportunity as often as you can.

Working with and against your preferences

As you'll know if you work with any personality tools, when people have different preferences or strengths to you it can be more challenging to work with them or to work like them. It's similar with intelligences; you'll have exercises, routines, tools and techniques you've been using for years and they work really well for you. But are they always working as effectively for your learners? If you have a strong linguistic preference, perhaps you liked English or languages at school, you write a blog, you enjoy reading, then you may be offering these delightful experiences to your learners. I know I have a terrible tendency to offer everyone a book as soon as they say they're interested in something – 'Oh I know just the book that you'll enjoy' say my linguistic, interpersonal preferences as I leap across to my bookshelf and thrust a book at them, thanks to a body physical intelligence that kicks in. I see them wince slightly and then remember 'Oh no, not everybody likes books. What would suit this person more?'

Try to design exploratory learning activities that suit multiple intelligences, or in the course of a learning session vary the activities so that you're meeting different intelligences at different times. Explain to people they'll find some activities really suit them and others they'll find more challenging but they'll possibly find their colleagues excel in them. Some topics, information or skills will lend themselves more naturally to particular intelligences. If you're teaching football it probably makes more sense to get out and kick a football, but for some learners they'll also benefit if you give them some theory to back up what they're trying on the field or perhaps they'll get better understanding if they have time to talk it through once they've practised. Just because you've only ever seen Excel spreadsheets trained by sitting someone at a computer and logically talking them through the functions doesn't mean that's the only way to do it. Harnessing the multiple intelligences can increase your creative design capabilities enormously.

Summary

Here are the highlights from this chapter:

- People need to make sense of the information that enters their heads. It seems that different people process information differently based upon their natural tendencies, their experiences and the information itself.

- Harness the Multiple Intelligences to increase your design and delivery skills.

- Working with people's preferences makes them feel more valued and they engage more.

- Howard Gardner proposes eight intelligences:

  1 Linguistic

  2 Logical–mathematical

  3 Visual–spatial

4 Body/physical

5 Musical

6 Interpersonal

7 Intrapersonal

8 Naturalist

- Use these intelligences to adapt what you do to appeal to more people and allow them to harness their natural strengths in learning.

- Increase your own creative design and delivery skills by adopting multiple intelligences as a framework to make sense of learning.

- Remember to work outside your own preferences.

References and further reading

Armstrong, T (2009) *Multiple Intelligences in the Classroom*, ASCD, Alexandria, VA

Dweck, C S (2007) *Mindset: The new psychology of success*, Penguin Random House, NY

Gardner, H (1987) The theory of multiple intelligences, *Annals of Dyslexia*, **37** (1), pp 19–35

Gardner, H (2006) *Multiple Intelligences: New horizons*, 2nd rev edn, Basic Books, New York

Myers, C A, Wang, C, Black, J M, Bugescu, N and Hoeft, F (2016) The matter of motivation: Striatal resting-state connectivity is dissociable between grit and growth mindset, *Social Cognitive and Affective Neuroscience*, pp 1–7

Pluck, G (2015) [accessed 2 July 2015] The 'street children' of Latin America [Online] https://thepsychologist.bps.org.uk/volume-28/january-2015/street-children-latin-america (archived at perma.cc/5MBF-2B6F)

Saxe, G (1988) The Mathematics of Child Street Vendors, *Child Development*, **59** (5), pp 1415

Strauss, V (2015) [accessed 2 July 2015] Howard Gardner: 'Multiple intelligences' are not 'learning styles' [Online] http://www.washingtonpost.com/blogs/answer-sheet/wp/2013/10/16/howard-gardner-multiple-intelligences-are-not-learning-styles/ (archived at perma.cc/798D-Q3VN)

Washington Post (2013) https://www.washingtonpost.com/news/answer-sheet/wp/2013/10/16/howard-gardner-multiple-intelligences-are-not-learning-styles/?noredirect=on&utm_term=.4e32f8b7ae52 (archived at perma.cc/ACW6-P5JZ)

Wikipedia (2015) [accessed 2 July 2015] Neil Baldwin (Keele University) [Online] https://en.wikipedia.org/wiki/Neil_Baldwin (archived at perma.cc/XH2Z-L4FS)

Zeki, S, Romaya, J, Benincasa, D and Atiyah, M (2014) The experience of mathematical beauty and its neural correlates, *Frontiers in Human Neuroscience*, 8 (68)

09

Meaningful memories

From encoding to forgetting

I've never met you before – have I?

Can you imagine what it's like to have been to a place hundreds of times and yet be utterly convinced you've never been there before, you don't know any of the people who you're talking to and you're sure you've never been asked to participate in any kind of memory experiment.

HM is one of the most widely documented people in all of memory research; pick up any textbook on memory and you'll find him in there. Since he died, a fascinating book (*Permanent Present Tense*, 2013) was written about him by Professor Suzanne Corkin, the researcher who spent much of her life working with him and studying his memory, and who introduced him by his name at last, Henry Molaison. Henry had his hippocampus removed when he was in his early twenties as a treatment for severe epilepsy and it's thanks to him that we know so much about memory. Because his hippocampus was removed Henry was unable to create any new memories and even many of his old ones were destroyed or at least significantly damaged.

Henry worked with Suzanne and her colleagues for about 30 years, regularly visiting her laboratory building, working with many people over and over again, but he was unaware that he had met them before or been to the laboratory and greeted them anew each time he saw them. But they were able to establish that, at some unconscious level, part of his memory was still working because he felt Professor Corkin was somehow familiar to him and decided that perhaps he'd known her at school. He was also able to learn skills such as 'mirror writing' without any awareness that he'd ever done it before; once he'd practised for a week or so he was surprised at how good he was at something he believed he'd never done. Professor Corkin also suspected that, like many of us, he may have had some element of selective memory because he was pretty good at remembering how many cigarettes he'd smoked.

What is memory?

Many aspects of memory are still largely a mystery but, as memory is so vitally important for learning, this is your opportunity to explore some of those mysteries and, more importantly for you, to see how you can make sure people have a strong memory of what they learn (see Figure 9.1 for an overview of the chapter). You'll explore different types of memories and triggers for laying down and later recalling memories. You might find out some things you didn't know about memory and I hope you will find some ideas to stimulate your thinking and, perhaps, to change your practices around learning – not just in the design and delivery of learning programmes but also in the wider environment of learning and development.

Figure 9.1   Memory and learning

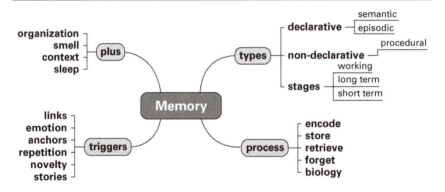

The key player in this memory game is the hippocampus. If you struggle to remember the word then imagine a large grey hippo with a pair of red reading glasses on its head, peering out of a small green camping tent, laid out on freshly mown grass. The hippo is calling in a squeaky voice, asking you why it can never remember where it's put its glasses. This is a silly thing to ask you to remember, but, if you don't already use silly images to aid your memory, as you read this chapter start to unpick why silly images conjured up in your head will help you remember better, and what that might mean for your learners.

Despite the amazing amounts of research, the process of creating memories is still not clearly understood and there isn't one unifying theory.

To understand a bit more about what happens, first have a think about several types of memories because it seems they behave a little bit differently.

Types of memories

Can you talk about what you remember?

If someone asks you who the UK Prime Minister is you can probably tell them. If someone asks you to tell them about your last holiday you can probably tell them about that too. But if someone asks you to tell them how to ride a bike or how to read you can probably start to find words to describe it but it's much harder to actually tell them about the experience. This is the difference between two types of memory – declarative or explicit, and non-declarative or implicit memory. Declarative (explicit) memories are almost what they sound like – you can declare them and talk about them; whilst non-declarative (implicit) memories are much more unconscious or subconscious and are things you've learned that you find harder to put into words. These types of implicit and explicit memories are processed differently in your brain and it's really worth thinking about this because it may alter the way you help people learn if you understand that they are different things you may be trying to do.

Explicit memories split further into semantic memories, those pieces of information that you just know (for example, the Battle of Hastings was 1066 or that the hippocampus is the seat of memory), as opposed to episodic memories, which are the memories of specific events, situations or experiences both autobiographical and general. It's possible you may remember the exact moment when you learned the hippocampus is the seat of memory (episodic) but it's more likely to just be one of those facts you know (semantic).

When you can't describe your memory

Implicit (non-declarative) memories include procedural memories: those memories of procedures that we do unconsciously and regularly so that we've effectively forgotten how we ever knew them. We may even find it hard to think of them as memories as they often just seem like a skill you've learned rather than a memory. However, at some point as you learned to ride a bike you were encoding and storing the complex skills, movements and coordination needed to do this. Now when you need to ride a bike you pull the memory out of all those different areas even if you're not aware of it.

How you process memories

I've already mentioned that you have declarative and non-declarative memories so you're going to read about declarative memories in this chapter and then more about non-declarative memories and habits in the next one on practice and testing.

Declarative memory processing is recognized to have four stages: encoding, storage, retrieval and – equally crucially for learning we also need to remember – forgetting. In real life it's nothing like as well ordered as this, but here goes…

Encoding

First of all you need to receive the information in whatever external format it arrives in your brain and change it into electrical patterns for processing. This encoding happens automatically without you necessarily having to consciously remember, particularly if there are strong emotional, multisensory, novel and attention-grabbing elements. An event like the most amazing holiday you ever had just stays with you, whereas the trip you specifically took to work yesterday as opposed to any other day is much harder to recall because it doesn't have so many of those unique elements to it.

Other types of encoding may seem like harder work; trying to remember the six points of your company mission statement so you can teach it next week is going to require some serious attention on your part. This is a deliberate encoding and feels more like 'learning' than the other sort of memory which just feels like 'experiencing'. The amount of attention you pay to something will affect how well you encode it so you probably didn't pay any attention to the journey to work yesterday because you know the routine and instead were able to put your attention to the training about the company mission statement. (You might want to go back to Chapter 7 on attention to refresh this.)

As information comes into your head it spreads out across your brain into different areas. Some parts of your brain are highly specialized and only process that sort of information. For instance, as you read earlier, in your visual cortex there are individual neurons that only react to information about horizontal lines, others that are only interested in corners or specific colours. And yet what we see is a whole picture because somehow our brains put all the information together to make it seem whole – this is one of the big mysteries of memory, called the binding problem, and is going to be important to remember when you come back to thinking about how you recall memories. How you encode memories is a big piece of how 'sticky' your memories are later and you'll explore some practical techniques later in this chapter.

Working memory through to long-term memory

One of the destinations of the new information will be your working memory, which somewhat confusingly used to be called short-term memory. Working memory is a slightly more realistic description of what is really a psychological construct, ie a model that psychologists use to try to describe something they don't quite understand entirely. Structurally, it seems that your dorsolateral prefrontal cortex, responsible for executive planning amongst other things, is involved. Your dorsolateral prefrontal cortex is heavily connected to other cortical and subcortical areas including your hippocampus.

Working memory is a sort of temporary storage area for information that you use before the journey to long-term memory begins. It has been extensively studied by Alan Baddeley (2009) of Bristol University who has a three-part model for how working memory operates:

1 The central executive sitting in your frontal cortex coordinating the information coming into your brain, focusing your attention, and tying it up with retrieval of old memories.

2 The phonological loop which seems to consist of Broca's area, a language processing area in your left hemisphere and a phonological stage or inner voice sitting in the left temporal lobe. You can hear your phonological loop sometimes when you've been immersed in a thought and someone interrupts you. You ask them to repeat themselves but as they do so you realize that you had heard what they'd said and you can replay it before they repeat it. It seems to last for only about two seconds.

3 The visuospatial sketch pad holds images in mind and is tucked away in your right occipital lobe. This has a much shorter time span than the phonological loop.

Working memory lets you hold information in your head for a short time in order, literally, to work with it; but it's very limited. If I ask you to count backwards from 100 you can probably start to do it, but if I ask you to continue to count backwards whilst recalling the six wives of Henry VIII you're probably going to fail at one task or another. You just can't manipulate that much data in your working memory which is one of the reasons that multitasking degrades your performance.

Storage or consolidation

Useful information coming into your brain needs to be stored somewhere but it's not quite as easy as saying there is one place where your memories are stored.

We know the hippocampus is vitally important for memory because it was Henry Molaison's lack of hippocampus that led to his problems. However, it seems the hippocampus may be more of an organizer than a warehouse worker. Your hippocampus doesn't just store information and then go and get it out when you ask but instead moves memories about to multiple different places and coordinates a very complex process of sorting, moving, shuffling, resorting, until such a time as it feels it's got the best fit. Rather than being stored in the hippocampus, information seems to be stored in the brain in the relevant areas in which it was originally processed; visual information is stored in the visual cortex and auditory information is stored in the auditory cortex. But this means memories are highly distributed across your brain because, on the whole, memories include multisensory, emotional and cognitive elements and this causes neuroscientists a big headache. How can we integrate all those different factors into one seemingly whole memory? This is currently one of the major ongoing areas of brain research.

The episodic memories of your life seem to shuttle for a long time between the hippocampus and your cortex; you store them, retrieve them, put them back again with a constant exchange of information between the cortex and hippocampus as you use those memories (Hupbach *et al*, 2007). An interesting patient known only as HK seems to be only the second person reported as having hyperthymesia: an ability to recall almost all of his autobiographical memories which may be due to a larger amygdala than normal tagging his memories with rich emotions (Jarrett, 2012; Ally, Hussey and Donahue, 2013). Occasionally unusual cases are reported of people who seem to have no significant episodic memories of their own despite having normal memories for facts and functioning perfectly adequately (Jarrett, 2015; Palombo *et al*, 2015). These people also struggle on visual memory tasks and to imagine future events which backs up the notion that memory and future imagination share similar processes. There's even a school of thought that thinks the main purpose of memory is actually to imagine and plan for the future which is a skill that seems rare in the animal world.

Eventually episodic and semantic memories seem to be lodged in your cortex which is when a memory is said to be 'consolidated' but it can take anything from a few weeks to decades. Procedural memories appear to sit mainly in the cerebellum, implicated in balance and some elements of motor control, but procedural memories also need the hippocampus to work hard in organizing them and you'll explore that more when you read about habits.

Over and over again researchers have demonstrated the value of sleep to performance and learning but it's sleeping after the encoding that's important – you don't encode information whilst you're asleep but it is vital for the storage. The neurotransmitter acetylcholine acts like a switch on your memories: during the day acetylcholine levels in your hippocampus are relatively high and information is sent from the cortex to the hippocampus but when you're asleep the hippocampus starts to send information back into the cortex – acetylcholine levels are correspondingly lower. It may be that during the day the higher acetylcholine levels partially suppress excitatory feedback connections which allows you to encode new fresh memories without older ones interfering. At night there is greater and wider electrical activity in the hippocampus which may spread back up to the cortex and help your memories to consolidate. Remember this information about acetylcholine because you're going to meet a whole new set of neurotransmitters relating to sleep and learning in Chapter 13.

Consolidation starts within the first few hours of learning but it can take many years for a memory to be, in any sense of the word, stable, but as you'll see when you read about retrieval it may be that your memories are always shifting. Your memories about you, facts, your life, your experiences are definitely not as solid as you might like to think they are. Once you start getting your head around memory you may never again be able to hold a convincing argument about what happened in the past because you'll see that you're just creating the story afresh each time.

Retrieval

Recall as you might imagine is also complex and isn't simply finding the memory and neatly pulling it out. Whilst memories are quite fresh (hours to days) they are relatively coherent and it's as if you were to retrieve a file from a newly organized office. You will find it where you put it and all the pages are there and in the right order. However, quite quickly these memories 'degrade' and, in the same way that memories were pushed all over the brain when you encoded them, you now have to retrieve them from all over the brain.

Memories are easily disrupted and can be distorted even when you think they are long term and therefore stable. When you remember something your brain pulls in information from across your brain and effectively reconstructs the memory afresh. As you retrieve all those pieces and put them back together again they become labile and unstable and are open to being affected by new data that comes in or other old memory fragments. Studies have shown how experimenters can manipulate memories quite easily and in fact it may be that the process of consolidation happens all over again – not surprisingly it's called reconsolidation.

Imagine you decide to recall getting on a bus last week. You effectively ask your hippocampus to go off and look for as much information as it can about that particular instance of getting on a bus. Depending on how many buses you get will affect the sort of information your hippocampus is able to locate. Now, say you were sitting on the bus next to a lady in a red coat yesterday but you sat next to a lady in a blue coat the week before. As you pull in all your memory fragments the lady in the red coat may just be a stronger memory trace, because it's fresher, than the lady in the blue coat and that trace might displace the blue coat trace. Having remembered last week's bus trip you put all the information back again, possibly whilst you're asleep and that acetylcholine switch sends the information from your hippocampus back into your cortex. Next time you remember last week's trip the red-coated lady has replaced the blue-coated lady. This is how you find yourself telling your friend how odd it is you always seem to sit next to a lady in a red coat. As you can see it's this kind of memory recall problem which causes difficulty for police investigations but perhaps it's also the cause of many personal disagreements over the years: 'I definitely remember it was a lady in a red coat I was sitting next to last week!'

Julia Shaw in her book *The Memory Illusion* (2017) explains some of her research where she implants false memories so that people believe, for instance, they had actually shop-lifted when they were young, even when they hadn't. You'll be glad to know she also helps them to 'forget' after the experiment. Our ability to create memories serves us well but can be a disservice too because we can never be sure they are entirely accurate; however strongly we believe they are. Julia says, 'We can merely collect independent corroborating evidence that suggests that a memory is a more or less accurate representation of something that actually happened.'

One way to try to keep your memories 'fresh' and more representative of the way they were originally created is to repeat the memory regularly whilst it's new and you'll find out more about the importance of review and repetition to effective learning in Chapter 11.

Forgetting

Surely you don't want to ask learners to forget; your job is to help them learn and remember. However, forgetting is vitally important to learning and to mental health. Those people who suffer from post-traumatic stress syndrome effectively can't forget, and this impedes their life because they'd like to forget. Research now shows that it's much harder to suppress or forget memories that are strongly emotional and this has cast serious doubt on the 'repressed memories' theory.

There are other reasons it's useful to know about forgetting too. If you're about to teach a new procedure what you may have to do at the same time is to ask people to forget the previous procedure. A colleague of mine, Jonathan Stevens, teaches touch-typing in a very innovative and successful way. His biggest challenge is to get people to forget their old habits of horrible typing techniques in order to touch-type effectively, not only speeding up their typing speed but also often correcting years of painful necks and shoulders.

One piece of research from Germany shows it may be possible to help people forget by telling them to do it (Dreisbach and Bauml, 2014). Subjects learned to give specific key presses to specific words chosen at random until they were 100 per cent accurate. They came back the next day and one half of the group were then trained on a new 'key press' task and they found that the key presses they'd learned the day before kept interfering in their new learning so they didn't perform as well. The other half of the group were told that the computer had crashed overnight and had lost all their sequences so they could forget everything they'd learned and just start again. This group performed significantly better on day two despite actually doing the same tasks as the first group. Researchers surmised that they chose to forget what they'd learned because it wasn't relevant anymore. Clearly on this task the learning was still quite new so it may be easier to disrupt it with a simple order to forget it.

If you put this into a real-world scenario, it may have implications for what happens when people go back to work after a training course. Regularly people go on a training course and come back with some nice, new, fragile information in their memories. Occasionally they are literally told to forget

– 'well you can forget all that fancy stuff you learned on the course and get back to some real work'. Or it may be more implicit; all the contextual cues around them are for their old habits which makes it much easier to remember the old habit and to forget the new one.

Other Voices

Ann Grindrod, *Simply Learning, UK*

Ann's Story – Unlocking the Key to Memory – Long-Term!

As a trainer, what's the key thing you want learners to take away from their learning? You might suggest a range of things – enjoyment, improvement, confidence, knowledge, etc – and all these answers are important. However, to me, the key thing any trainer needs their learners to take away from the learning is a memory of what has been learned, and preferably for the long term! But it's now very well documented that memory of learning is extremely variable and this is not good news for your clients or your learning sponsor, who will want a clear return on their investment. And of course memory loss is also not good for you!

So what prevents memory formation? There's lots of things, but for me it first became noticeable during my teenage years. At school, most topics were lectured; students were always sitting down; and there was a critical culture – not great for experimental natures! There was also no teaching about 'how to' learn – just a lot of exam cramming. This was combined with a difficult home life, where my independent thinking was not encouraged, learning was not actively supported, and I was given few opportunities to learn from a wider range of people and cultures. I ultimately decided that I was not 'academically' inclined, and although I did reasonably well in a few subjects, on the whole my memory of most academic subjects was pretty poor. When I left education at 16, albeit thankfully, I felt that my prospects were limited.

However, in my choice of careers, I suddenly developed a superb memory, for my work and the lives of the many customers with whom I interacted. Looking back, the factors which aided my memory were: really enjoying my work; gaining knowledge I could immediately apply; working in teams; meeting others from different backgrounds; and everyone (managers and customers) having high expectations that I, and the teams I led, could achieve what was needed, every day. My superb memory lasted well into my late 40s until, following a prolonged period of stress, and re-entry into education part-time, I woke up on the morning of a professional exam, to realize that a lot of my memory had gone, and I could not remember a thing about one of the major exam topics!

I know now that the hormones released during prolonged periods of stress, particularly cortisol, inhibit the growth of new brain cells in the hippocampus, which prevents new memories being made, or existing ones being accessed. Even though my stress was all positive, nine months of working with no breaks took their toll, and I remember how my mind felt 'strange', my concentration was poor, and my recall was highly variable! And thus began my brain friendly journey towards the key (for me) to learning and memory long-term – the discovery of brain maps, variously called mindmaps, spidergrams, model maps, even cognitive cartography! Now known to have been used in varying forms by many of the world's recognized 'geniuses', they contain what to me are the three fundamentals for building a superb memory – imagination, association, and organization.

Brain maps are designed to emulate how the brain naturally works and the most effective maps can become visually stimulating creations through the use of colour, symbols, lines, emphasis, novelty, images, and key words. My discovery of this whole brain alternative to linear thinking meant learning and exam revision became much easier for me, and my recall improved so much that I gained a 96 per cent pass at my next exam; a near-perfect memory!

As a trainer, variations on brain maps transformed my life forever! I used them to plan for client meetings, draw up agendas, quickly record lots of information at meetings, develop tutor notes for learning sessions, provide interesting learning plans, remember the material I was delivering and, best of all for my clients, design creative learning review mechanisms, which helped my learners to achieve up to 100 per cent retention of what they'd learned; a superb memory for them too! And away from work, I started to use maps in every aspect of my life: food shopping, household management, project planning, and arranging holidays, to name just a few. My maps may not always make sense to others, as they're individual to me, but they help me remember so much!

Now I am immersed in another stressful phase of my life, involving elder care, and as I have also reached my sixth decade, I have an increasing awareness of the effects of cognitive changes in later life. Sadly, I have felt the effects of cortisol release on my brain function once again, as different aspects of my memory seem lost to me currently. However, this time around, I recognize what's happening, and thanks to my knowledge of how to support my brain to work more effectively, I am putting strategies into place which are already working, and which I trust will help my brain to function effectively for several more decades to come!

How to help your learners remember

It's all very well having all this great information about how memory works but unless you've got some practical ideas about helping people remember then it's all just neuroscience! How can you make it easier to encode, store and retrieve memories, so people apply them to improve performance?

Rich embroidery

One of the big shiny keys to memory is to encode things more richly, with more gilded decoration and noisy fanfare so that you have many more access points to pick up that information later. It's like the difference between trying to pick up an egg with no shell that slips through your fingers or picking up a knobbly piece of wood with twigs and leaves on it as well – there are lots of easy 'handles' to pick up the information.

1. Links

When you're trying to remember something new it's so much easier if you can link it to something you already know because you're working on stitches that are already in your tapestry. You're building on the networks of neurons that already exist rather than having to start building new wobbly ones:

- Ask people questions about what they already know and then thread the new learning onto those current ideas. Asking questions fires up neurons in an effort to find the answer. The relevant neurons are then active and you can hang new information onto those excited neurons.
- Refer to everyday situations that we can all relate to.
- Ask about work situations that relate to the topic in hand.
- Relate ideas to popular TV, films, books, etc.
- Encourage people to choose their own links.

2. Emotion

Emotion is to memory what Juliet is to Romeo – without the emotional content, ideas lack any life. Business can be seen as rational, measurable and objective which somehow seems to filter down into believing that information has to be rational and objective too. But humans don't work like that; you use emotions to give strength to data so you can measure it subjectively and intuitively as well as objectively. You recall information more easily when it's emotional, but you may not always recall the information you intended to remember and sometimes your emotional memories may literally lead you down the wrong roads.

I visit a friend in Luton only occasionally and I almost always take the wrong turning at a particular T-junction near his house usually causing me to get emotional and call myself stupid. So if emotions strengthen memory why don't I remember the correct way? It turns out it's partly because I let my brain tag the incorrect route with a stronger emotion than the correct route, plus there's a crucial lapse of time. When I first went the wrong way it made me feel anxious, lost and late – I had to turn around and go back once I realized it was the wrong way. But the emotion of relief that I was now going the right way wasn't as strong as the anxiety/fear in the first place and I was paying less attention because I now knew which way to go.

Because it's usually about a year before I revisit Luton the memory trace isn't particularly strong because I've done nothing to strengthen it in all that time. So, as I approach the junction my brain calls up all the information relating to that junction, including an emotion, and I remember being there before. But the actual emotional memory has faded and all it gives me is a slightly stronger link to the incorrect route which therefore feels more 'familiar' – so it must be the right way. And yet again I choose the wrong way and have to turn around again. Of course I curse myself again for being a fool and so I retag the incorrect route with a strong emotion, barely paying any attention to the correct route. Guess what happens about a year later... This feeling of familiarity can be a challenge for recalling all sorts of information when there are emotions and longer timescales involved.

How could I change this pattern? To pay much more attention to the correct road, when I choose it, and to give myself a huge cheer for getting it right. Negative emotions tend to carry more weight than positive ones because they are the ones that keep us out of danger, so I'll have to work doubly hard on praising the correct choice. This could be relevant for your participants too – help them pay more attention to and connect stronger emotions to correct choices to balance up the emotional memory equation. Most of all help people feel the emotions that go with the topics you're talking about – dry data doesn't stick.

3. Anchoring learning

Anchors are a specific way of using the sort of associative learning you read about in Chapter 4, connecting neuronal networks that are already strong and well used. Effectively you repeatedly link two specific ideas together so that the presence of one reminds you of the other; you're actively practising Hebb's Law (cells that fire together wire together). You'll remember that I have previously mentioned linking chocolate to the basic structure of the brain and repeating and repeating this association. Many years later, people still tell me that they always think of the brain when they see a bar of chocolate. As long as you link the ideas together sufficiently you can create anchors to all sorts of things: objects, music, ideas, smells, phrases. Anchors can also be physical, such as pinching two fingers together to link to a particular emotional state that you may want to recreate later, or counting ideas off on your fingers.

4. Repetition, repetition, repetition and meaning

You've already read about how repetition is required if you want to keep a memory fairly accurate. Anyone who, like me, learned their times tables by chanting at school knows the power of repetition on memory. Only yesterday someone asked me what 11×12 was and was surprised that I knew the answer without even having to stop to think – 132. You may have your own particular poem or speech you learned at school that as soon as you start it you can finish it – your neurons know which connections to make without you really putting much conscious effort into it. People can memorize meaningless strings of information, if necessary, through repetition but meaning makes things even easier to remember. Hermann Ebbinghaus was one of the fathers of psychology and famously learned multiple meaningless strings of information discovering that if you do nothing active to review your memory you'll forget most of the information. His famous curve of exponential forgetting from 1885 can be roughly described by the following formula:

$$R = e^{-\frac{t}{s}}$$

where R is memory retention, S is the relative strength of memory, t is time and e is a mathematical constant.

It's this often replicated study that is the basis of the idea that you forget 80 per cent of what you've learned within 24 hours. When you learn without meaning and without repeating the memories later you are very likely to forget most of what you learned. You'll read more about the importance of reviewing, repeating and getting neurons to refire in Chapter 11 on reviewing.

5. Novelty and meaning

Make information stand out in people's heads against the mass of everyday information. Novelty works because it raises our attention levels and causes a momentary frisson of discomfort, even fear, because you don't necessarily know how to react to the new situation or information. This lets your amygdala tag the information as important to remember just in case you come across it again. Novelty for novelty's sake isn't enough for training and especially for learning at work – meaningful, valuable information combined with novelty is going to give you a return on your investment whereas novelty alone is really a frivolity.

6. Stories and meaning

Which is easier for you to remember? This haiku poem from Basho Matsuo, the first great poet of haiku in the 1600s:

An old silent pond ...
A frog jumps into the pond,
splash! Silence again.

Or this 'poem' I wrote with the same number of characters:

Bno stpd bhwx wqlipas
Poiw kglqb iqnc jkaic ewsr
Pdiue toidn mndxzb ygt

Humans have been remembering stories since time began and I expect you probably regularly tell stories, even if you don't necessarily label them stories. Sometimes trainers tell me that they don't use stories and then go on to tell me an anecdote about someone else who tells stories. Anecdotes, metaphors and analogies are all stories in their own way. Stories are memorable because they're emotive, use multisensory language, have a structure that helps to prepare our brains to recognize what's coming and often they cause heightened attention because of a dilemma or some novelty factor. They also give meaning to information and we find meaningful things easier to remember than non-meaningful things. You'll come across stories again in Chapter 12.

7. Organization and chunking

Before you go on to read about some other ideas to help memory retention, have you noticed anything about the first set of six 'memory aids' that would help you to remember them? Did you notice the acrostic (the first letter of each memory aid) spells out LEARNS? Links, Emotion, Anchors, Repetition, Novelty and Stories. You can easily use this LEARNS mnemonic as a checklist to see how sticky your learning designs are.

Acrostics are a useful way to remember information because they create links and meaning between information that isn't necessarily obviously linked. Numbers can also help to organize information and improve recall because at least you know how many pieces of your puzzle you have to fill.

Anything that helps us to organize information into meaningful 'chunks' can help with learning and recall, but chunking is most powerful when learners choose their own categories to put information into. So giving people opportunities to organize and sort information will make it more meaningful and easier to recall as well as delivering the information in chunks in the first place. Sometimes as trainers you may end up sorting and categorizing information in an effort to reduce cognitive overload, but in fact it might be better for learners' memories if you let them do the work for themselves. Sometimes the process of learning can be contradictory.

8. Smell

Smell is often underestimated as a tool of learning, particularly in organizational environments, where people aren't inclined to think about smell as something that belongs at work, unless you work in a perfumery of course. Smell is particularly powerful for memory when there's an emotional context to the memory or it's an autobiographical, episodic memory that's being recalled. Smell is less successful for retrieving facts, ie semantic memories. Receptors in our nose are stimulated by the arrival of a chemical, ie a smell, and they start to fire excitedly and communicate with the neurons in your olfactory bulb which sits nearer to the hypothalamus than your other sensory processing areas. Unlike your other sensory receptors your olfactory receptors are exposed directly to the outside world; visual receptors and auditory receptors are buffered by your cornea and your ear drums so there's already a slight barrier to communication. On top of that, all the other sensory messages have to pass through the thalamus before they connect to relevant cortical areas but the messages to your olfactory cortex don't have to take this indirect route; they just go straight there to be processed. A key destination for information about odours is your amygdala, so smells directly stimulate emotions, which as you know already, strengthen memories. Information about smells also goes to higher cortical areas like the orbitofrontal cortex which is relevant in decision making. Does this mean you'll make your decisions based on smell alone? It's unlikely, but smell might add weight to your decision and is definitely going to strengthen your memory.

If smell is such a strong evoker of memories then it could pay to use it more at work; studies regularly show that students who link particular smells to particular topics are more easily able to recall that information in exams. But remember it is most effective when linked to episodic and emotional material so creating smelly, emotional and storylike links to dry, dusty information is going to optimize your chances of remembering it.

Context

As well as remembering richly embroidered information, another key to remembering well is context. We've all done it – had to go back downstairs to remember why you came upstairs in the first place. Is it the physical activity that stimulates the brain with a better flow of oxygen? Or, more likely, it's going back to the same physical environment that reminds you of what you were about to do. This is similar to context-dependent learning. The classic experiment for this was when Godden and Baddeley (the same Baddeley who defined encoding, storage and retrieval) studied the effect in 1975 with divers who were asked to remember 36 unrelated, two- and three-syllable words (Godden and Baddeley, 1975). When tested later their recall was better on land if they'd learned on land and better underwater if they learned underwater.

The effect also seems to extend to our mental states, our mood and even our level of intoxication. Whilst alcohol will usually make learning worse, students who learned five word sentences whilst 'under the influence' were able to recall it better when 'drunk' than 'sober' (Goodwin *et al*, 1969; Weingartner *et al*, 1976). Learning was superior though when students were sober rather than when they were drunk; so you only need to have a drink to find your keys if you were drunk when you put them down.

What does this mean for training? Would we be better running training courses at work rather than in hotels or special training rooms? Quite possibly – wherever you can recreate similar conditions for learning as will exist back at work when the person needs to recall what they learned and apply it. Whilst you might not have access to flight simulators or virtual reality you can perhaps use actors/colleagues to recreate realistic situations and use real case studies from your business rather than invented ones. Take a leaf out of sports trainers' books and ask people to visualize taking their new learning into the workplace – visualization causes us to activate similar pathways in your brain as those used in actual performance. Rather than teaching abstract theoretical constructs, make discussions, conversations and exercises concrete and relate to the real world that people experience at work. Remember you can create context through the physical, environmental, psychological and emotional environment.

When to sleep on it

When is a good time to learn something, and should you sleep on it to enhance your learning? You've already read that sleep is vital for memory but what you learn and when you sleep might be important. Procedural learning (the skills you do rather than talk about) seems to be most effective just before sleep. It's thought we may dream about the skills and effectively practise them in our sleep. On the other hand learning facts or information, which is dependent on 'declarative memory', seems to be more effective if the learning starts in the afternoon, about seven and a half hours before sleep, though the evidence from this research is slightly less robust.

One thing I've found particularly helpful for learners is to explain to them that receiving information is only the start of the learning process and that if they feel 'full' of information at the end of a day they will feel more comfortable the next day after they've slept on it. The first thing this does is to reduce their anxiety levels and my experience is that the next day they say the information now seems to have settled into their brains. Sleep has become a huge area of research with regular new discoveries so you can find out more in the chapter devoted entirely to sleep and learning.

Summary

Here's a partial summary and your opportunity to put your memory to the test and see what you can remember from this chapter. The answers are at the end of the book on page 285 but before you peek remember how much better you will remember it if you recall or even guess first:

1 Memory is incredibly complex and is not entirely understood.

2 What part of your brain is vital for memory and exchanges information backwards and forwards between your cortex, limbic system, cerebellum, and multiple other brain structures?

3 You have different types of memory: declarative and _____.

4 Name the main two types of declarative memory.

5 You also have emotional memories and _____ memories which are non-declarative.

6 What are the three stages of memory described by Alan Baddeley?

7 Use rich encoding to help information stick in long-term memory.

8 When are your memories mainly consolidated?

9 When you recall information you pull information from many sources and effectively rebuild it afresh each time.

10 Forgetting new information is easier than forgetting old information.

11 What's the mnemonic you can use to design 'sticky' learning?

12 Organization, smell, context and sleep also enhance memory.

References and further reading

Ally, B, Hussey, E and Donahue, M (2013) A case of hyperthymesia: rethinking the role of the amygdala in autobiographical memory, *Neurocase*, **19** (2), pp 166–81

Baddeley, A, Eysenck, M W and Anderson, M C (2009) *Memory*, Psychology Press, Hove

Corkin, S (2013) *Permanent Present Tense: The unforgettable life of the amnesic patient* (Vol. 1000), Basic Books, New York

Dreisbach, G and Bauml, K (2014) Don't do it again! directed forgetting of habits, *Psychological Science*, **25** (6), pp 1242–48

Ebbinghaus, H (1885) [accessed 1 September 2015] Memory: A contribution to experimental psychology [Online] http://psychclassics.yorku.ca/Ebbinghaus/index.htm (archived at perma.cc/9UYW-8Q26)

Godden, D R and Baddeley, A D (1975) Context-dependent memory in two natural environments: on land and underwater, *British Journal of Psychology*, https://onlinelibrary.wiley.com/doi/abs/10.1111/j.2044-8295.1975.tb01468.x (archived at perma.cc/PQ3P-JDJY)

Goodwin, D, Powell, B, Bremer, D, Hoine, H and Stern, J (1969) Alcohol and recall: state-dependent effects in man, *Science*, **163** (3873), pp 1358–60

Hupbach, A, Gomez, R, Hardt, O and Nadel, L (2007) Reconsolidation of episodic memories: a subtle reminder triggers integration of new information, *Learning and Memory*, **14** (1–2), pp 47–53

Jarrett, C (2012) [accessed 2 July 2015] Total recall: the man who can remember every day of his life in detail [Online] http://digest.bps.org.uk/2012/05/total-recall-man-who-can-remember-every.html (archived at perma.cc/66TU-7LD7)

Jarrett, C (2015) [accessed 2 July 2015] Some perfectly healthy people can't remember their own lives [Online] http://digest.bps.org.uk/2015/06/some-perfectly-healthy-people-cant.html (archived at perma.cc/TL78-WCE9)

Palombo, D, Alain, C, Söderlund, H, Khuu, W and Levine, B (2015) Severely deficient autobiographical memory (SDAM) in healthy adults: a new mnemonic syndrome, *Neuropsychologia*, **72**, pp 105–18

Shaw, J (2017) *The Memory Illusion: Remembering, forgetting, and the science of false memory*, Random House

Weingartner, H, Adefris, W, Eich, J and Murphy, D (1976) Encoding-imagery specificity in alcohol state-dependent learning, *Journal of Experimental Psychology: Human Learning and Memory*, **2** (1), pp 83–87

Testing, experimenting, habits and practice

10

Punish the correct answer

Most of us who work in a learning and development environment would like to think of ourselves as helpful people who want to inspire others to learn successfully and effectively. We spend time, energy and resources on creating pleasant and stimulating learning environments and we believe people should, and can, enjoy learning. You may believe it's appropriate to reward people for getting the correct answer; we give out degrees because people get the questions right in the exams; at school we give ticks and gold stars when work is correct. Even at work we reward people with smiles, 'good answer', or gaming points when they get an answer right.

However, a study from 2006 shows that perhaps what you ought to be doing is punishing correct answers (Finn and Roediger, 2011). Yes, you read that correctly, and it is seemingly in contradiction to the advice in the last chapter on providing positive memories. You should perhaps punish correct answers because it seems to improve people's memories for what they learned – at the testing stage. In this particular experiment people were asked to learn some Swahili/English word pairs and were then tested on their recall. When they got an answer right they were shown either a neutral picture or an unpleasant one. When they were retested later the group who'd seen the unpleasant pictures had better recall of the word pairs than both people who'd seen neutral pictures and those who'd merely reviewed the word pairs passively.

Now, as with many psychology experiments this was an artificial situation and it doesn't necessarily mean that we should all start punishing our learners for getting things right. But it does yet again show how important emotional links are for learning, even negative ones. Performance was improved because the increased arousal felt by the people who saw the unpleasant images attached itself to the learned topic and was more effective than having no emotions attached. The other important lesson from this study was the importance of recalling information as part of the learning process rather than just passively reviewing the information again, ie testing improves your learning. The researchers didn't test the effect with positive images which again demonstrates the narrowness of scientific studies and why you really have to look at a range of different results and studies – meta-analysis.

Why it's important to test, experiment and practise whilst learning

In Chapter 9 on memory you came across the process of consolidation where neuronal connections are strengthened when they have recently been used which helps us learn new skills, knowledge or even attitudes. The opportunity for active recall makes learning stick for the long term; just exposing people to information is insufficient for learning to be really effective. One of the key messages from psychology is the benefit of testing for recall rather than merely refamiliarizing yourself with the material, which seems to create overconfidence. If you remember back to the story of me feeling confident about which direction to take in Luton it's a similar sort of problem. When you see the material you've seen before your brain registers it as something familiar and that familiarity tells you that you're confident you've seen it before – which you are but you're not going to necessarily be competent at recalling it.

In this chapter (described in Figure 10.1) you'll explore why to test learning and how, where and when to do it.

For trainers

As a trainer there is value in testing your learners because it means you can check whether they've got hold of the right end of the stick and whether you've done your job effectively. For some training this may be crucial because knowing exactly how to defuse a bomb in a real-life situation may make a significant difference compared to having read about it in a book.

Figure 10.1 Why, how to and why not test

For other areas of learning there may be less at stake but it's still useful to be confident that learners have gone away with the right skills, information or knowledge and that they can use it in relevant situations.

To improve performance

Testing has been known to be an effective tool as part of learning since the first documented empirical study in 1917 by A I Gates where they showed learning was enhanced by recitation. Another study in 1992 by Carrier and Pashler showed that testing wasn't just another chance to practise but that it produced better results; learners who actively tested their knowledge during practice could remember more information than learners who spent the same amount of time just studying the information. It has been demonstrated repeatedly that retrieving information is more effective than merely being re-exposed to it. This all makes sense because learners have to make the effort to recall that information from wherever it's stored which reconsolidates the memory, rather than just checking whether it's familiar. You'll remember from Chapter 9 on memory that something that's familiar may be a false friend.

At work, significant amounts of time and energy are spent with senior managers presenting their vision of the future, or the company structure or the systems architecture over and over again, when they would probably find if they merely kept quiet and asked the audience to tell them about it people would remember the information better. Learning is improved by active testing but, as you'll read later, testing may not always be as effective as it could be.

To increase confidence and motivation

What other reasons are there for learners to test their learning apart from it improving their performance? One key factor is the confidence it can give them to see their progress and the added benefit of showing them that learning is a slowish process and not a magic wand that trainers and educators can wave. Have you ever had that feeling of frustration when you're learning something new and not making progress? My squash game is like that at the moment as I'm going through these coaching sessions and I know from talking to my coach that I'm not the only one losing games as I struggle with a new serve. When I'm in a game my serve keeps going wrong but when we're back in the safety of a coaching session and I carefully test my lob serve I can get it right, and that progress motivates me to continue practising. Now I just need to practise sufficiently to use the lob serve effectively in a game; but at least the testing shows me I've not become entirely incompetent.

To make adjustments

Testing lets you make adjustments to your new skills or new knowledge, hopefully in safe situations where you can make mistakes without serious consequences. When you learn something new those new neural connections aren't as strong as you need them to be so they are prone to interference from old habits and you probably also need to make fine adjustments. This is going to be true about learning a new motor skill like a sport or learning to be a neurosurgeon but is also the case for other less obviously physical activities. Have you ever watched a colleague come back from a training course and practise their new-found behavioural skills? I used to meet someone regularly who had fairly recently been on a communication skills programme and it was positively painful watching her practise and test out her skills; they weren't natural to her. It was almost comical watching her consciously rehearsing what to do when she met someone new and then see her going through her 'build rapport' routine; shake hands with required firmness – check; make eye contact – check; mirror body language – check. Later when I met her again these skills had become automatic and she greeted people without having consciously to go back through her checklist.

I'm sure you already suggest to your learners who are practising new skills that they do it on safe ground first such as negotiating with your toddler before going in to talk to your boss about a raise in salary. Practise in an environment where you can check, adjust, replay and check again until the learning becomes automatic.

To change habits

Think about your brain and compare the differences between a well-established neuronal network with cells that have been firing together for years and the wobbly neuronal network that is tentatively being created thanks to the really useful training programme you attended yesterday. When you're back at work and you're thrown into a situation where you could use your new learning, imagine what's going on.

For a start, you normally spend a lot of time operating on autopilot; a situation occurs and you just respond automatically; a stimulus appears and your habitual response kicks in. Robert Cialdini describes this very effectively in his book *Influence: Science and Practice* as the 'click-whirr' mechanism that you can see in baby birds when they see a parent with food. They're wired to respond that way; and we have similar strongly wired behaviour too. Our habituated responses are strong; they've served us relatively well until now and to break those habits takes effort, energy and resources.

First of all you're going to have to recognize it is a situation where the new learning could be effective, then you have to suppress all that activity that your well-wired pathways have started and go looking for the new wobblier pathways. The new task is likely to activate far more of the pre-frontal cortex in order to pay attention to what's going on and the prefrontal cortex is energy hungry. Recognizing that you've got a new skill to implement will increase your attention and arousal levels so suddenly you've got more stress hormones moving around your brain and body and stress hormones are known to reduce performance on cognitive tasks. So even if your new skill is physical you've just made it more cognitive by being so painfully aware of what you're doing.

As you learn a new skill it's not going to be as perfect or as well-honed as someone who's an expert. When you're learning you're going to have to make lots of adjustments and correct errors. The prediction of error seems to happen in your right prefrontal cortex but the detection of errors may be done by the anterior cingulate gyrus which is connected both to your cortex and your amygdala thereby responding to emotional and cognitive components of learning.

Neuroscience of habits

The formation and breaking of habits has gained a lot of attention in recent years and many new discoveries are shedding more light on the process inside our brains. Charles Duhigg in his book *The Power of Habit* (Duhigg, 2013) suggests that habits can't be broken and can always lurk ready to pop up again, sometimes when you least want them. Conversely, it's also hard to learn new habits whether you're trying to replace an old one or just start something entirely new.

There is a strong dopaminergic pathway between the frontal cortex and the striatum (one of the basal ganglia) and this is heavily implicated in the making and breaking of habits. As you consciously learn and practise something your goal-directed behaviour is mainly directed by the orbitofrontal cortex (OFC – an area of the prefrontal cortex mainly responsible for decision making). Because of the strong connections between the OFC as you achieve your goal or receive a reward for the action the striatum releases dopamine so you feel rewarded and want to repeat the behaviour. But as your behaviour becomes habitual the levels of dopamine, at a cellular level, drop so you don't get the same reward any more. So, after a time management course you get back to work and practise your new routine of only checking your e-mails at lunchtime and get the reward of feeling virtuous and making those phone calls instead. But after a little while that reward is less 'rewarding' and if the habit hasn't become fully engrained then it's really easy to slip back into the old routine because that in itself has some reward associated with it; perhaps the sense of 'being busy' that checking your e-mails gives you.

A recent study (Gremel *et al*, 2016) suggests that less well-known neurotransmitters called endocannabinoids may be the ones that effectively change a conscious cortical activity into a habitual unconscious activity. Endocannabinoids are linked to physical activity and are one of the factors responsible for a 'runner's high'. It seems they begin to reduce activity in the OFC so that your actions become more unconscious and less goal-directed and harder therefore to change. These researchers predict that this discovery will make endocannabinoids as famous as dopamine and endorphins.

Along with that discovery is another (Martiros *et al*, 2018) showing how a habitual pattern of behaviour is marked in the striatum as a specific sequence and is one reason why it's hard to break persistent habits. If you think for instance of a habit like brushing your teeth there is a relatively complicated sequence of behaviours that lets you pick up the brush, spread on the toothpaste, brush in multiple directions etc. When the habit is new the striatum fires consistently throughout the pattern of connected behaviours but as the sequence is repeated day in and day out the firing becomes clustered at the beginning and end of the task and this pattern becomes much harder to break.

Habits usually have a trigger or cue, a routine and a reward and you can break a habit by changing any one of them. Sometimes the trick is to identify which part you have the most influence or control over.

Changing habits and CARS

Evidence-based research indicates it takes anything between 16 days to eight months to break a habit but the average is about two months – not 21 days as sometimes reported. If you fail occasionally it won't ruin the effort – carry on with the chosen behaviour and you'll get there. But be aware the old habit is probably still lurking so here is a framework to help you or your colleagues change your habits:

Cues – the things you encounter regularly that you have linked to particular behaviours – you need to identify your cues to certain behaviour patterns.

Actions – the things you do in response to the Cues – you need to change these actions into new habits.

Rewards – what you get as a result of the Actions – you may find the reward remains the same or you may require a new reward.

SIMPLE ideas – to improve your success at building new habits:
- S – Small steps – don't try to change everything at once but start with small, easy-to-implement changes.
- I – Increase your efforts as you find the changes are working; you may want to try new connected habits or extend the current one.
- M – Missing an action; if you miss an action occasionally it won't affect your habit formation. You don't want to get emotional about having missed it because that may well reinforce the old habit; you simply return to the required action and if possible reward yourself again. Often, it's sufficient simply to be pleased you've returned to your new habit; it's not hard to provoke your brain into a dopamine release.
- P – Practise regularly – all habits need lots of repetition to diminish the previous habit and build new strong pathways (remember neuroplasticity).
- L – Link to other similar habits to improve your chances of being successful. So for instance you might want to learn a new language.

Language apps are really useful because you probably already have the habit of checking your phone in the morning so you simply add that to your routine.

- **E** – Environment – change your environment so you don't experience cues for previous habits that might undermine the new one. Imagine you want to spend more time at work moving rather than sitting. Change your desk to an adjustable standing desk and as you leave at night make sure it's in the standing position so when you arrive in the morning it's just as easy to stand as sit.

How to test

Testing is a key part of learning because it lets us see where we're going wrong, what we're doing well, and to make adjustments; but it's not the end of the learning journey – it's just a part of it and it can upset things when it's not done well.

A few years ago I was lucky enough to go to a wine tasting course with one of my daughters. It was an excellent day out and we learned a lot about wine; where it came from, what wine went with what food, how to tell a Sauvignon Blanc from a Chardonnay, and other useful and delicious things. The bonus was we got an official certificate at the end to prove we had learned something. Now, I don't know about you, but surely the most important part of wine tasting is the skill of being able to tell your Shiraz from your Merlot rather than the semantic memory that Shiraz is the same as Syrah and comes from the Rhône area of France. Having spent the day pouring, peering at, smelling and tasting wine we had to do a multiple-choice test that merely tested our familiarity with some facts. The things that were new to me and I really was learning weren't included in the test. Eighteen months on I had to Google that information about the Shiraz grape being the same as Syrah even though I have a certificate to prove I passed the test.

Across education and training there is a tendency to test people's semantic memory or their knowledge of facts. We most commonly still do this in written tests but a lot of what we learn isn't semantic knowledge. Thinking back to Howard Gardner's Multiple Intelligences you'll begin to see why this is not necessarily helpful to all learners or for all types of learning. Being able to describe a skill (declarative memory) is not the same as being able to do it (non-declarative memory) Gardner believes it's better to measure intelligence by observation of action in the real world. Real-world tests might be better for your learners too.

If you are able to influence learning techniques in your environment then please think about how you test learning and what you're testing. Someone may be able to write a superb essay for their MBA on running a business, but would you put them in charge of your most important business unit without some further real-world experience and testing?

Next you're going to look at some ways to test as part of the learning process.

Teach someone else

Summarizing and integrating information creates lasting memories because you have to recall the information. And a really good way to do this is to teach the information to someone else. You may remember the study from Chapter 5 on motivation where the researchers found that just expecting to teach something later improved learning. Two groups were asked to study a passage of text for a later test. One group were told they would have to teach the text to another group who would then be tested. This group were able to recall more of the passage, their recall was better organized and they could correctly answer more questions. Neither group actually did any teaching but both were tested so the difference in performance was down to their expectation they were going to have to teach. That's definitely an example of a science experiment proving what good trainers already know – the best way to learn something is to teach it or at least expect to have to teach it.

Drawing as a test

Drawing information as a way of testing also seems to make learning more effective. There have been differences seen as to the benefits of drawing in learning depending on what's being taught and you may remember some of those experiments you read about in Chapter 6 that suggested drawing could improve learning; though those experiments were done with children so it's always possible the evidence could be different if adult learners were tested.

Looking back at the research about recall versus recognition, this seems to be further evidence that having to get the information out of your head and manipulate or use it in some way is superior to continuing to put it back in through just looking at it again. Personally I think this has significant implications for information delivery at work because often people are given information at a meeting and then somehow it's expected that they will just know that information forever. How often have you heard someone say 'I've told them again and again but they just don't do it'? Perhaps you could try telling someone and then asking them to go and map out the process or draw the organizational chart for themselves.

One of the added benefits of drawing was that students reported enjoying learning more when they could draw. This was dismissed in the original journal article as almost irrelevant to their research but, of course, if people enjoy learning something they are more likely to come back for more. Very few people ever say 'That was a really miserable experience and I'm just itching to go back and repeat it'.

Can neurofeedback improve practice and testing?

The type of practice you get does seem to have an effect on how well you can master a skill, and some interesting research about neurofeedback seems to show that you may be able to master a skill much faster if you closely copy what experts do and get feedback as to what's actually happening in your brain. Neurofeedback is a relatively new technique whereby you can measure electrical brain activity and see or hear the feedback in order to reduce or increase particular responses in your brain. It seems that it may be useful for learning some motor skills, such as target practice for archers, and has been tested on musical performances, dancing and acting. It's been shown, for instance, to help actors perform better by showing them how to get into a more productive 'flow' state. However, it's not yet been shown to be particularly helpful in attention-related or cognitive tasks and even the manufacturers of the neurofeedback equipment recognize that far more serious scientific research needs to be done to meet some of their claims for performance enhancement.

Practice – the 10,000 hours myth

You may have heard that in order to be good at something you need to practise, practise, practise – possibly whilst you were learning an instrument at school. Malcolm Gladwell in his book *Outliers* (2009) suggested that in order to become an expert you need to practise for 10,000 hours. This idea became popular and is either hugely inspiring or hugely depressing depending on the time you have available to you. If you've got a handy 10,000 hours then you could become a virtuoso violinist, perhaps even without much real talent, but if you're a bit short of time then you're never going to become good at anything, however much talent you have.

Fortunately the 10,000 hours has been debunked. Even the original researcher Anders Ericsson, a Florida State University psychologist, has said that it's not just simple repetition that creates expertise because you also need feedback in order to adjust your execution to get it right. It seems the quality of the time you invest in the practice, the more deliberate you are about it, and the feedback you receive are equally as important as the amount of time.

And you can't cram all your practice into the shortest time possible because as you already know your brain needs downtime – time to recover and consolidate what you've learned. It seems world-class experts limit themselves to no more than four hours of *focused* practice per day.

Creating real-life or virtual environments

In April 2015 a BBC report mentioned an initiative by an educational consultant to let children use Google whilst they were in exams because this was how they would genuinely work at home whilst revising and later when they had to use that knowledge in the workplace. I can imagine some people were choking on their cornflakes that morning but it's worth considering the merit of the suggestion. Context-dependent learning has been shown repeatedly to work – remember the 'drunk students' in Chapter 9 on memory? If people learn by using Google or, of course, another search engine, and they have to use that learning later in a similar environment then it makes sense to test them under the same conditions. In a research laboratory if the testing was done under hugely different conditions to the original learning you'd have peer reviewers shouting about the lack of consistency in the experiment.

The same thing could be said of learning and testing at work. If the topic of the training is 'Customer Support' then the best place to do the training and for people to test their skills could quite possibly be with customers. One way to replicate this, or get as near as possible, is to use actors to create realistic scenarios rather than have the rather forced role play that most people seem to find embarrassing. When faced with a seemingly realistic customer, people are better tested and less embarrassed.

Pilots are trained on realistic events using virtual simulators, UK lifeboat volunteers are tested in huge training tanks where artificial storms can seem awfully real and doctors are trained on neurosurgery using virtual simulations. Personally I'm quite pleased to hear all these people are tested out on simulations before they get to fly me on holiday or remove a vital organ. I'd be far less happy if they'd just sat a written exam. In the three years between the first and second edition of this book virtual reality has already become much cheaper to design and implement and it's likely to become a more familiar tool in organizational settings.

Here's another of our 'Other Voices'. Read Darja Mirt's story about how she tested her learning about Brain Friendly Learning principles in a real-life environment.

Other Voices

Dr Darja Mirt, *DVM, PhD, Slovenia*

Using Brain Friendly Learning for more creative workshops

As a manager I often run team meetings and short workshops and I was interested in how Brain Friendly Learning could make these more creative and effective. Following the workshop I worked on applying the concepts learned for an important one-day meeting with my team that I needed to prepare. We were together from afternoon one day till lunchtime the next.

I planned the event starting with an informal walk in nature as a relaxed and easy way to talk as a team. We had special team T-shirts for the occasion and a nice dinner together in the evening.

The next day we had the formal part of our meeting. I made the style and format completely different, including no laptops.

I had small gifts for each person as a thank you for their work during the year, each chosen for the person. I brought a railway model, 100 pieces that they put together to represent the journey we had been on during the past year. They were surprised by this, but really enjoyed it and while putting it together we discussed our experiences, successes, challenges and learnings during the past year. The process made it very relaxed and they were very honest and open, sharing stories and feelings and telling each other what they appreciated and giving a lot of respect to each other.

I also had some Euro image chocolates that they got when sharing the stories and examples of achievements and some 'brain' erasers when we talked about challenges.

They really appreciated the honest and open feedback they gave each other, which was a very positive experience with some learnings, positive feedback and even a few 'Aha moments', even for me.

At the end of the meeting I asked for their feedback and they were very satisfied, appreciating the different design and approach. Their comments included:

'This is really a different meeting to what we have had so far, I didn't expect a senior management meeting like this.'

'I hardly can imagine other departments able to speak this openly to each other as we did now.'

'It was good that we met and had this opportunity to reflect, remember all that we did/achieved together, especially now in this uncertain time.'

Overall I was satisfied with the outcome and especially that I managed to run an important meeting with sensitive topics through a completely new approach. What a good feeling!

Why sometimes testing gets in the way of learning

Reducing intrinsic motivation

One of the joys of learning when you don't have to is that lovely feeling of learning for learning's sake – your motivation for learning is intrinsic. Interestingly, when learners are rewarded for their learning they can perform worse. Once tests become something to strive towards as a reward for learning it is possible that they become an extrinsic motivator rather than an intrinsic one. Other rewards for learning that you may be familiar with are bribing someone to do well in an exam: I'm not talking about the sort of bribery that gets you sent to prison but the sort when you tell your 17-year-old that you'll buy them a car if they pass their driving test first time or your 18-year-old that you'll pay for their holiday if they do well in their A levels.

Learning to pass the test and therefore have the reward of a pass or a high mark may convert intrinsic to extrinsic motivation and reduce their long-term learning. People who learn for tests tend to have a medium-term memory for the test but don't retain that knowledge or skill much beyond the test.

Increasing stress during recall

For most people their most significant experience of testing was probably at school or university or a formal qualification later in life. How do you feel about exams – those significant tests of your learning? And what do you now remember about what you learned for those exams?

Possibly not very much, partially perhaps because it was a long time ago and you've learned a lot since, but perhaps because you were at least marginally stressed when you took those exams? Even the coolest of cucumbers and the most prepared exam sitter (note that phrasing for later when we talk about language and senses) usually feels a certain tension as exam time approaches; the waiting in the corridor with a bunch of other nervous people, the unnatural quiet of the exam room, the strict faces of the invigilators and all those rules about what you can and can't take in. The chances are your adrenaline levels were high and so were your cortisol levels. Both adrenaline and cortisol are needed to help you handle stress appropriately but a) both hormones evolved at a time when being under stress usually meant you had to fight or run away and b) they help under short-term conditions of stress but they are not particularly good for you over the longer term. In a study in the *Journal of Cognitive Neuroscience* in 2013 (Ackermann *et al*, 2013) scientists found higher cortisol levels didn't have a particularly detrimental effect as people were learning or encoding information but it did seem to decrease their recall, particularly if they were more inclined to be stressed anyway. Their results suggested it was the change in cortisol levels that had a particular impact on retrieval; so people who already had strong baseline responses to stress, ie they were stressed more easily, found it more difficult than less stressed people to recall memories in stressful situations like exams.

If this is the case, why do we persist in putting people through stressful exams that are not particularly like the situations in which they will have to apply their learning?

Even my Wine and Spirits Society exam felt stressful despite the fact I really didn't care whether I got a certificate or not. Still, whilst I can't quite remember where the Shiraz grape grows most readily, I can still tell a Shiraz from a Merlot when I taste them so I did learn what was important.

Tests of learning

In our 'Train the Trainer' programmes we want our learners to go away with as many new and stimulating ideas as they can. We encourage them to steal our ideas but we also believe that creating their own ideas and testing their own creative skills is a valuable part of the programme. It gives them greater flexibility and far more options than they've used before.

Here are some ideas about testing culled from these brain-friendly 'Train the Trainer' programmes where we ask them to devise 52 ways to test learning – a different way for every week of the year:

Quizzes, crosswords, anagrams, puzzles, variations on TV game shows, jigsaws, create or build models, write essays, produce a video, radio programmes, podcasts, written exams, spoken exams, draw ideas, practise on dummies, case studies, real-life scenarios, write a song, poem or rap, devise questions to ask another team, build a replica, body sculpture, write a log, write a diary entry, draw a cartoon strip, teach someone else, sort and categorize information, fill in the blanks, tweet, devise a metaphor, create a game, make a flowchart, work with actors, do an experiment, recitation, brain storm, do a presentation, operate the machinery under safe conditions, virtual environments, explain to a colleague, mindmap, blog, teach on a webinar, make a set of postcards, discussion, interview each other, analyse a situation, work with a customer, action learning sets, contribute to forums, fill fortune cookies, make buttons, choreograph a dance, bandage a volunteer...

I'm sure you can easily devise some more tests based on what you teach. Use the multiple intelligences as a starting point for ideas and don't be limited by what you've seen or heard before.

Summary

You could choose to test your learning from this chapter by writing or drawing your own summary.

But if you feel you want some support here are the highlights:

- Testing is a key point of the learning process and active recall beats passive recognition every time.
- It helps you as a trainer to check that the learning is going in the right direction and to make adjustments if necessary.
- Learners get the benefits of improved performance, higher confidence and motivation, time to make adjustments and change their habits.
- You can test learning by many means apart from exams including drawing, teaching someone else, neurofeedback, making it as realistic as possible.
- Testing can get in the way of learning if it reduces motivation or increases stress.
- Add your own ideas to the list of 52 Ways to Test Learning.

References and further reading

Ackermann, S, Hartmann, F, Papassotiropoulo, A, de Quervain, D J-F and Rasch, B (2013) Associations between Basal Cortisol Levels and Memory Retrieval in Healthy Young Individuals, *Journal of Cognitive Neuroscience* [Online] http://www.washingtonpost.com/blogs/answer-sheet/wp/2013/10/16/howard-gardner-multiple-intelligences-are-not-learning-styles/ (archived at perma.cc/AJV7-5JR7)

Carrier, M and Pashler, H (1992) The influence of retrieval on retention, *Memory and Cognition*, **20** (6), pp 633–42

Cialdini, R (2001) *Influence*, Allyn and Bacon, Boston, MA

Duhigg, C (2013) *The Power of Habit*, Random House, London

Finn, B and Roediger, H (2011) Enhancing retention through reconsolidation: negative emotional arousal following retrieval enhances later recall, *Psychological Science*, **22** (6), pp 781–86

Gates, A (1917) *Recitation as a factor in memorizing*, The Science Press, New York

Gladwell, M (2009) *Outliers: The story of success*, Penguin Group, London

Gremel, C M, Chancey, J H, Atwood, B K, Deisseroth, K, Lovinger, D M and Costa, R M (2016) Endocannabinoid modulation of orbitostriatal circuits gates habit formation, *Neuron*, **90** (6), pp 1312–24, https://www.cell.com/neuron/fulltext/S0896-6273%2816%2930157-X (archived at perma.cc/J7QJ-5MKS)

Martiros, N, Burgess, A A and Graybiel, A M (2018) Inversely active striatal projection neurons and interneurons selectively delimit useful behavioral sequences, *Science Direct*, **28** (4), pp 560–73, https://www.sciencedirect.com/science/article/pii/S0960982218300332 (archived at perma.cc/W7LG-2M4E)

Nestojko, J, Bui, D, Kornell, N and Bjork, E (2014) Expecting to teach enhances learning and organization of knowledge in free recall of text passages, *Memory and Cognition*, **42** (7), pp 1038–48

Review and reflect 11

Getting rid of the magic wand

The Truly Terrible Training Course

Occasionally, for a bit of creative fun, my colleagues and I have thought about designing a 'Truly Terrible Training Course'. I will confess that the idea started in response to a particularly difficult couple of days in a training room but more often we do it as a reverse psychology style exercise where we get people to turn everything they've learned about designing fabulous learning on its head. It gets people laughing (releases endorphins and reduces stress levels), challenges assumptions and encourages people to see learning from multiple viewpoints, activating their frontal cortex.

We ask people to design a Truly Terrible Training Course from the points of view of the learners, the trainers and the organization. A regular suggestion is not to review any learning once the information has been shot at people through 1,000 PowerPoint Bullets; I did say it was a Truly Terrible Training Course. Not reviewing means the truly terrible trainers can finish and go home early so they're happy, at least in the short term. But the learners who aren't asked to review can't see the point of what they've learned and forget it almost immediately and the organization is furious because they've wasted all that money and nobody remembers anything so they can't do their jobs properly. The organization calls in the trainers and fires them because they're so inept, so now the trainers aren't happy either.

This chapter is about reflecting on and reviewing learning so that it does stick; this is one of the most valuable, but often neglected, areas of learning design and delivery, and may be one that requires a culture change in your organization.

Why you need to review – what it feels like when you don't

You've probably experienced learning a new skill or piece of information, and potentially found it really interesting or useful but then a day or so later you come to think about it again and somehow it seems ephemeral; you can't quite remember the information though you've got a general feel for it. You are certain there are six parts to the really useful learning process that you've just read about but you just can't bring back to mind the middle two elements.

Perhaps some of those pieces of information were really stimulating for you, strongly multisensory and were definitely relevant to you. You probably spent time exploring them and maybe even told someone about them when you got home so you definitely encoded them in your memory and could recall them initially, so what's gone wrong now? Why are the details you need so faint? The evidence shows that you need to review repeatedly and space your learning out over a longer period in order to really retain it with any success.

In this chapter you'll read about what happens in your brain when you review learning, how to review effectively, and you'll think about some of the challenges that prevent effective reviewing in the real busy world of work and what to do about it. You'll uncover some crucial timings that will make learning stick and who you can involve to spread the load. After all it's not you as the trainer who needs to change your brain – it's your learners, and they can get help from all sorts of places. Figure 11.1 provides a visual mindmap.

Figure 11.1   Review and reflect

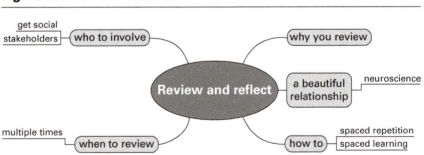

How long do you need to remember this new information for? There may well be information you want to remember for a significant length of time, and other information you need to know really well for now, but you know you're going to need to replace it with something else later. Imagine how actors have to learn their lines. Whilst the play's running they need to be word perfect but once it's finished they want to replace that knowledge with a whole new set of lines and don't really want interference from the first set of lines (see back to Chapter 9 on memory to remember how important 'forgetting' is to your continued learning and healthy cognitive function). If it's a new process at work that's taken a long time to implement and is a fundamental shift in your way of working, then you may need to remember it for years or more. If it's the new company organization chart, then the chances are it may be out of date in a few months so you don't need to remember it for quite so long. Other things like driving a car, or riding a bike, are skills you want to hang on to for pretty much the rest of your life.

Reviewing is a vital part of strong memory consolidation – revisiting and repeating the learning over time helps to strengthen the neuronal pathways and it's also an opportunity to break old habits and create new ones.

As a committed professional you probably want to pack maximum value and learning into any learning event and you're probably under pressure to cram a lot of information into a short time, particularly if it's a programme that people have invested a lot of time and money into. Sometimes you get to the end of your session with very little time left. It's tempting to leave out the review and just hope that the learning happened but the end-of-session review is just the start of a vital part of the learning process. So in addition to the well planned, lengthier review that you'd designed when you planned the session, have a few quick and effective review methods up your sleeve.

Reviewing – the story of a beautiful relationship

One way to think about the power of reviewing is to consider learning to be a bit like relationships between people; the forging of new neuronal networks starts like any new relationship when two neurons who haven't met before are introduced to each other. When you're learning, the desired end result is to create patterns of strongly connected neurons; because they fire together they eventually wire together (remember Hebb's Law) and become stable partners.

On the first introduction your neurons are a bit hesitant, timid and want to be polite but they don't want to commit to anything at this stage; they'll want to meet a few more times until they feel more sure of each other. When they meet again they are more comfortable, conversation flows more easily and they begin to think this new friendship may be going somewhere and it could be worth making a small commitment to keep in touch. So they exchange mobile phone numbers; they can contact each other again if they need to. After a few more meetings they're feeling really comfortable together, communication is easy, rapid and smooth and they decide to start being seen together regularly; they talk all the time on the phone; they're texting each other but they still could see other neurons if they wanted. Eventually they are seeing so much of each other they decide to move in together and start buying pots and pans together. Time passes and as long as they keep talking and resist the temptation of more alluring connections they find they are celebrating their golden wedding anniversary.

Now this is the story of a beautiful long-lasting relationship, but imagine all the other scenarios that could have happened along the way if they hadn't kept meeting, if they'd failed to swap mobile numbers, if some other neuron had come along and offered them something more exciting and recruited them into another network, or if they'd just drifted apart because they just weren't seeing enough of one another.

Reviewing – the neuroscience of the beautiful relationship

What actually happens isn't quite the same but I hope the analogy sticks. The neurons connect across the gap between them (synapses) and exchange neurotransmitters in order to stimulate (or sometimes suppress) electrical signals along their long axons, but initially the signals between them are relatively weak and not very fast (see Figure 11.2). As neurons fire repeatedly the connections strengthen and they fire together more easily. This is because as the neurons connect together the fatty cover around the long axons, called a myelin sheath, changes which allows signals to be transmitted more quickly and efficiently. As networks develop those myelin sheaths become thicker and act as insulation so that the messages can be transmitted quicker and quicker (up to a limit of course). Neighbouring myelin-producing cells, called oligodendrocytes, are the ones that recognize neurons are repeatedly firing together and wrap myelin around the axonal wiring.

Myelin is the white matter in your brain and makes up about 50 per cent of your brain mass. It's laid around your axons a bit like a string of sausages, and it's thought that the myelin sheath may allow the signals to travel faster because electrical impulses leap more quickly between the 'sausages' to

Figure 11.2 Neurotransmitters moving across the synapse

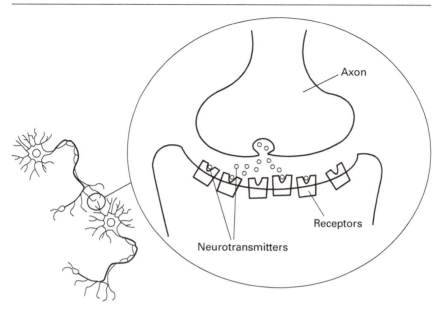

uninsulated areas (called the Nodes of Ranvier) than if the signals just ran from one end of the axon to the other (see Figure 11.3).

Figure 11.3 How myelin affects signal transmission

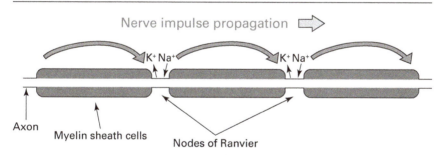

A study published in *Science* (McKenzie *et al*, 2014) found that myelin production was needed for learning new motor skills in mice, but when scientists blocked the production of myelin once the skill was learned it didn't affect the mice's performance; once something has been learned new myelin is not required. At the time of publication the team of scientists at UCL Wolfson Institute for Biomedical Research hadn't tested whether this process only affected motor learning or whether it would be the same for cognitive skills too. This is another example of a lovely piece of neuroscience that may be representative for all types of learning but so far the evidence is only available in the very specific condition of mice learning to run on a complex wheel with irregularly spaced rungs; and we just don't know yet whether it's true of all learning.

Back to the beautiful neuron relationship: it's going to be meaningful and the learning is going to be useful for the long term. The neurons will eventually make a commitment to stick together through thick and thin and it's going to take quite an effort to disrupt them. Just like a relationship that's been going on for a long time, if you decide to split up it can be a wrench. Old habits and relationships are stronger bonds than new ones and it's going to take a pretty significant attractive new piece of learning to come along and disrupt those old familiar bonds.

How to build the relationship

To get to this level though there's got to be a bit of effort. It's unrealistic to expect two people to meet, get married the same day and then have a long and meaningful relationship and it's not much different for neurons. So you need to review your learning in order for it to stick; you need to ensure your neurons meet regularly in these new patterns for sufficient time to develop the relationship, otherwise they'll easily be distracted by other new, shiny ideas.

You'll find conflicting information about specific times to review information but there's sufficient evidence to say that reviewing at regular intervals after the learning does work to ensure learning is permanent and not transitory. It may be that some of these meetings need only be brief in order to keep that flame alive, but they need to happen.

Spaced repetition

As you've already discovered in Chapter 9 on memory, different types of memories are processed and stored differently and memories are effectively created afresh each time you remember. Every 'rehearsal' of a memory embeds it deeper until it's consolidated and until then learning can be easily disrupted by other information or experience.

Stretching learning across time and making information or learning stick for the long term makes intuitive sense and is well backed up by the evidence. Way back in 1885 Hermann Ebbinghaus showed that spacing your learning over a longer time period was far more effective than trying to cram information into a short space of time. But Hermann Ebbinghaus and multiple researchers since were doing 'experimental learning', ie the sort of learning of very specific items that you can do in a laboratory but isn't really what most of us encounter in a workplace learning situation. However, despite the difficulties of doing this sort of research in the real world, there is sufficient evidence to suggest that short bouts of reviews over a longer period of time will yield far better rewards then trying to digest large amounts of input information quickly. Figure 11.4 illustrates how much more information is retained if you review regularly.

Figure 11.4   The importance of reviewing

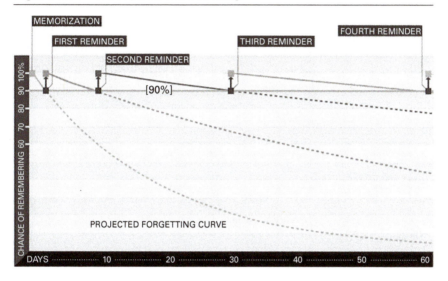

Fortunately you don't need to spend a long time at each subsequent rehearsal of information, though the learning will also be more effective if you recall information rather than merely repeat your exposure to it. Read on for some practical ways to review information in the real world rather than the laboratory.

A study from 2007 by Doug Rohrer and Harold Pashler looked at the relationship between the time at which you should review what you learned compared to how long you want to remember it for. They suggested that you should review materials at a point which is about 10–30 per cent of the time for which you want to remember it. For instance, if you need to sit an exam in 6–8 months then reviewing the material after about a month is optimal, but if your exam is only 11 days after the learning session then you should review it a day later.

Their suggestion is that reviewing whilst the material is still really fresh in your memory doesn't necessarily work as well as reviewing and testing yourself at this 10–30 per cent period because the information hasn't started to get into your long-term memory, so it can give you false confidence that you really know something that is still only in a newly-formed state. However, these results may be the difference between actively recalling to review and merely revisiting material without active recall and as usual this was one experiment done in a particular situation. I think the weight of evidence shows that if you left it for a month before any sort of review much of that material would already have faded. So perhaps a better approach would be to spend the early part of your time actively recalling and practising your learning, and review again at the 10–30 per cent period.

Spaced repetition seems to be one of the best researched, most important ingredients for effective learning and yet is often left out of the learning recipe. One of the enormous benefits of digital learning is that it can be used really effectively as a tool for spaced repetition. For a comprehensive review of the research on spacing learning look for the work of Will Thalheimer (Thalheimer, 2006) who is on a mission to bring evidence-based practice to the fore.

Spaced learning

This is a very specific form of learning reported in the *Journal of Frontiers of Human Neuroscience* by Paul Kelley and Terry Whatson (2013). Content is repeated three times with two 10-minute breaks in which students do distractor activities, often something physical like juggling. Their method was based on the neuroscience finding that long-term potentiation starts to happen within minutes when repeated stimuli are separated by timed spaces; long-term potentiation is the persistent strengthening of synapses based on recent patterns of activity and is one of the cellular foundations of learning. Effectively it's when your neurons are talking well together and a small conversation produces a larger reaction than when they first met. Think of a really good friend who knows you so well that from a look on your face they recognize what you need is a cup of tea, a piece of cake and a good two hours of conversation.

Kelley and Whatson put their spaced learning theory to the test with a biology course and found that students using this method performed at the same level as two control groups – one group using 'one-hour spaced learning' and the other having a four-month teaching programme. You may be surprised to read that there was no difference in performance because if that's the case then what's the point? The obvious implication is that the learning was much more effective per hour of instruction. This type of learning is being feverishly tested, including in UK schools, and seems to have excellent potential for learning about information, although whether it is applicable for soft skills or behavioural training remains to be seen.

The challenge of reviewing in the real world

Laboratory studies tend to ask learners to learn one specific thing which isn't true of a learning situation at work. You might be on a long intensive learning programme when you're going to be expected to make fundamental changes in the things you do and the way you think; you might be on a workshop for a few days and expect to encounter multiple new ideas; or perhaps you're doing a short piece of e-learning amongst your other activities. Whatever sort of learning you're doing time is likely to be precious, and whilst you're taking in the new stuff everyone recognizes that you're learning, but once it comes to reviewing you might hear people approaching it differently. 'Well that is just repeating what you've already done'; 'Surely you're a quick learner – you don't need to go over it again and again, do you?'; 'That course you went on was supposed to teach you everything – why can't you remember it all?'

Training isn't a magic wand. You can't just expect people to go on a training course and then come back 'fixed' or having learned everything they need to. As you've noticed as you've read through this book, learning is a messy, long-winded, easily disrupted process and it's hard work for your brain. If you've ever read *Thinking, Fast and Slow* (2011) by Daniel Kahneman you'll recognize that our brains are quite lazy – we don't want to do more with them than we can help because they are so energy-hungry. Familiarity with material is your brain's own way of tricking you into thinking you know 'stuff', but until you've really consolidated your learning – created networks that can fire together regularly and efficiently – you haven't really learned something. And neither have your learners or your colleagues. Reviewing is so easy to ignore but fortunately it's also quite easy to slip it in under the border guards so long as people know they've got to do it. One of the first things you need to do with your learners is to teach them about the power of reviewing. Explain to them that you don't have a magic wand and that the learning is up to them and it's going to take some time and effort.

Good reviewing is vital to all effective learner-centred learning. Learning doesn't all happen in an e-learning package, a virtual reality game or at a workshop – it happens in multiple places and different times and it happens in people's heads and bodies. Creating multiple opportunities for rediscovering, reflecting on and reviewing learning – whether it's skills, information or behavioural learning – all contribute to the learning process and this is where digital technology can be a huge benefit because it can be so readily available.

Your next 'Other Voice' is from Sandra Lace who has been really excited by the deeper level of learning her participants achieve from having a different environment and reviewing effectively before, during and after training events. She's had to overcome some hesitancy amongst her colleagues who thought that senior managers might feel 'silly' being physically involved in learning. Her experience has been that the senior managers enjoy the deeper and richer experience that reflecting and reviewing effectively gives them and they are more open to changing their behaviours. All her colleagues are now convinced about the benefits of creating a brain friendly environment and reviewing learning. Here's Sandra in her own words.

Other Voices

Sandra Lace, *Head of Training Academy for an international bank, Latvia*

After many years working as a trainer and consultant of leadership development I have resolved my inner dilemma: how to influence managers' *meta* level thinking to strengthen learning and influence changes in behaviour. My observation was that managers are good at asking questions, sharing experience, reflecting on group tasks and making links between discussed learning points and real-life situations. But they have difficulties reflecting on their own behaviour during the task or learning process: how he/she influences group members and how the process can be influenced by different kinds of attitude or unsaid messages. I know from my experience if this *meta* level is activated then managers can more easily transform learned competences into actions and strengthen new habits. The Brain Friendly Learning methodology gave me convincing examples and creative ideas about lifting training to a new level. The other part of implementing this methodology in development programmes is subjective: in a trainer's courage to try, to overcome their own stereotypes and assumptions about what training participants – 'high level and serious managers' – like and dislike.

I wanted to put together Brain Friendly Learning methods and have the courage to create joyful and productive training which activates three levels of learning:

1 Doing tasks and reflecting on what was done – what are the takeaways?
2 Reflecting on the process of how the task was done – what are the learning points for everybody?
3 Influencing meta-level thinking and reflection on feelings, interaction and collaboration.

To ensure the desired results I do step-by-step activities; use pre-reading materials sent by e-mail or mobile app; create some fun using leadership games (mobile app). I am not afraid to create a colourful and creative atmosphere in the training room with many 'work-stations' and use short and simple tasks which can seem child-like at the beginning but develop, and tasks with movement. It helps to experience a process instead of speaking and thinking about it.

I have experienced positive surprise from the participants about the room, equipment and pre-tasks which creates open and cooperative learning. They give feedback which confirms managers' openness to creative methods: for example, writing a Twitter message, using mnemonics, creating a poem, or blog of the day. My favourite methods are to 'mindmap' with different objects to reflect on the day, and Twitter messages to colleagues about the main learning points. To learn serious leadership competences doesn't mean to do it in a cool and unattractive atmosphere. I try to use everyday resources in the brain friendly methodology: infographic, Instagram, blogs, etc to combine with mnemonics and brain psychology. I often use the 'manager's hat method' to separate participants' roles during training: participants do and analyse all tasks from one perspective, then they do meta thinking with the 'manager's hat' on their head.

Using these methods has created brilliant results; the methods really work to create willingness to make changes in behaviour. As a result the managers make small changes and find success motivates them to try the next steps to implement their learned competences in work-life.

How and when to review learning

Begin the session with a review of what people already know. One way is to get people to draw a concept map of everything they already know. Show everyone how to create a cognitive cartograph (another name for a mind-map). Give each person a little time to reflect on and capture what they already know. Then ask people to work in pairs to generate more ideas by sparking thoughts from each other; this can lead to more recalled memories or people learning something new from their colleagues. Finally encourage everyone to contribute to a large concept map on the wall (sheets of flip-chart paper or a roll of newsprint) so that everyone can see all of the information they already have on the topic. This will give you, the trainer, a clearer picture of the current knowledge levels in order to pitch the rest of the sessions appropriately. It will also give everyone a chance to get an overall map of what might be covered during the learning and to start warming up those relevant neuronal networks – it becomes a review, an overview and a start to learning at the same time. If you're designing digital learning then start with a test of current knowledge levels. You can decide whether you provide the answers now or you merely use it as a reflective exercise and the answers are revealed later.

Whilst delivering content deliver it fast and take regular 10-minute review breaks, based on the spaced learning results. Deliver the information in a multisensory way, then break and ask people to do something physical and entirely different to the content delivery method. Then repeat the content again but this time encourage people to challenge and explore it, another 10-minute break and a third repetition of the content but with the emphasis on learners applying the content. E-learning can do this really well because it's easy to break into small chunks; you may need a mechanism to encourage people to move away from their computers and then return so they are physically distracted too. Or some other type of online activity unrelated to the learning could be used instead.

At the end of an activity encourage people to spend a few minutes working socially to discuss what the session has meant to them, and what they will do with that knowledge. Perhaps create pictorial handouts with a timeline for people to build up their own individual action plan. Give a creative title to that space of time, eg Oxygen Check, so people know when they've finished an exercise there'll be time to reflect. Give people flexibility about how long they spend reviewing by tying reviews in just before a break so people have the option to take longer if they prefer, but don't let them skip it.

At the end of session review the whole day or whole programme. Encourage participants to create their own reviews based on the Multiple Intelligences. Many trainers swear by slide presentation software like PowerPoint or Prezi and others just swear about it. Death by PowerPoint is something no one wants to suffer; however, a slide review can be an excellent way to recall learning. Use the colourful, graphic, low-text-content slides that you've already designed for your training. Add in some story-telling text to lead people through the chronology of the day and prompt them with suggestions and reflective questions such as 'You started by exploring some fascinating neuroscience'; 'You now easily recall the six steps of the learning process'; 'What do you plan to do differently?' Then create an automatic slideshow by turning the slide transition to automatic with a delay of about 9–10 seconds. Use some alpha-wave-inducing music and then let your participants sit back and relax to review their learning. It's amazing how much gets covered and forgotten even in short sessions so it's a valuable reminder just before you ask people to write their action plans.

A review at the beginning of every subsequent day of a multi-day workshop will get everyone back into the appropriate state for fresh learning and after a good night's sleep people are better able to build on what they learned the day before. Remember Hermann Ebbinghaus's Forgetting Curve (see p 191 for illustration) – if you aren't seeing people the next day, make sure you have set up a review 24 hours later because it is a critical period for long-term learning.

Create a quiz or a wordsearch to get everyone thinking, ask people to create their own logical flowchart, to build a model, discuss their most valuable takeaway, sort questions and answer cards; be creative about using different reviews and giving people choices. Put a review activity in an envelope or e-mail marked 'Not to be opened until tomorrow' and you'll create curiosity too – you'd be amazed how keen people are to peek inside those envelopes.

One week, one month, two months, three months and six months

The evidence for spaced repetition shows there are critical periods for review that make a difference. When you do short reviews regularly at these time intervals retention of information is maintained. Once you get to about six months that information or skill is pretty well consolidated; you can't be certain you'll remember it forever but there's a much better chance than if you don't do anything. Create a schedule for these reviews and use the wonder of digital technology to deliver those reviews.

Encourage your participants to devise their own reviews too. On modular programmes, whether digital or face to face, there may be a period of two or three weeks before the sessions so select a different group each time to invent an interactive review for everyone else. They will tend to take a lead from you, the trainer; if your reviews have been interesting and involving, theirs usually will be too.

Who to involve

Using social connections

When we connect socially with others we release neurotransmitters such as oxytocin, the nurturing hormone. As part of the review cycle, reignite those social bonds and encourage learners to continue to support each other. Some of this can be really simple; write a short e-mail with some prompt questions and ask your learners to reply, copying in all the other participants, so they can see what challenges and wins other people are having. For instance:

- What was your key 'takeaway' from the training?
- What's been your biggest success after the training?
- What has started fading from your memory and needs revisiting?
- What barriers have you come across and how have you got round them?

Pick up the telephone to your participants and ask them how they're getting on. Organize a webinar where everyone shares their updates. Use digital sharing platforms to upload supporting materials to discuss.

Create social forums either using social media platforms already in general use or bespoke in-house systems.

Take up ideas from social psychology about social proof, the idea that people are influenced by the actions of similar others and explicitly tell learners that most people like them participate in this important part of the learning process (so long as it's true, of course).

Include other stakeholders in the review process

Managers, colleagues, suppliers and even customers can be included in reviewing learning.

You're probably already familiar with concepts like having study buddies, creating action learning sets or cascading learning back by delivering key points after a training session. All these are really effective ways of including other colleagues in learning and at the same time being a useful review of learning.

You might choose to involve suppliers and customers because they are more likely to be pleased that you are developing your people rather than displeased. You could ask your learners to feed back to their customers what they've learned and what difference they believe it will make to the customer. You'd tell your customers you had an Investors in People award so why not tell them about what you're learning too?

Consistently you'll hear the vital importance that managers play in supporting learning back in the workplace and on how well people implement what they have learned, which of course reflects on the return on investment in training. So what can you do to make sure managers recognize the importance of review and make them a significant part of it? You probably can't expect every manager to sit down everyone who's done some training to ask about what they learned and what further support they need. Managers are busy people and it's easy for them to imagine that the training was done by the Learning and Development Department – you've waved your magic wand and now it's complete.

You can make it easier for them, and more likely to happen, by doing simple things like creating a manager's brief with an overview of the training highlights. Send this to the learners and their managers a week after the training session to initiate a 10-minute conversation about what was learned and how it will be applied. You can't guarantee they'll sit down and share but you can increase the likelihood if you make it a simple but required part of the learning process. Another option is to invite managers along to a final presentation at the end of the training programme and ask the learners to present back what they learned. This has multiple benefits like reviewing the learning, building relationships and gives learners more confidence to test new ideas back at work because they know their managers know what their new skills are. Additionally it's sometimes a useful refresher for managers who may well have had the training in the past and sometimes it's a way to give managers training without them knowing that's what you're doing. They get to learn something new without having to admit they didn't know. Design an overview version of some digital learning for managers for similar reasons.

Give them an emotional hook too. Get their buy-in by making them feel valued and build their credibility and authority by making them feel like an important part of the process. This can give you greater influence with them for the future. Being in Learning and Development is sometimes just like being in Sales and Marketing because you're selling ideas and concepts. Use ideas that marketing might use like focusing on what the majority of people are doing rather than the minority. Even today some managers will make excuses about being too busy to develop their people, but don't worry about them. Instead make it the norm for managers to be involved by shining the spotlight on those managers who do support learning in this way – and tell the rest of the organization about it. This will help create a culture in which learning thrives and is supported by all and some of those 'too busy' dinosaurs may eventually join the rest of the pack.

It's much easier to build spaced learning into a programme if you're already immersed in a continuous learning culture; for instance, genuine application of the 70/20/10 model where more of the learning will happen informally than formally. But it is important for learners, managers and stakeholders to understand this review process so that it's not left to chance or the vagaries of work schedules.

Top Tips

- Use the multiple intelligences as a framework for reviews that reflect different topics and different people.
- Make reviews short and snappy so that they fire up neuronal pathways but aren't too time-consuming.
- Get people to actively review and recall their learning rather than passively review it.
- Schedule the reviews so they become part of the normal process in your organization.
- Educate your learners so they know you don't have a magic wand – it's their neurons that have to connect and stay connected rather than yours.

Summary

This summary is a way of reviewing what you've just read in the chapter so read it to fire up those neuronal networks again:

- You need to review because memories decay quite quickly if they're not actively kept fresh.
- You're trying to build and maintain a long-term and lasting relationship between neurons through improving connectivity.
- Connectivity between neurons is enhanced by myelin – a fatty, white cover around your axons.
- Spaced repetition builds long-term memory better than cramming.
- Reviews are better as active recall rather than passive review.
- Spaced learning is a specific way of reviewing and learning information – repeat input three times with 10-minute diversions between repetitions.
- Build a culture of reviewing to get over the challenges of reviewing in the real world of business – schedule reviewing to be part of the process.

- Review immediately, 24 hours later, one week, one month, two months, three months and finally at six months to create lasting long-term learning.
- Exploit social connections and involve other stakeholders.
- Help learners learn by explaining what they need to do – you don't have a magic wand.

References and further reading

Innovation Unit (2015) [accessed 2 July 2015] Spaced Learning: Making Memories Stick [Online] http://www.innovationunit.org (archived at perma.cc/C5N4-QZFZ)

Kahneman, D (2011) *Thinking, Fast and Slow*, Allen Lane, London

Kelley, P and Whatson, T (2013) Making long-term memories in minutes: a spaced learning pattern from memory research in education, *Frontiers in Human Neuroscience*, 7 (589) https://www.ncbi.nlm.nih.gov/pmc/articles/PMC3782739/ (archived at perma.cc/9HAJ-RQ82)

Kimura, F, and Itami, C (2009) Myelination and isochronicity in neural networks, *Frontiers in Neuroanatomy*, 3 (12)

McKenzie, I A, Ohayon, D, Huiliang, L, de Faria, J P, Emery, B, Tohyama, K and Richardson, W D (2014) Motor skill learning requires active central myelination, *Science* [Online] http://www.sciencemag.org/content/346/6207/318.abstract (archived at perma.cc/PKJ3-KX8T)

Rohrer, D and Pashler, H (2007) Increasing retention time without increasing study time, *Current Directions in Psychological Science*, 16, 183–86

Thalheimer, W (2006) *Spacing learning events over time: What the research says*, http://q-mindshare.com/assets/spacing_learning_over_time__march2009v1_.pdf (archived at perma.cc/EDT5-VMLH)

Stickier stories and food for thought 12

There's been a debate going on for years as to whether you should give people handouts or other material before you present it to them yourself. People argue that if the audience has read ahead they won't listen when you come to present your information. But what does the research suggest? One study in 2009 (Marsh and Sink) tested how much students remembered from a lecture. They received notes before, during or after their lecture and were tested on their memory of the lecture, immediately after and a week later. It turns out that test performance at both tests was pretty much the same regardless of when the notes were given out – so there was no advantage to waiting until the end to give out notes.

The researchers observed that students who'd received notes before the lecture took fewer notes but their conclusion was notes were more of a distraction than a 'deep encoding task'.

Giving out notes early on appears not to have a negative effect on how well people remember and the researchers suggested that 'students still benefited in the sense that they reached the same level of learning with less work'. With many people already having significant cognitive overload, making learning less work is a positive result. And those people who seem to be studiously scribbling notes whilst you talk may actually just be distracting themselves.

My view is that particularly with adult learners we need to treat them like adults and let them make the choice about whether they want to read ahead or whether they'll wait until the appropriate moment. Looking ahead may help them create some initial hooks to hang more complex ideas on as they come to them. So long as the learners learn what they need it really doesn't matter whether they learn it listening to you, reading ahead for themselves or talking it through with colleagues. Each exposure to a piece of information increases the likelihood they will learn it.

What you'll cover in this chapter

This chapter is about some fascinating areas, each of which could be a chapter or a book in its own right, but time is pressing so you're going to connect with them to unearth some pragmatic insights you can use quickly yourself in designing and delivering sticky learning. You'll cover why stories might be so much more sticky than facts, what sorts of environment make a difference to learners, some ideas to stimulate creativity, how the language you use might affect what people do and how to create an earworm (see Figure 12.1).

Figure 12.1   Ideas from this chapter

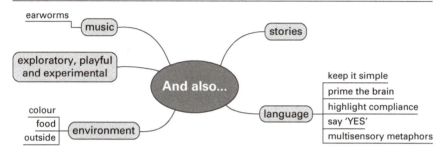

Stickier stories

As you're probably already aware, stories are great for learning and there is abundant research showing how learners benefit from stories and how they stick. But let's just unpick a little bit of what goes on in people's brains when they are hearing or reading a story rather than just being exposed to facts.

When you experience the world your senses send messages to your brain to be processed by the relevant areas. When you remember information your brain obligingly goes off and searches for those pieces of information again and reconstructs them in just about the same way so that you can remember the original event. Similarly, if you imagine something your brain dutifully marches around seeking out the information it can find in its memory banks to construct the imagined situation. It's hard for your brain to tell whether that event is real or imagined which is why false memories can be constructed and hallucinations seem so real. And later in this chapter you'll find out about how when you even think about a sensation, such as texture, your sensory cortex fires up in much the same way as if you were actually feeling it. In an article in *Scientific American* in 2014, researchers showed that wrist strength could be increased just by thinking about moving your wrists – not as strong as if you actually did the exercise but measurably stronger (Mosher, 2015). So a good story can stimulate your brain in a way that a plain fact or stand-alone data just can't.

Imagine someone is about to teach a new fire safety policy your organization has implemented and starts the session along the lines of:

> 'We're going to learn about the new Fire Safety Policy. It's very important that you read, understand and comply with the policy because it saves lives. Here is the policy...' and they show the new policy on a slide.

How much activity is going on in their audience's heads relating to the fire safety policy? In the 'Policy only' column of Table 12.1, tick off any areas of the brain that you think will be particularly active when looking at the policy on a PowerPoint slide.

Now consider a slightly different scenario where you start along the lines of:

Table 12.1 Stories or facts exercise

Brain system	Function	Policy only	Story and policy
parietal lobes	reading		
left frontal cortex	logic/procedure		
reticular activating system	attention		
hippocampus	memory		
amygdala	emotion		
Broca's and Wernicke's areas	language processing		
occipital lobe	vision		
temporal lobe	hearing		
motor cortex	movement		
olfactory bulb	smell/taste		

I'd like to tell you a story....

One Thursday morning in 1952 a French chef, Raymond Lempereur, was just putting the finishing touches to a delicious Mousse au Chocolat at Croxteth Hall near Liverpool. He found himself recalling his days in the French Resistance during World War II, starting and putting out fires, when he realized the burning he could smell wasn't his imagination or his cooking. A real fire had started in the Queen Anne wing and he immediately ran to the phone to raise the alarm and started getting everyone out of the building.

The fire brigade arrived swiftly amid the clanging of bells, the frightened shouts of people escaping from the burning building and the crack and hiss of the fire itself.

The restoration of Croxteth Hall took more than 60 years to complete and though Monsieur Lempereur knew it had started he sadly died in 2013 so he didn't live to see the new wood panelling, new windows, lighting and major redecoration works on one of the jewels of Liverpool's heritage. He did know that his quick thinking and action had saved anyone from being hurt, the Hall from being burned to the ground, and meant the priceless collection of 200 paintings did not get destroyed in the blaze.

As you tell the story you show an old black and white picture from the *Liverpool Echo* in 1952 showing a lone firefighter staring forlornly at a burned-out shell of a building. As the story finishes you move to the fire safety policy slide.

Which brain areas do you think might be stimulated by this story and the picture? Complete the rest of Table 12.1. When you've finished, read on to see a completed version of the table (Table 12.2).

Clearly this is a simplification of what happens when you see and hear a story but it does illustrate why telling stories is so much more engaging than talking plain facts.

You can use stories for more than just creating greater engagement too because they have structure. You can use them to help people remember specific data, especially if you want people to remember information in a sequence or need to link seemingly unrelated data. The story structure provides a framework to drop the information into and the more curious, novel and richly embroidered the story the more easily it will be remembered.

Table 12.2 Stories or facts: suggested answers

Brain system	Function	Policy only	Story and policy	Comments
parietal lobes	reading	√	√	
left frontal cortex	logic/ procedure	√	√	
reticular activating system	attention		√	Which gains your attention?
hippocampus	memory		√	Which is more memorable?
amygdala	emotion	?	√	How emotional is the policy?
Broca's and Wernicke's areas	language processing	√	√	
occipital lobe	vision	?	√	How visually stimulating is the policy?
temporal lobe	hearing	√	√	
motor cortex	movement		√	Motor cortex is activated even by words describing movement
olfactory bulb	smell/taste		√	Similarly for olfactory cortex

Other Voices

Larry Reynolds, *Trainer and writer*

Making it memorable with stories

How many people died when terrorists hijacked and crashed two aircraft in New York on September 11th, 2001? Unless you are quite unusual, you probably can't remember the exact figure. Your cortex, the part of the brain mainly involved in processing abstract data, isn't that good at remembering facts and figures, unless you make a conscious effort to repeat the learning. The official figure is 2,996. But I bet you can remember perfectly where you were when you heard the tragic news of 9/11. This is quite a feat of memory for something that happened more than a decade ago. This is because your hippocampus – the part of your brain involved in processing places and events – is much more effective at creating and recalling long-term memories.

Whilst it's misleading to say that certain functions only happen in certain specific parts of the brain, it's certainly true that some areas are more implicated than others. The link between the hippocampus and places and events was nicely demonstrated by researchers at University College in London who put taxi drivers into an fMRI brain-scanning machine. They discovered that the hippocampus of a London taxi driver is indeed physically larger than yours or mine, because London cabbies spend a great deal of time learning and thinking about places and events. They call it 'the knowledge'.

Do you find it easier to remember the contents of a policy document, or a scene from your favourite novel or movie? Once again, the parts of your brain involved in processing abstract facts in a policy document are far less effective than the parts involved in processing a story – especially a story that is multisensory, as most good stories are. The implications for trainers are clear. If you want people to remember stuff, use fewer abstract facts, and more stories that involve places and events.

I often deliver a course called Courageous Conversations. It's designed to help managers at work to have those tricky conversations that they know in their heart they need to have, but keep avoiding because they are worried about how it will go. Giving feedback is one kind of courageous conversation. When I first began to deliver this kind of training many years ago, I'd generally start with the principles of giving feedback – make sure you know the facts, be clear about what you want the person to do differently next time and so on. It worked moderately well.

Now I do it quite differently. I begin by telling stories: How I once tried to give my partner some feedback about her driving and what happened; some feedback my first boss once gave me and the effect it had. Then I invite people to share some of their feedback stories – good and bad. Out of these tales emerge some rules of thumb about how best to give feedback. We practise and refine these ideas through role-play and further sharing of stories.

This approach is more fun, because people like telling and listening to stories. It's more memorable, because the parts of our brain that handle stories and events are better at creating long-term memories than the parts that deal with abstract data. And it's more effective because the stuff we're talking about is far closer to the participants' real experiences.

Language and learning

Whilst you've been thinking about stories let's also just uncover a few interesting nuggets about language and some research that's relevant to a learning environment.

If you were to do any sort of search on the neuroscience of language you'd come across thousands of journal articles with increasingly complex and complicated titles and even more complex and complicated language once you'd got into the articles. This may be fine for research scientists but complicated language is definitely not very helpful for you or your learners and I'd argue scientists are not doing themselves any favours if what they want to do is communicate their great research. When you are designing or delivering learning you want to use straightforward language so you can communicate even complex information clearly.

So here are five neuroscience nuggets that will help you to make your language and messages more accessible.

1. Keep it simple

Whilst it may be tempting to sound clever and use long words and complex sentences people actually think you're more organized and have a better grasp of the facts if you explain things simply. An experiment in 1978 with students at Bangor University gave them two pieces of prose to read, both of which described the same information – but one was written in an over-complex, highly academic style and the other was written pretty much as you'd say it out loud (Bardell, 1978; Turk and Kirkman, 1978). Students rated the writer of the simpler style as more organized, more knowledgeable and even gave them characteristics that they couldn't imply from the information, such as they were more likeable. When you are nervous or less sure of your facts you have a tendency to talk or write in a more formal and complex way which can get in the way of your message.

Sometimes people bury the important information at the end of a sentence. Remember how working memory is limited as to what it can process at a given time. If you leave the point of your sentence until the end, your listener or reader has to hold the entire thought in mind whilst you get to the point. You tax their working memory. Put the key point first when you're writing, particularly if it's something that people really must do. If you exhaust their working memory they may not get to your important 'must do'. Here's an example of what not to do:

> The first and most important rule of woodworking is to wear appropriate safety equipment. Whilst hearing protection is necessary for some very noisy tools such as routers and surface planers, and latex gloves may be necessary when applying finishes, there is no time in the wood shop that you should be without your safety glasses. Put them on when you enter the shop, and don't take them off until you leave. Your eyesight is too important to take chances.

How far did you have to read before you found out the key message of wearing safety glasses? It could have been written:

> **Always** wear your **safety glasses** in the wood shop.
> - Put them on when you enter the wood shop.
> - Keep them on until you leave.
> - Your eyesight is too important to take chances.
>
> Use **hearing protection** when using noisy tools such as routers and surface planers. Wear **latex gloves** when applying finishes.

2. Prime the brain with what you want

Whilst we're talking about what not to do, have you come across the concept of priming? Priming suggests that things in the environment of which we are unaware can cause us to react in particular ways; for instance, if you take a warm drink from someone you are more likely to rate them as a 'nice' person. Sometimes you may be communicating an unintended message and the simple way to do that is to use negative language.

How often do you say 'Don't forget to...' or write 'Don't hesitate to contact me'? What are you really saying? People struggle to process a negative thought because it makes more work for the brain; effectively you have to fire up all the connections related to that word, then suppress them and whilst suppressing them you're effectively thinking of them again until you can replace that thought with something else. But if your working memory is full of messages like 'don't think of a pink elephant' then it's not got much capacity left to find something else to think about.

This next piece of research (Earp *et al*, 2010) demonstrates that telling people what you don't want may increase the behaviour you are trying to avoid. In the study they tested two groups of smokers; both of whom were asked to look at photos and decide whether they were taken by amateur or professional photographers. What they didn't know was that the photos either had inconspicuous 'No Smoking' signs or the signs were edited out. The presence of the 'No Smoking' sign, whether people noticed it or not, significantly increased the tendency to approach 'smoking-related stimuli'. Whilst the researchers stress they need to do more real-world research it seemed the 'No Smoking' sign was more likely to promote smoking than having no signs.

Why is this important for you? When designing instructions, tell people what you want them to do rather than what you're trying to avoid. 'Remember to do your 24-hour review' is likely to be more effective than 'Don't forget your 24-hour review'. If you're teaching something that's prohibitive are you potentially increasing the behaviours you are trying to eliminate? What messages may people be seeing before they come to meetings or workshops, or after they've completed an online programme, that are in direct contradiction to what you want them to learn? How can you constructively use priming to deliver your key messages?

3. Highlight compliant behaviours

It's human nature to notice what's different and what stands out but sometimes by highlighting the anomalies or pointing out differences you may be failing to influence the people you're talking to. Anyone working in training recognizes the challenges of getting people to engage in training, encouraging managers to support training and of people ducking out of training when something more 'exciting' or operationally urgent appears. In reality of course only one person left the training and the other 15 stayed for the whole day but we have a slight tendency to talk about that one. Perhaps it's drawing attention to these behaviours and the language that's used that is potentially making the situation worse.

Evidence from multiple social science studies shows that we are influenced to do what those around us are doing; this is called 'social proof'. Instead of pointing out irregular behaviours, if you highlight what's working you may be better able to influence people to comply. As an example, you may have seen notices at your doctors telling you how many people missed their appointments. These signs are designed to shame you and prick your conscience so you make an extra effort to keep your appointment. However, research has shown that informing people of the number of missed appointments is not an effective strategy for increasing attendance. A study with Bedford NHS by Steve Martin *et al* (2011) of Influence at Work, and BDO, showed that notices truthfully highlighting the number of people who turned up for appointments contributed to a reduction of 30 per cent in the number of 'no-shows' for NHS appointments and it's been calculated that this could save up to £250 million if it was replicated across the NHS. This principle of 'social proof' suggests we look to see how others are behaving in order to decide how we should behave. In other words we tend to follow the crowd.

When you feel included your reward-related brain areas including the ventromedial prefrontal cortex and the posterior cingulate are activated, releasing stress-reducing chemicals such as oxytocin, so is it any wonder we like to be part of the crowd? I know there will be somebody reading this book saying 'I don't like to follow the crowd' or 'I like to be different' and you're right – some of the time that makes good sense – but I challenge you to observe your own behaviour and just notice how often you do something because that's the social norm or what most other people around you are doing.

Back to the language you use: instead of writing e-mails focusing on how many people didn't complete their training or who isn't supporting colleagues it may be more influential to turn your language around to focus on the majority of people who are doing the 'right' thing. Publish figures and tell stories about the higher percentages of people who do complete their training or turn up on time or managers who do make it easier for people to learn on and off the job.

When you're asking for prework to be sent back, point out that most people have their prework returned by the deadline. Send e-mails thanking people for completing the prework and copy everyone in. If you can use statistics then use them – but make sure they are true because this is about influencing and not manipulating. When you're communicating with people think about how you can make them feel included and release some stress-reducing oxytocin for them.

4. Say 'Yes' rather than 'No'

Are there particular words to avoid in life? Well it seems that 'No' may be one of them if you want to help people think better, improve their cognitive abilities, reduce their stress and improve your communication. Flashing the word 'No' three times to people in an fMRI scanner creates a sudden release of stress-producing neurotransmitters that doesn't happen when they see the word 'Yes'; these hormones have an effect on how well people process information as well as their emotional state. In their book *Words Can Change Your Brain* (2014), Andrew Newberg and Mark Robert Waldman talk about the power of positive language to improve people's thinking, communication and ability to deal with the world. However, there is a challenge because positive words don't have the same power to change your brain as negative ones so you need to use far more positive words to counteract the negative ones. Based on work from Positive Psychology they suggest you need to say at least three positive things for every negative one, and this includes negative body language such as frowning as you speak. You might like to try the 'Yes and…' exercise as a way of practising responding positively rather than negatively. Work with a partner and whatever they say respond with 'Yes and…' and build on whatever they say. They then say 'Yes and…' in response to you, and so you continue. As an exercise it's great fun and promotes creative thinking and as a more permanent growth mindset it's a way of acknowledging the value that everyone can bring to a conversation.

5. Metaphors touch your multisensory brain

You may already be warmed up to the concept of talking in multisensory language and, if not, you'll begin to see how often our senses creep into our language. We are so heavily dominated by our senses that they worm their way into everyday language, both as sensory metaphors, but also in the words you commonly see, hear or write. Think about well-known phrases or sayings you know that are visual: 'Do you see what I mean?' How often do you hear phrases that are related to sounds? 'Does this chime with you?' How about words or phrases that are physical and help you 'grasp' what I'm talking about? Read back through this paragraph and see how many words I used that have a sensory element to them; words like 'warmed', 'talking', 'see', 'creep', 'worm', 'say', 'write', 'chime', 'grasp'. Most of the sentences could have easily been written using different senses whilst still conveying the same meaning.

There's now increasing evidence to show that sensory language may indeed be more interesting and more memorable to your listener or reader because it stimulates more areas of the brain than just the language process-ing areas. Students in an fMRI scanner were asked to listen to sentences containing textural metaphors such as 'a rough day' and sentences that were matched for meaning and structure but without any textural metaphor. They took slightly longer to process the textural metaphor but the areas of their brains that were previously identified as registering real textural input by touch, the parietal operculum, showed increased blood flow. When you use multisensory language you are indeed creating wider neuronal stimula-tion than when you use non-sensory language. If wider stimulation helps to create richer experiences, then you are improving people's ability to learn and remember by using that sensory language.

This may also help to explain why concrete language is easier to under-stand and process than abstract language – it may actually 'touch' parts of your brain that usually respond to real stimuli so you've got a richer picture for concrete language than abstract language which almost 'floats' with nothing to hang onto.

Other Voices

Krystyna Gadd, *Founder of How to Accelerate Learning, UK*

Using Clean Language to create a safe environment

One of my five secrets to accelerated learning is to pay attention to the environment. Not just the physical environment, but the emotional and social environment too. This has led me to think very carefully about how I set the classroom up (physically) and also how I contract with the learners, to make it a safe and stimulating place to learn. What prompted me to think deeply about the environment, some years ago, was a challenging delegate I had on a nine-month-long programme. This individual was probably the most difficult I have had to deal with. What made them 'difficult' was a mismatch between their expectations and mine.

The individual and their specific issues do not warrant any great debate or description even, but the encounter made me reflect deeply about how I 'contract' with learners. It made me consider how to set and manage the expectations of the learners:

- of me, as the facilitator;
- about the programme;

- concerning their own behaviour as the learners;
- how they interact with each other.

Making a safe environment for learners to learn has always been an important factor for me when setting expectations. If the environment is safe, then the learners will trust me as the facilitator, to stretch them beyond where they are just now to create new insights into a topic. A positive environment will help to achieve this and it is borne out in a CIPD (2014) paper '… the fact that negative moods can impede thinking and insight…'. Various permutations of 'How shall we work together' seemed to help somewhat, but it never seemed to work quite as deeply as three specific questions, that originated from Clean Language.

These are the questions and the originator is Caitlin Watkins, in her book *From Contempt to Curiosity*:

1 In order for this (event) to be of value to you it has to be like what?

2 In order for this (event) to be like that, you have to be like what?

3 In order for you to be like that, others have to be like what?

The questions are pre-written on a flipchart and my role is purely to read the questions out in order and to record the answers. I write exactly what they say, rather than my interpretation. I do not comment on any of their responses, other than thanking them and only ask 'Is there anything else?' if they are quiet. Once finished I ask for a volunteer to take the flips away, type them up and then get everyone to sign.

The effect of asking these three questions has been remarkable. There have been three specific things, which I have observed:

- The learners discuss at quite a deep level the meaning of what has been said. For example, they may ask 'what do you mean by "challenging"?'

- They seem to bond quickly as a group, giving them a shared understanding of what is expected and what they should expect of each other (including support).

- There seems to be a deep trust that develops with the facilitator. This, I think, is as a result of asking 'What do you expect?' without the usual prejudging of what that might be.

These three observed outcomes have convinced me to continue the use of these questions in both long and short programmes.

Whilst we're talking about the environment

Do you remember the story about the Truly Terrible Training Course from Chapter 11 on reviewing? One of the things we used to fantasize about in order to create a hideous workshop of no value to anyone was about what would make for a really awful place in which to learn. You may have worked there yourself. I've seen some dark dungeons and tiny cupboards and been told 'This is our training facility'. There are trainers amongst you who may have to train in manufacturing areas, on building sites, on the roads in the middle of the night, in cupboards in retail parks and any variety of non-specialized training areas. Sometimes you really don't have a choice and yet some people never think to question the venue or the layout they are given even when they could. There is ample evidence to show that the environment has a significant effect on how you think, how you feel and ultimately how you learn. Here are a few thoughts about learning environments.

Colouring your judgement

Colour is hugely important to all of us and can change our behaviour and our thinking. Wearing red makes sports teams more successful and can increase their levels of testosterone making the wearer feel and appear more confident. A red environment can reduce analytical thinking, whilst red light makes you more aware of your environment and time seems to pass more slowly when compared to blue light. Warm colours, such as orange, red and yellow make you think the temperature is warmer than it is and cool colours tend to make you feel cooler. Green environments seem to be better for creative thinking and even a view of green plants seems to be relaxing. You may think this is all very confusing so decide to choose a white environment to make it simpler, but that may make your learners simply bored. Perhaps in the ideal world you'd design an environment where the colours could be changed depending on type of thinking required and I do know of occasional venues where you can control the colour of the light. In the meantime be aware of the colour of the environment you're in because you may have to do something to work with or counteract the effect. If you're designing a learning environment then make sure you've checked out the impact of colour on your users; people with visual or reading difficulties can find certain colours or contrasts much more difficult to process. It may put them off learning altogether, make them procrastinate or delay or waste energy in processing unnecessary complexity.

Bringing the outside in and taking the inside out

Natural light boosts attention levels so select rooms with natural daylight; open the blinds and let the light shine in. If you can influence the design of your environment replace ordinary light bulbs with blue spectrum light bulbs which are more like daylight. The best place to get natural light is outside so if the weather allows you to take people outside then devise ways to learn in the great outdoors. I have a client who regularly teaches financial awareness and budgeting in their company car park – not only does it get the learners' attention but it also raises awareness of the Learning and Development team because everyone else in the organization wonders what they are up to. A view of the outside has been found to make people feel more refreshed but if you can't have a real view then experiment with a video loop of an outdoors scene, though this is not as refreshing as the real thing.

What you put inside you

All types of different nutrients seem to have an effect on our brains but there are massive amounts of misinformation about which foods are 'good' for your brain and which aren't – you could write a book on this alone. Omega-3 fish oils were hailed as the big brain food for a while but some of the claims made for their effects on your brain seem to have been overexaggerated and later studies show they may not be quite the superfood that was originally thought. You certainly need fat in your diet because your brain is composed of so much fatty tissue: myelin. You can probably find a claim and counter-claim made for almost any variety of food you like, some of them seemingly valid and some definitely financed by vested interests, so when you hear a piece of research I suggest you go back to those questions you read about in Chapter 3 and just ask yourself whether it seems reasonable. You might even ask, what's your gut feeling about the research?

Some findings published in *Nature* in 2012 link the bacteria in your gut with possible developmental changes in brain structure as well as the processing of neurochemicals (Cryan and Dinan, 2012). Stressed mice fed on microorganisms from the guts of relaxed mice showed changes in behaviour and brain chemistry, and one group of scientists showed that healthy women given particular probiotics showed small changes in their anxiety brain circuits. This research is very much in its infancy still but could certainly add credibility to some old phrases such as 'food for thought'.

Being exploratory, playful and experimental

You may have heard that creativity lives in the right side of your brain but I hope by now you're already seeing that it's very rare that a single part of the brain is responsible for a single activity or particular type of thinking or processing. Creativity is, like most other brain 'activities', extremely complex and there's far more we don't know about it than we do know.

When you're being creative it depends on what type of creative thinking you're doing at the time as to which parts of your brain are playing the strongest role.

Rather than creativity being located in your right hemisphere research now suggests that it's a complex network of activity. We're possibly using three particular networks when we're being creative: the executive attention network, the imagination network and the salience network. All three networks show complex interactions between both left and right hemispheres, conscious and unconscious thinking processes, cortical and subcortical regions, and different networks may be more dominant as you go through different creative thinking states.

Regardless of exactly where creativity happens in your brain, how can you encourage creative thinking in your learning environments?

Encouraging people to try new and different things helps their brains be more plastic and open to ideas, so here is a brief list of things that have been shown to increase divergent and creative thinking. Feel free to add in your own:

- laughing;
- hugging;
- group brainstorming – standing up;
- brainstorming on your own before sharing;
- horizontal eye movement exercises;
- being bored;
- dreaming;
- working in a blue office;
- walking;
- being distracted;
- living abroad;
- working when you're feeling groggy;

- being slightly drunk;
- working with new people;
- meeting new people;
- distancing yourself from the problem;
- building on what you know;
- playing.

Other Voices

Helen Ashton, *Senior Learning Consultant, First Class learning and development*

'We have booked the boardroom for your day'

My heart sinks at these words. I ask if the tables can be moved and the reply is 'No it doesn't move. It is a beautiful solid oak one-piece table and we never move it' and my heart sinks further again. On the surface of it what does it matter that the participants will work round a boardroom table all day? But my experience shows that it does make a difference to energy levels.

I understand there are many factors that may impact on the energy level of a group but in making my observation about room layout I draw on my experience from delivering one particular workshop for the same client. They are a national organization and workshops are delivered around the country at their different sites. The layout, size and flexibility of the rooms vary between sites. My preference is for U-shape of chairs with a table in the room for group work. It suits this programme making it easy to move around for group work and we can use the floor space for walking through models and processes.

Sometimes it is not possible to create the layout I want and I have to work with a room that might be cramped and sitting round tables. I personally find the lack of freedom to move more tiring and I can feel my energy levels are lower than when I have space to move and move around. I have had a sense in the past that participants have felt the same, less willing to move and 'stuck' in their chair and table territory. However, recently I was in the same site two weeks in a row. Having checked the room layout in advance I had been told the large boardroom table didn't move and worked round it. Despite being a great group of people they were flagging by the end of the day and comments on the feedback said the day was too long. The next week I was there for two days running the same workshop for two more groups, in the same room. The thought of that room for two days made me determined to do something with 'the table' and so I moved it to one side of the room. The difference in my energy levels and those of the group was staggering. They moved in and out of groups easily, and comments about the length of the day – nil!

Musically speaking

I am not a musician and have always admired people who can sing, play an instrument or compose. Music clearly affects our emotions and can be a useful tool in creating different emotional environments in a learning situation. What I'd really like you to think about here is how music can be used to get a message to stick, and at the risk of being really annoying I'd like you to think about 'earworms'. Which snippets of music get stuck in your head and go round and round and round until you want to bang your head to tip them out? What is it about earworms that make them so 'sticky', and can you use them to help people remember information? One researcher suggests that it's to do with the length of notes and the intervals between them that makes them stick; notes that are close to each other on the musical scale and then each note is held for a moment before the next (like the chorus of Abba's *Waterloo*) seem to be prime candidates to create earworms. So if you're more musical than me you could experiment with writing short musical sequences with words to reflect your key learning points and if you play them often enough you'll have your own earworms. Can you infect your learners with them too?

Summary

This is necessarily a very brief overview of some additional areas of neuroscience that you might find interesting as someone who wants to create the best physical, emotional and cognitive environment for learning. If they interest you then do go and explore them further and, better still, experiment with them in your world.

- How and why stories are more memorable than facts.
- Five neuroscience nuggets about language and learning.

- Keep it simple.
- Prime the brain with what you want.
- Highlight compliant behaviours.
- Say 'Yes' rather than 'No'.
- Use multisensory metaphors to stimulate more of your sensory cortex.
- The environment and learning:
  - Colour – choose colours to change moods.
  - Bringing the outside inside.
  - What you put inside you may affect your thinking.
- Being more exploratory, playful and creative.
- How earworms might help information to stick.

References and further reading

Bardell, E (1978) Does style influence credibility and esteem?, *Communication of Scientific and Technical Information*, **35**, pp 4–7

Cryan, J F and Dinan, T G (2012) Mind-altering microorganisms: the impact of the gut microbiota on brain and behaviour, *Nature Reviews Neuroscience*, **13** (10), pp 701–12

Earp, B D, Dill, B, Harris, J, Ackerman, J and Bargh, J A (2010) Incidental exposure to no-smoking signs primes craving for cigarettes: an ironic effect of unconscious semantic processing, *Yale Review of Undergraduate Research in Psychology*, **2** (1), pp 12–23

Marsh, E and Sink, H (2009) Access to handouts of presentation slides during lecture: consequences for learning, *Applied Cognitive Psychology*, **24** (5), pp 691–706

Martin, S J, Bassi, S and Dunbar-Rees, R (2011) Commitments, norms and custard creams – a social influence approach to reducing did not attends (DNAs), [Online] http://www.bdo.co.uk/__data/assets/pdf_file/0008/186443/NHS_Bedfordshire_-_Case_Study.pdf (archived at perma.cc/9DJF-6JQ8)

Mosher, C (2015) [accessed 2 July 2015] How to Grow Stronger Without Lifting Weights [Online] http://www.scientificamerican.com/article/how-to-grow-stronger-without-lifting-weights/ (archived at perma.cc/W3BB-TKJU)

Newberg, A and Waldman, M R (2014) *Words Can Change Your Brain: 12 conversation strategies to build trust, resolve conflict, and increase intimacy*, Penguin Group, London

Turk, C and Kirkman, J (1978) Do you write impressively?, *Bulletin of the British Ecological Society*, **9** (3), pp 5–10

Sleep and learning

13

To sleep, perchance to dream.

A dangerous activity

Are you aware that you regularly undertake a very risky learning activity but remain completely oblivious of it? It's usually at night when you're most likely to put yourself in harm's way and most of us do it willingly, sometimes desperately waiting for it to happen. From an evolutionary standpoint it seems very strange that you would stop keeping an eye out for information about potential food, mates, prey or enemies and instead shut yourself off from all external stimuli in order to concentrate only on what's going on inside your head. But of course, you're not concentrating consciously, because you're sleeping.

Whilst you're asleep you become unconscious of the outside world and for part of the time not only do you cut yourself off from all potential warnings of danger, but you are also completely paralysed, becoming unable to respond to danger, even if you were aware of it.

Every animal on the planet seems to show some form of 'sleeping' activity even down to insects and nematodes. How they sleep varies in terms of length of time, day or night sleeping and whether they sleep standing up or lying down. There are animals such as some migratory birds and water-living mammals that manage to keep moving whilst sleeping because only one side of their brain sleeps at a time. Clearly sleep is a universal need but what exactly is it and why is it such a vital learning activity?

Overview – what you'll cover

You've already read a bit about sleep throughout the book but this chapter is going to take you on a deeper dive into that strange part of a third of our lives that we usually pay little attention too – except when we're not able to do it.

There's still a huge amount about sleep that is vastly mysterious and hotly debated. Whilst it's been a relatively underexplored area of neuroscience there's a growing interest and new discoveries being made all the time but as with most of what we find out about our brains it usually throws up more questions than it answers.

Figure 13.1 presents the mindmap for the chapter. We'll start with defining what sleep is and isn't and some ideas about the different stages of sleep. You're going to find out what parts of the brain help to regulate both sleep and waking, the neurotransmitters that have an impact and, of more relevance to you, the vital part sleep plays in learning; particularly memory consolidation and sense making.

Figure 13.1   Sleep and learning

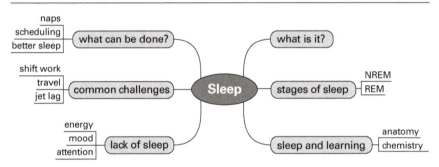

We'll look at some of the challenges of lack of sleep, particularly in a modern 'always on' world and the impact that has on effective learning amongst both adults and children. You'll find out about napping and microsleeps and what you can do to work with them rather than let them get the better of you.

Finally, you will get some ideas to help your learners and yourself to sleep better. However, this is one area where as a designer or facilitator of learning you may have less direct influence and it's a bigger issue for individuals, organizations and educational practice.

What is sleep?

We all sleep, so have some idea of what sleep is but what do we really know about it? How is it different to being unconscious under anaesthetic or because you've been hit on the head? What happens whilst you're asleep?

Sleep is different from other types of unconscious activity in that it's completely natural and is a regular, rhythmic activity controlled both by circadian rhythms in your brain and body and a homeostatic system of chemicals. Circadian rhythms occur naturally, seem to be linked to the earth's rotation and are built into many of your body's processes. The sleep cycle, like other circadian rhythms, will persist even without the stimulus of light and dark and the most accurate estimates measure it at an average of 24 hours and 11 minutes (Czeisler *et al*, 1999). Previous estimates were found to be inaccurate because subjects had access to electric light which prolongs the circadian rhythm. The homeostatic system is a balance between a system of wakefulness and sleep controlled by hormones and neurotransmitters with adenosine playing a particularly important role in 'sleep pressure'. The evidence is unclear as to whether one controls the other but seems currently to weigh in favour of the homeostatic system having more influence over the circadian system than vice versa. Cortical regions are affected by both systems but sub-cortical regions are more heavily influenced by the circadian rhythm.

Not everyone has the same requirement for sleep but the data suggests the average is about 7.5 to 8 hours per day. Matthew Walker in his book *Why We Sleep* (Walker, 2018) describes long-term studies suggesting that people, such as Margaret Thatcher and Ronald Reagan, who famously survived on a few hours each night, may function well in the short term with reduced sleep hours, but they are storing up problems for themselves such as dementia or Alzheimer's disease as they age.

Sleep is a multipurpose tool for repairing your brain and body cells, clearing up debris in the brain, promoting better function and, significantly for us, plays a huge role in memory and learning. Memories of what you learn are encoded and recalled whilst you're awake but sleep is vital for both consolidating, storing and making sense of what you've learned.

Stages of sleep

For a long time people thought the brain simply switched off during sleep and nothing really happened all night long apart from a few dreams, but in the 1950s, a researcher, Eugene Aserinksy, used EEG to measure his own son's sleeping patterns and showed that we have multiple different phases of sleep throughout the night (Brown, 2003). With his surprising findings the science of sleep was ignited. (You can read an excellent full-length version of this story in the *Smithsonian* magazine.)

Between those first feelings of falling asleep until you wake up again you go through five different stages every night which are split into two categories: Rapid Eye Movement (REM) sleep when your brain is at least as active as during the day; and Non-Rapid Eye Movement (NREM) sleep where it's doing more recovery. You may sometimes find only three stages of NREM sleep described because the American Academy of Sleep Medicine (AASM) has combined Stages 3 and 4 but we're going to stick with all five.

NREM sleep

You pass through gradually deeper stages of between 5–15 minutes each, from Stages 1 to 4 of NREM sleep and then into REM sleep, all taking about 90 minutes. Then you start again with the same cycle, so in a good night's sleep of eight hours you probably go through about five cycles. However, as with many things in your brain, it's not as simple as it seems because you tend to experience more deep sleep (NREM) in the first half of the night and more REM (dreaming) sleep in the second half.

Additionally there are significant changes with age; so whilst a baby experiences about eight hours of REM sleep at birth, you're probably having about two hours of REM in your twenties but by the time you're in your 70s you're down to only about 45 minutes. This has an impact on learning as you'll see when we explore what's happening in the different stages.

During the different stages your brain reveals different patterns of brainwaves related to different activities at each stage and you covered them briefly in Chapter 2. What do you remember?

Stage 1 NREM – as you drift off to sleep your brainwaves start to slow down and you'll experience first alpha and then theta waves. During this stage you may have dream-like experiences, more like daydreams and strange illusions of falling or hearing things. These are called hypnogogic hallucinations. Research from Cambridge University Gates scholar Sridhar Jagannathan shows the average person, without any sleep problems, takes between 5 and 20 minutes to fall asleep (Coughlan, 2018). To help yourself fall asleep more quickly, create a regular sleep habit with rituals and routines including reducing your core body temperature before you go to bed.

Stage 2 NREM is when you start to generate 'sleep spindles'; bursts of waves with a frequency of about 10–12 Hz that last for at least half a second (sometimes they are called sigma waves). They are not clearly understood by sleep scientists but are very important for learning, especially for declarative memory; remember that's the sort of memory you can describe so it's your semantic memories and episodic memories. It's thought the spindles correspond to transfer of information from short-term memory in your hippocampus to your frontal cortex and are important for integrating new knowledge with what you already know. Sleep spindles increase in quantity if you've been learning something new and some people suggest they may be a physiological marker of 'intelligence'.

You'll remember you read about 'WEIRD' subjects for research. Perhaps they should be called WEIRDM because for much of the earlier research the overwhelming bulk of human guinea pigs were young male students and women's results may have been overlooked in the aggregate results.

Women typically have twice as many sleep spindles as men and have an advantage when it comes to tests for episodic and semantic memories, smell memories and also memories for faces. Oestrogen seems to increase sleep spindles and some scientists propose a waxing and waning of memory during the menstrual cycle. However, more research is required to make this a conclusive finding.

The number of sleep spindles you experience declines with age which may be why 'it's harder for an old dog to learn new tricks'. Recent research has demonstrated that applying an external, oscillating current just as you enter slow wave sleep can induce more sleep spindles and did improve declarative memory for a group of students. Perhaps a cure for memory decline with age is on the way; however, this stimulation was under closely controlled laboratory conditions so is not to be recommended at home.

Stage 3 NREM is a transition between the lighter sleep stages and really deep sleep. It's characterized by the appearance of delta brainwaves which then persist into Stage 4 deep sleep or slow wave sleep.

Stage 4 NREM is when it's hardest to wake someone up but is the sleep that refreshes you the most and tidies up your brain. Your brainwaves are at their slowest, breathing slows, temperature decreases. When experimental subjects are deprived of sleep for more than one night this is the type of sleep their brains immediately try to recover.

You can help yourself sleep more soundly during NREM sleep by obvious things such as reducing noise, having a dark room or wearing an eye mask and earplugs.

You'll recall that long-term potentiation happens in your synapses when you are awake; neuronal connections that are repeated become more likely to fire again. During Stage 4 sleep it seems that those strongly stimulated, potentiated, synapses are maintained whilst weaker ones are filtered out; it's as if your brain is deciding what to keep and what to throw away. Some people suggest this is what gives us that 'insight' that often happens when you sleep; you go to bed puzzling over a problem or feeling overwhelmed by new information but somehow by the time you wake up it has started to crystallize and become clearer. It's a time of 'sense making'.

Another important observation for learning is that the most active parts of your brain when you're awake also have the highest levels of delta waves in this stage. If you are woken up during deep sleep it usually takes a while for your cortical brainwaves to 'speed up' again which is why you feel particularly groggy and unable to think clearly.

Deprived of this deep sleep, amyloid proteins and free radicals build up causing damage to your brains and, as mentioned previously, are associated in the long term with dementia and Alzheimer's disease (Ow and Dunstan, 2014).

REM sleep

REM sleep is particularly associated with dreaming and EEG measurements show your brain is particularly active. Most of us dream even though we don't always remember our dreams. For many years, and still today, some people believed we could interpret our dreams to better understand our personalities and deepest thoughts. However, there's very little evidence that our dreams have any potency for predicting the future (beyond the consideration that the purpose of memory may be prediction) or for seeing into our deepest darkest psyches. This part of your sleep cycle is, however, particularly important for learning non-declarative skills and habits.

There's a nice story in Mathew Walker's book *Why We Sleep* about an insight from talking to a concert pianist. The pianist tells him that despite being an expert pianist, when he's learning a new piece his playing is clunky and deliberate. 'But' explained the pianist 'when I wake up in the morning I can simply play the piece perfectly.' His brain practises the sequences whilst he sleeps enabling him to express his skills fully the following day.

Normally you have about 20–30 minutes per sleep cycle of REM sleep and during this phase your motor cortex is as active as if you were awake and attempts to send coordinated patterns of information to your muscles. Fortunately for you, your muscles are paralysed thanks to the effect of GABA and another neurotransmitter, glycine that need to work together for the paralysis to be successful. Without this paralysis you would act out your dreams which can be extremely dangerous for you and those you sleep with.

The evidence for skills learning comes from many experiments where, typically, researchers ask subjects to learn finger movements or sequences and then test them before and after learning. They vary the conditions so people are either asleep or awake between tests; following normal sleep patterns and varying the time of day of the tests. Subjects who sleep between tests always show more improvement than those who remain awake.

On the face of it it's not a very interesting skill to learn but of course most of us use these skills every day when we enter pin codes or phone numbers. Often when people are asked for a phone number or pin code they need to 'dial' it with their fingers because the information has become a non-declarative, procedural memory rather than a declarative memory. Recently I needed to tell my husband my pin code and could remember all the numbers but simply couldn't remember the order until I looked at a card machine. Then my fingers knew the pattern so I could 'act out' the sequence and give my husband the code. Of course, you're often practising more complex skills during this important sleeping stage of learning and it seems that if you practise these skills shortly before you sleep you're more likely to dream about them and get that extra little bit of unconscious practice.

Anatomy of sleep

At the start of the book you briefly read how various parts of the brain control sleep and wakefulness and most of the story of sleep is a balancing act between these different regions and the ebb and flow of hormones and neurotransmitters. You'll explore it in more detail now.

Your sleep pacemaker – suprachiasmatic nucleus

Deep within your brain is a small structure called the suprachiasmatic nucleus (SCN) that receives information about light levels directly from your eyes and acts like the pacemaker for your sleep/wake cycle. It's buried in the hypothalamus and matches your circadian rhythms with the light/dark cycle sending messages on to your pineal gland to produce or inhibit melatonin.

Hypothalamus, pons, medulla and midbrain – keeping you quiet

The hypothalamus and a group of other sleep control centres in the brain stem, the pons, medulla and midbrain all have sleep-promoting cells producing GABA which suppresses different attentional systems in the hypothalamus – this is part of the homeostatic balance between sleep and wakefulness. During REM sleep it's the pons and medulla that send quietening signals to your muscles to stop you moving.

Thalamus – the gatekeeper

All sensory information, except smell, is filtered through the thalamus whilst you're awake but when you're asleep, rather than being a selective gatekeeper allowing information in, the thalamus turns into a draconian night-club bouncer and prevents external stimuli from reaching and stimulating your cortex. However, this night-club bouncer clearly has ideas of its own because when you move into REM sleep once again the thalamus starts to allow sensory information into your cortex, feeding into your dreams.

Cortex – weird dream maker

Your visual cortex, as you know, is the largest sensory processing part of your cortex and its contributions to your dreams usually ensure they are highly visual. However, the frontal cortex is pretty inactive whilst you sleep. It's not paying attention to what's logical or real, leaving you open to accepting the highly improbable events that often take place in dreams.

Chemistry of sleep

Homeostatic sleep pressure and your neurotransmitters

The balance between sleep and wakefulness is a delicate one and is controlled by a number of neurotransmitters that either promote sleep or wakefulness or sometimes do both depending on their levels and when and where they are released (see Table 13.1). Some you've come across in other parts of the book particularly when you read about attention.

Melatonin

Melatonin is one of the main neurotransmitters associated with sleep and is significantly controlled by your circadian rhythm. Melatonin itself controls physiological sleep measures such as reduced heart rate, temperature and breathing. It is one of the chemicals people sometimes take to help them overcome jet lag and is being investigated as a preventative measure in Alzheimer's disease. Melatonin levels are inhibited by light so they fall during the day and then rise again once it starts to get dark. It takes about two hours for them to reach their peak, sending you off to sleep, and then

Table 13.1 Neurotransmitters for sleep and wakefulness

Sleep	Wakefulness
Adenosine – sleep pressure	Noradrenaline/norepinephrine – high alert
Melatonin – high levels promote sleepiness	Dopamine – motivation and reward
GABA – muscle suppression during REM sleep	Serotonin – precursor to melatonin
Galanin	Orexin/hypocretin – hippocampal cell growth
	Acetylcholine – encodes memories
	Histamine – promotes wakefulness

falling levels during the night help other brain areas to measure the amount of sleep you've had. Once melatonin levels are low enough you will start waking up.

Adenosine – sleep pressure

Adenosine is produced by the breakdown of adenosine triphosphate (ATP) which is a fundamental energy molecule for all your body's cells including your brain cells. ATP is stored as glycogen in your brain. The harder your neurons and glial cells work, the more your glycogen stores are converted to ATP, producing more adenosine. Increasing levels of adenosine make you feel sleepy; desperately sleepy. They induce a pressure to sleep and if you resist it the levels continue to increase until you eventually sleep. When you go into NREM sleep your brain is less active than when you're awake so it has time to recover and replace your glycogen stores and levels of adenosine gradually fall until you're ready to wake up again.

GABA and histamine

GABA suppresses muscle tone whilst you're dreaming so is important for keeping you safely inactive and may also inhibit histamine production which keeps you awake; so this is a classic balancing act in the homeostatic sleep mechanism. You're probably aware of anti-histamine tablets, often taken for allergies, and how they can make you sleepy. This is because they reduce the uptake of histamine in your brain and the purpose of histamine is to keep you awake. If you're bitten by a mosquito at night it raises your histamine levels so not only does it itch but the histamine keeps you awake too. In terms of learning, histamine at appropriate levels promotes learning but higher levels of histamine can impair memory retrieval; experiments with rats showed that high levels of histamine made them less capable of learning to avoid small electric shocks (Tasaka,1994).

Galanin

The role is not fully understood but galanin-producing genes are stimulated when people are prevented from having REM sleep so it probably helps to promote REM sleep and may have a role in heat loss; lower body temperature is associated with better sleep patterns.

Noradrenaline/norepinephrine

This is another example of the complicated homeostasis model. We normally associate noradrenaline with vigilance and high arousal but it also signals the pineal gland to produce melatonin. Too little and you don't get sufficient melatonin production so can't fall asleep; too much and it keeps you awake anyway so it's another Goldilocks neurotransmitter – you need just the right amount at just the right time.

You know the importance of emotions for learning and noradrenaline plays an important part in processing emotional experiences during REM sleep. When something unpleasant happens you produce noradrenaline making you feel physiologically stressed. However, when noradrenaline levels drop at night replaying unpleasant experiences with these lower levels of noradrenaline lets you store the memory without the overwhelming stress that you may have felt at the time. It's not so much time that heals bad memories but possibly your dreams. People with post-traumatic stress disorder (PTSD) have been helped to overcome disturbing nightmares with drugs to lower their noradrenaline levels whilst they sleep.

Dopamine

When this reward neurotransmitter is registered in the pineal gland it prevents noradrenaline release, reducing the production and release of melatonin so you wake up.

Serotonin

Like many neurotransmitters serotonin has multiple functions depending on levels and site of impact. For a start it's one of the precursors to melatonin so is required for sleep. But when it's at high levels in the dorsal raphe nucleus in your brain stem it is associated with wakefulness, unless you end up with an accumulation in which case it puts you to sleep. You may be beginning to see why sleep research took so long to take off and is so complex.

Orexin

Orexin is another neurotransmitter produced in the hypothalamus and improves learning and memory potentially by enhancing new neuronal cells to grow in the hypothalamus. It's been associated with spatial learning, for which the hippocampus is vital, and improves mood which you already know supports learning. Animals with reduced levels of orexin are worse at associative learning through smell.

Acetylcholine

This neurotransmitter is mainly associated with attention and during the day it promotes the transmission of information from your sensory cortices through to your hippocampus but at night with falling levels the information transfer shifts direction out of your hippocampus and back into long-term storage in your cortex. It's particularly important for storing declarative memory.

Lack of sleep and learning

You've found out about what happens in your brain when you're sleeping and how it's so vital for laying down memories as part of learning, but sleep, or more often loss of it, impacts on other aspects of learning. There has been far more research done on complete sleep deprivation rather than partial sleep deprivation but as many of us regularly suffer partial deprivation for a multitude of common reasons that's what we'll focus on here.

Partial sleep deprivation means losing sleep relative to your normal amount. Acute partial sleep deprivation is when this happens for just a night occasionally, as can happen to many of us for any number of reasons.

Chronic partial sleep deprivation is when you continue to do this for weeks, months or years, which is also worryingly common.

All sleep deprivation impacts on mood, attention, working memory, decision making and vigilance. The recovery process for cognitive function takes longer after chronic sleep deprivation than after acute total sleep deprivation. Chronic sleep restriction may cause long-term changes in brain functions that are not reversible and anyone who reads Mathew Walker's book *Why We Sleep* is likely to lose at least a little sleep worrying about the impact of any sleep deprivation at all.

Physical and mental energy

Lack of sleep means lower levels of glycogen and therefore ATP. This is the energy source of all cells in your body so not only is it harder to think but even your muscles feel tired. Because your brain uses a high percentage of your body's available energy it suffers faster than the rest of your body. Your frontal cortex doesn't have the energy it needs for working memory to function so all cognitive tasks are affected and you may not even be aware of it until you've made noticeable errors.

Motivation levels

Your mood is significantly affected by how much sleep you get and you can probably testify yourself how being deprived of sleep makes you feel less motivated, less able to think positively, more likely to be irritable, angry or hostile. And you're more likely to feel depressed. If feeling this bad isn't enough, sleep loss increases activity in the amygdala but decreases connectively between the amygdala and the frontal cortex so you perceive things more negatively and have less ability to control your reaction.

Sadly you will also miss out on the effects of positive experiences too. Sleep-deprived people are less friendly, less empathetic and don't feel the positive mood they would normally get from an achievement. Trying to learn something when you feel like this is just going to be a lot more difficult.

Reduced attention

Everyone knows how hard it is to concentrate the day after a late or disturbed night. Directed attention is vital for learning and so when you don't get sufficient sleep learning becomes harder; either you miss information, are poorer at sustaining practice or, worse still, if you're learning something practical you may make errors or have accidents due to lack of attention.

Lack of sleep means levels of adenosine are not sufficiently reduced so you're attempting to stay awake with a stronger sleep pressure than normal. The likelihood of impaired attention is, not surprisingly, particularly noticeable when tasks are boring or repetitive. If something is new or extraordinary your attentional mechanisms can override the sleep pressure.

Lack of vigilance

Vigilance is the ability to sustain concentration over a long period of time and is essential in many technical jobs. When you're learning you also need to sustain your concentration over time. Sometimes this sustained concentration, like cramming for an exam, or swotting up on a new topic, can be what leads to the sleep deprivation in the first place, creating a downward spiral. The less effective you are at sustaining concentration the more you're going to do poorly and therefore feel you need to do more revision or study for longer. Certainly staying up late cramming for exams is not the way to embed that information in your brain or to help you perform well in the exam the following day. And, even if you were to perform well, your lowered mood level means you won't be able to appreciate it.

Access to previously remembered information is reduced

Much of our learning is supported by building on what you already know but unfortunately when you're sleep deprived it's harder to recall what you remembered before so you can't create effective links to new information.

Decision making

Many learning tasks involve some kind of decision and being sleep deprived affects decision making in a range of ways. You're more likely to find it difficult to use new information in complex tasks, to have more rigid thinking and to keep returning to the same thinking or actions (called a perseveration error). Lack of sleep is also likely to make your decisions more variable and more risky.

Microsleeps

These are very short sleeps of a few microseconds and we're often not aware of them. But if you've ever driven along a motorway when you're tired you're sure to have experienced them. You're just as likely to have experienced them in meetings and I'm sad to say training sessions too; those moments when you notice you've missed something, perhaps felt your eyes shut or that disconcerting feeling of your head dropping. You're more likely to experience a microsleep when you're tired but they are exacerbated by lack of engagement, boredom, a warm room… sometimes the conditions associated with a poor training environment or dull e-learning.

Common challenges

Lots of people suffer from insufficient sleep but there are a number of areas where learning at work and lack of sleep come into conflict:

- People working shifts often have to work unusual hours in order to fit into standard training programmes. This is doubly challenging if they are already chronically sleep deprived (common for shift workers). It's the equivalent of asking 9–5 workers to attend a training course all night after a day of work.

- Face-to-face training may involve travel for trainers or participants and often both. Many people arrive at training programmes at a standard start of 9 am saying, 'I had to get up at 4 am to catch the early train/plane/bus'. They are not in peak learning condition and will find the learning more difficult than their peers who live down the road.

- It's popular, and sometimes cheaper, to run training programmes abroad, particularly in global organizations. The effects of jet lag on learning are obvious to anyone who's flown across time zones and it's because your brain is still stuck in the circadian rhythm from where you came. If you travelled east you lose time and sleep and it takes one day for every time zone crossed to reset your circadian rhythm. If you travelled west it takes one day for every 1.5 time zones crossed. Most people are probably returning by that time so need to reset again on their return. Regular time zone travellers rarely function at their best.

- Learning programmes with overnight stays often include elements of team building, socializing or networking which can mean a late night for participants. This prevents them consolidating what they learned on the first day and makes them less alert and open to learning on the second.

- There are significant differences in sleeping habits of younger and older people and typically younger people are more likely to be owls than larks. Early starts to school and university days are damaging young people's ability to learn. Dr Paul Kelley, who you came across in the spaced learning chapter, has done a huge amount of research on this and his book *Body Clocks* is an insightful read with a strong call to alter school hours and business hours. He's kindly given us permission to reproduce part of a chapter here as one of our 'Other Voices'.

Other Voices

Dr Paul Kelley, *Honorary Associate, Sleep, Circadian and Memory Neuroscience, Learning and Teaching Innovation Portfolio, The Open University*

School start times

The essential problems with early school start times are well known. Adolescents need anywhere from 8 to 10 hours of sleep each night to ensure the best health and optimum academic performance, depending on age and inter-individual differences, yet most get far less. Adolescent sleep restriction is clearly linked to early school starts as on non-school days adolescents have wake times two or more hours later. This finding has been confirmed in Korea, Europe and North America and is not substantially affected by cultural factors. Why school times should remain so early is not clear, and there has been little research into much later start times. A simple answer appears to be to move school starting times two hours later, but that is only a rough estimate rather than an accurate proven solution that takes in to account the age of students. This type of solution would require the application of scientific methods and research in education, which in this area have previously been somewhat lacking. In 2007, Paul established the UK's first Trust School, with the aim of translating scientific research into educational practice using evidence-based methodology. By 2009, the Trust School's innovative approach to education attracted the attention of *Horizon*, the BBC's flagship science programme, for their episode on chronobiology called 'The Secret Life of Your Body Clock'. As part of filming, Horizon conducted student academic performance tests at 10.00 and 14.00. The students' results were 24 per cent higher in the afternoon than in the morning. As one student remarked, 'It's going to affect teenagers all over the world when people realize teenagers learn better in the afternoon, I don't see why they shouldn't come to school later too.' The *Horizon* programme, which also made the case for later school start times, was aired in 2009 and watched by over 2 million viewers.

Paul was convinced that the school's start times needed to be considerably later than 09.00. Research into the issue over the previous 10 years suggested that the best solution was probably a core learning session for all students between 11.00 and 15.00, and then independent sessions on both sides so that individual students could choose learning times that were optimal for their chronotypes. His first objective, however, was to move the start time later for students of 13–16 years of age. These younger students needed later starts that synchronized with their biological times, though not as late as older teenagers. A range of different research by Roenneberg suggested that a 10.00 start would be most appropriate for the majority of students of this age, and so to improve students' health, and after consultation with parents and students, the school's start time was changed from 08.50 to 10.00.

In the wake of research from the United States indicating that later start times would improve results, the change was very much under scrutiny when examination results were announced a year later in 2011. In the UK, educational success was measured by the percentage of students achieving good examination scores that met a national standard for 16-year-olds, covering all the main subjects. Some education administrators were certain that the results would go down with later starts, whereas the scientific community was quietly confident they would go up, as in the United States. Of course, no one really knew.

The examination results went up, but more than anyone expected, with 18 per cent more students achieving the national benchmark for good results. Many commentators praised the impressive improvement and use of sleep science to enhance education. A lead article in *The Times* declared, 'It is heartening to see education responding to the sort of evidence-based research that revolutionized medicine 100 years ago.' The changes also brought health benefits, students quickly adjusted to the later times, and parents were able to see differences in their children. Liam McClelland, 14, said, 'I'm getting an extra hour's sleep and I just feel much more awake. I used to be so careless in the morning: really simple things like when I was pouring milk or something, I'd miss the bowl. Now I feel happier in lessons, when before I was so tired I used to rest my head on my hands. I don't get so many headaches either.'

Extracted from *Body Clocks* by Paul Kelley and Sian Griffiths (Kelley and Griffiths, 2018). Reproduced with permission.

Unfortunately, despite the compelling evidence from this research, and more, about the impact of a later school time on students' results and their health, the local authority in this case made a policy decision to return school hours to normal.

What can you do?

Naps, sleep pods – pros and cons

Some organizations are famed for having sleep pods on site where people can catch up on some lost sleep. Whilst they are seen as very forward thinking some research suggests they may not always be the perfect solution. Sleep expert James Wilson in an article in *The Independent* (2018) says installing nap pods is 'one of the worst things you can do', and can exacerbate insomnia. 'Naps knock bedtime back. Using a nap pod sounds like the right thing to do, and people are doing it because they don't know any better, but it's not right for everyone.'

Other napping research, however, suggests napping is useful for different cognitive and motor skills. A power nap of only 10–15 minutes means you stay in the early stages of sleep so recover quickly and feel rested if you need to do something physical but a longer nap of 50–60 minutes may help 'clear the desktop' making it useful for complex mental processing like studying. And a full sleep cycle of 90 minutes including a REM stage will boost creativity and perception. So it looks as if you need to decide what you want to learn and nap accordingly.

Certainly if you're feeling sleep pressure a short nap can help to reduce the levels of adenosine so you function better until bedtime.

There are of course cultures where napping is much more acceptable and considered normal. Since moving to Spain I enjoy a regular short nap of 15 minutes after lunch which seems to perk me up for the afternoon. Try it out for a week and see how it works for you.

What can be done at an organizational level

Organizations need to become more aware of the human cost and the ineffectiveness of learning when people are tired. Here are some suggested solutions:

- For face-to-face sessions make sure people with long journeys have overnight accommodation so they arrive fresh or start later in the day.
- Split learning programmes into shorter sessions interspersed with sleep opportunities – this is where digital learning to support face-to-face sessions is really valuable. For face-to-face programmes spread shorter sessions across more days and nights.

- Shift workers need time to adjust their circadian rhythm before training programmes or give them access to learning during their normal working hours.
- Create a culture where the restorative value of sleep is valued more highly than staying late in the office or responding to messages at midnight.

What you can do to help your learners

- Teach them about sleep so they can help themselves.
- Plan your training/ learning around the types of things you want people to learn. It may be more effective to have two half days of training than one full day giving people the time to consolidate before learning more.
- Give people opportunities to nap during learning programmes. Doing a guided visualization allows tired people to nap and others to reflect.

What you can do for your own learning

There's a mountain of advertised products to help you sleep better and therefore learn better but many are poorly researched, inaccurate and may actually cause more disturbance with unnecessary light or sound. A genuine sleep monitoring experiment in a laboratory to determine how you sleep will have you wired up to measure at least 20 physiological signs of sleep which are monitored by experts all night; whereas the sleep app on your phone is really only able to tell whether it, rather than you, moved at night.

Sleep is a habit like any other and you can build a new sleep habit over time. Some of the following ideas may sound like things your parents told you but 'sleep hygiene', as it's termed, is an important factor in improving your learning capabilities. Perhaps you won't manage to do all of these sleep promoting ideas every day but if you're revising for exams or have something important to learn for work it's worth paying attention to your sleep for a period before, during and after; giving your brain its best chance to learn effectively:

- Regular bedtime and waking-up time helps your brain to maintain appropriate levels of brain chemicals and because your brain can't tell the difference between weekdays and weekends it's better to keep to the same times all week rather than try to binge sleep at the weekend.
- Turn off all blue-light-emitting devices at least two hours before you sleep (I know that one sounds cruel – no mobile, no TV, no tablet...). Your

devices use short-wavelength-enriched light, meaning it has a higher concentration of blue light than natural light which disrupts melatonin levels and reduces the quantity and quality of your sleep. You can also buy filters and most modern phones have a night-time setting.

- Use special light bulbs designed to mimic the natural light patterns of night and day.

- Studies found 30 minutes of blue-light exposure in the morning improves working memory and reaction times and can promote sleep later – a walk on a sunny day will do it just as well as special light bulbs.

- Reduce your inner core temperature because you'll go to sleep faster and sleep more soundly. A warm bath makes the blood flow to your extremities reducing your core temperature so is a sure fire way to get a better night's sleep.

- Reduce light pollution with black-out blinds or eye masks so that you follow the natural circadian rhythms of night and day as much as possible.

- Caffeine has an effect on your acetylcholine levels and whilst it can boost cognitive performance in the short term it also disrupts your sleep. The half-life of caffeine in your blood is six hours so a coffee even six hours before bed can keep you awake.

Summary

As you've read this chapter you've learned:

- Sleep is a natural process experienced by all animals.

- Sleep is divided into five stages of REM and NREM sleep, all of which are important for learning, memory consolidation and recovery of brain function.

- Sleep is controlled by a complex balance of circadian rhythms, neurotransmitters and hormones.

- Numerous parts of the brain control sleep and wakefulness.

- Lack of sleep impacts on learning because of changes in mood, attention, vigilance, decision making, working memory and memory consolidation.

- There are challenges for individuals and organizations in learning whilst tired.

- Some suggestions for improving quality and quantity of sleep.

References and further reading

Brown, C (2003) The stubborn scientist who unraveled a mystery of the night, *Smithsonian*, https://www.smithsonianmag.com/science-nature/the-stubborn-scientist-who-unraveled-a-mystery-of-the-night-91514538/?page=9 (archived at perma.cc/C75P-5TBT)

Coughlan, S, (2018) https://www.bbc.com/news/business-42945383 (archived at perma.cc/C36W-9HG2) https://www.ncbi.nlm.nih.gov/pmc/articles/PMC4286994/ (archived at perma.cc/2W2E-3MPQ)

Czeisler, C A, Duffy, J F, Shanahan, T L, Brown, E N, Mitchell, J F, Rimmer, D W, Ronda, J M, Silva, E J, Allan, J S, Emens, J S, Dijk, D J and Kronauer, R E (1999) Stability, precision, and near-24-hour period of the human circadian pacemaker, *Science*, **284** (5423), pp 2177–81

Deboer, T (2018) Sleep homeostasis and the circadian clock: Do the circadian pacemaker and the sleep homeostat influence each other's functioning? *Neurobiology of Sleep and Circadian Rhythms*, vol 5, June 2018, pp 68–77, https://www.sciencedirect.com/science/article/pii/S2451994417300068 (archived at perma.cc/QG32-QQ2H)

Kelley, P and Griffiths, S (2018) *Body Clocks: The biology of time for sleep, education and work*, John Catt Educational, Woodbridge

Marshall, L, Helgadottir, H, Molle, M and Born, J (2006) Boosting slow oscillations during sleep potentiates memory, *Nature*, doi: 10.1038/nature05278, https://www.ncbi.nlm.nih.gov/pmc/articles/PMC6057895/ (archived at perma.cc/9A7M-M2SR)

Ow, S Y and Dunstan, D E (2014) A brief overview of amyloids and Alzheimer's disease, Protein Science, **23** (10), pp 1315–31, https://www.ncbi.nlm.nih.gov/pmc/articles/PMC4286994/ (archived at perma.cc/DY5N-J9C4)

Tasaka, K (1994) The role of histamine on learning and memory, in *New Advances in Histamine Research*, Springer, Tokyo

The Independent (2018) https://www.independent.co.uk/news/long_reads/sleep-napping-sleeponomics-korea-sleepology-science-nap-pods-sleeping-a8534601.html (archived at perma.cc/KSV9-DF9J)

Walker, M (2018) *Why We Sleep: The new science of sleep and dreams*, Scribner, New York

Your brain and digital learning 14

The curious worlds of digital and learning

There is something curious about learning digitally because it appears that 'digital learning' may have less impact on your brain than other digital activity such as video games designed for entertainment rather than learning. It seems that games have noticeable, measurable and valuable impacts on some important learning skills.

People who play video games are immersed in rich, changing, interactive, engaging environments which seem to build skills that are often targets for more formal learning. Laboratory tests show players enhance their visual acuity, track objects better than most people and improve their levels of attention and multitasking (Bavelier, 2010). Most interesting of all, the varied environment, skills development and ability to think and react in new situations are highly transferable; the test activities in the laboratory are quite different to those they've been practising in the games but playing the games has noticeably improved the skills required for learning the new tasks in the lab. Some researchers suggest that the constant requirement in games to adapt to new environments and task demands have helped players simply to learn to learn better – a skill that is going to be more and more important with the rate of change most of us experience in work. These effects persist for the long term and can still be detected 6 to 12 months later (Green *et al*, 2010).

Conversely, digital learning programmes designed specifically to enhance learning for specific skills seem to have less short- and long-term impact on the brains of those who use the tools, whether adults or children. Games manufacturers may be able to teach us some lessons. One interesting idea from the study of digital gaming is this: rather than study the neuroscience and try to build learning based on that, unpick the digital games that are already found to produce results and then work out how and why they work. Of course I still believe understanding the neuroscience of learning is going to be valuable too.

What's coming up?

In this chapter you're going to find answers to some questions (see Figure 14.1). What's different, if anything, between digital and other types of learning? What's not 'brain friendly' about digital learning and what is? Plus you'll identify some practical ideas you can use to make digital learning more brain friendly:

- How digital technology affects our brains.
- Virtual reality learning – how real is it?
- Social digital learning – do we want it?
- Practical tips for designing and delivering digital learning.

Figure 14.1   Your brain and digital learning

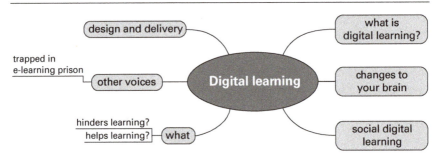

I'll start by declaring I'm not an expert in digital learning but my background in IT has left me with a deep interest in technology and how it can serve us to learn and train more effectively. I've been involved in designing, implementing and using digital learning and I'm usually a relatively early adopter or supporter of new technology, even when it is sometimes scary, exciting and challenging.

If you're an expert already in digital learning then I trust you will discover some new ideas to add to your armoury. If you're new to digital then I hope you'll see the value and benefits digital technology can bring to workplace learning and perhaps get started on your journey to embrace it.

What is digital learning?

Wikipedia has this description: 'Digital learning is any type of learning that is accompanied by technology or by instructional practice that makes effective use of technology. It encompasses the application of a wide spectrum of practices including blended and virtual learning.'

In terms of the tools used in digital learning, outside of your brain of course, there's a really useful list produced each year by Jane Hart of the Centre for Learning and Performance Technologies. The list has rapidly grown from 100 to 200 top tools and those are just the ones people vote as the most useful. Currently there are 35 different categories, split into four main areas: Instructional, Content Development, Social Tools, Personal and Professional Development Tools. I recommend a visit to Jane's website if you're trying to find a tool or even just trying to distinguish between different types (https://www.toptools4learning.com/ (archived at perma.cc/FL99-85Q2)). Each year more technology appears to add to the list so if you're an expert in digital and your favourite technology isn't mentioned in this chapter then I apologize, but this is a book about brains rather than tools.

We're all experiencing digital learning in many ways inside and outside of work. Simply 'googling' or 'youtubing' something can be digital learning, though isn't always. Alternatively, you may be actively learning a language through Duolingo or enrolled on a MOOC or listening to podcasts or audio courses. You might be immersed in gamification, using bots, working with artificial intelligence (AI) or virtual reality (VR). You may be learning from webinars, virtual classrooms or conversations on Skype or Zoom. We've all got access to the technology but are we always learning or are we merely being exposed to information or ideas without any long-term changes in knowledge, behaviour, skills, attitude or our brains? Just reading about something, answering some multiple choice questions or watching a video isn't usually sufficient work to call it learning any more than reading a book is learning; you may learn something but exposure isn't a guarantee of learning.

At the very end of his 2017 book *Learning Technologies in the Work Place*, Donald Taylor reminds us of something very important. He's written 14 really interesting chapters about the technology, the history, how it's used currently and the future, but his final sentence is this: 'Success in learning technologies depends on just one thing: the people.'

Whatever the technology, our brains are still the same damp, pink, interconnected, complicated tangle of cells and much of what goes on in it when we learn is the same, regardless of the tools. So a lot of what you've already read about effective learning applies just the same in digital learning. Sometimes we may need to be more creative about how we use the technology in a digital context but armed with a focus on results and the learner experience it's clearly possible to make digital learning as valuable as any other type of learning.

Some benefits of digital learning

- Accessibility – everyone can have access.
- Immediate – it can be in the palm of your hand and in context.
- Just-in-time learning – perhaps it's not even learning but the information is there when needed.
- Less time spent travelling, out of office and possibly more time to sleep.
- Collaborative and social – when done well.
- Global – everyone can have access to the same learning – it's even easy to translate.
- Personalized – you can choose what you want – so long as it's not 'sheep dip' digital training.
- Faster to redesign.
- Can ensure everyone gets the same information – though not necessarily the same learning.
- Can be cheaper – especially if designed for large numbers.
- Valuable for previews and for spaced learning – especially as part of a blended approach.
- Monitoring and assessment is easier.

The technology for digital learning is developing all the time and whilst there are still plenty of examples of non-brain friendly learning through technology, which is just as true of pencil and paper, there are huge opportunities to use digital technology really effectively.

Does digital learning affect our brains?

Of course we hope that digital learning affects our brains in that all learning affects our brains but does it actually change the way your brain works in a way that's different to non-digital learning? Are there measurable differences due to the use of digital technology that we can measure and that may have both positive and negative impacts on learning? This is not a comprehensive account of the changes that may happen in your brain as a result of digital activity but it does cover most of the important areas for learning.

Sleep

If you've already read the chapter on sleep then you know that the blue light from digital technology including relatively old technology like television, interrupts our sleep patterns and therefore prevents effective consolidation of memory. That's not necessarily a problem because there are plenty of filters for reducing that blue light, but that doesn't necessarily solve the sleep problem because technology disturbs you in other ways by stimulating your brain to be more active. Most of what we do on computers is designed to be interesting, engaging and to draw your attention, which is exactly the opposite of what you need for sleep when your brain needs to start winding down.

Attention

This brings us to attention. Digital technology of many sorts is designed to grab our attention and keep it. However, many of the attention-grabbing features are short-lived and work by constantly presenting changes in attention so we become better at paying 'continuous partial attention' but less effective at sustaining focused attention which is required for learning skills and processing complex information.

We have become poorer at reading deeper and more sustained information, says a five-year study from University College London (Carr, 2008). The researchers tracked how readers accessed articles through their online library facility and found that readers are now more inclined to skim articles, switch rapidly to other articles and rarely return to the same one. Whilst reading, per se, is not an inherited skill but a learned one, it has been the source of learning for most people for hundreds of years. These researchers and others suggest that we are not only changing what we read but how and why we read. We are more likely to read for facts and immediate information and less likely for thinking deeply, making inferences and connections. That may certainly have an impact on what and how we learn.

However, a question people often ask is whether our attention span has been changed by the use of technology. Frequently stories appear in the media suggesting attention spans are shorter, but currently there appears to be no significant research to say that use of digital technology has reduced our attention span. This is partially because attention spans are more strongly related to individuals and the task in hand so there is little intrinsic value in measuring 'attention span' itself or in researching it.

Distraction

One major challenge for digital learning, and it's clearly worse for poorly designed digital learning, is the opportunity for distraction. If your poorly designed e-learning system is sitting in almost the same place as hour upon hour of hilarious cat videos, then you are facing a losing battle, however much you use tracking technology to tell whether people have completed their online programme.

In a study at Stanford University students who said they used many different media at the same time were more easily distracted (Ophir *et al*, 2009). This was true of information in the environment but they were also distracted by irrelevant information in their own memories and found it harder to switch from one task to another.

Reduce distraction to a minimum by reducing load, making things relevant, emotional, as short as possible though no shorter and make your information easy to read. You'll read about some of the major things that lead to distraction in the 'Features of the digital world that don't help learning' a bit later in this chapter. Thank you to Julie Dirksen of Usable Learning for the interesting conversation about distraction that influenced my thinking.

Memory

Before the advent of digital technology most of what we learned we had to remember because it was hard work to look it up in an encyclopaedia or go and find the right book with the right information. Nowadays, however, it sometimes feels as if we don't need to remember anything because we can just google it and this is having an effect on our memories.

In a study entitled 'Google Effects on Memory: Cognitive consequences of having information at our fingertips' (Sparrow *et al*, 2011) the authors tested students on their memory for some trivial facts (memory researchers do this frequently). The students were told the information would be saved or it wouldn't be saved and then later tested on their recall. Not surprisingly perhaps, students who thought the information would be saved were less likely to be able to recall the information.

What the students were good at was knowing where the information had been saved; even down to being able to remember the specific folder the data was stored in. It's almost as if they were using the digital information as a prosthetic memory source in the same way as they may previously have asked friends, family or experts for information.

Other researchers suggest that the way we store memories may be affected by multitasking. For instance, in a study at UCLA students had to learn a fairly simple classification task (Wolpert, 2006). In some trials they were distracted and were effectively forced to multitask, whilst in others they were able to focus on the task undisturbed. fMRI scans from the trials showed a difference in how their brains processed and stored the memories. The focused task results showed more activity in the hippocampus as would be expected whilst the distracted task sessions measured more activity in the striatum, which is normally associated with learning procedural, non-declarative memories. The obvious difference in this learning was that when asked about the focused tasks people were able to explain their learning, whilst on the distracted tasks people struggled to explain what had happened or how they'd learned because their memories were non-declarative. It seemed the distraction of multitasking had given them less time to reflect as they learned, had made their memories less flexible and they had less insight into what they'd done. The researchers are not saying never multitask, only noting that multitasking whilst learning new material affects how you learn it and your ability to reflect consciously on the learning later on.

The study of changes to our memories based on the use of digital technology is still in its infancy but studies like this show that learning with digital technology can affect what and how we remember.

Creativity, mind wandering and learning

Creativity is often about linking unconnected ideas and because of this you draw from ideas pulled from multiple memory sources. One of the complications of technology changing our memories is we may have fewer memories to call on in order to think creatively.

Additionally with a lot of time spent using technology we tend to have less time simply to contemplate. Time spent not focusing and allowing our minds to wander is a valuable tool for reflection, creativity and learning. What used to be called 'day dreaming' seems to have been renamed as 'mind wandering' and it is a powerful tool for learning. Mind wandering is effectively when we turn off attention on a focused idea or thought and instead let our default network take precedence. You'll remember when you read about attention in Chapter 7 that your brain is quieter overall when you pay attention and activity is directed to specific areas. When your default network is at work the spread of activity across your brain is actually wider than when you're focused. This means you can make connections between unrelated things more easily, often leading you to have insights or solve problems that you couldn't do whilst you were concentrating. Whilst the use of digital technology may mean we don't pay such close attention to one thing at a time it also means we are continually paying attention to something and therefore not giving time to reflect, imagine, contemplate or mind wander. Perhaps for learning facts and figures this won't matter but those are also the things that we can leave to digital storage. Learning skills or learning to connect, apply or relate knowledge to your work may be more difficult without time simply to let your mind wander.

On the other hand some researchers argue that there is now more time to be creative because we've freed ourselves up from day-to-day tasks and that the availability of diverse information, ideas and concepts is literally within our hands. Tools and apps that inspire and allow people to create are multiple and easily accessible to everyone, so perhaps creative thinking isn't yet on its way out.

What sort of brain do you already have?

One of the conclusions that seems to be coming from virtual reality and immersive digital learning is that this type of learning is particularly useful for skills acquisition and habit building but currently has less impact for declarative or content-based learning. Plus, it may depend on what sort of skills you already have. In a University of Illinois study, students who already had larger caudate nuclei and putamen than others were more likely to improve their skills for playing a game called Space Fortress; whereas the size of their hippocampus was less important (Erickson *et al*, 2010).

As with many other types of learning it seems that if you're already equipped to learn something well you'll probably make better progress than others. However, the growth and changes in these brain structures still shows that we can all improve, regardless of where we start. I imagine it a bit like sport; I have short legs so I'm unlikely to be challenging Elaine Thompson, the 2016 Olympic gold medal winner for 100 metres. However, by learning better techniques for running and practising I can improve my running skills.

Digital social learning

Some people may have the impression that digital learning is a solitary activity as you work your way through an e-learning programme, read a book online or play a learning game. However, for many people digital learning is, and benefits from being, highly social.

There are those who believe we already have the best learning technology within our grasp which needs to be included as part of the digital package.

'Conversation is the most effective learning technology ever invented' – Jay Cross, an American futurist who popularized the term 'e-learning'. And others were early to understand the power of social media because of our innate need to be social. 'It's exactly the kind of thing that a hacker like myself would come up with because you're exploiting a vulnerability in human psychology… The inventors, creators, it's me, it's Mark [Zuckerberg]… understood this consciously. And we did it anyway.' – Sean Parker, the first president of Facebook (McCarthy-Jones, 2017).

These are two prescient statements from people with a big impact on digital learning and social connection. Jay Cross understood that conversation is hugely important to humans because we're social animals with an enormous need for social connection and Sean Parker, along with other social media entrepreneurs, recognized that our desire for social connection is both a strength and a weakness: one that can be exploited by those with the knowledge to do so.

Our brains have evolved to respond to other people. One of the concerns levelled against digital activity is that it is solitary, with a stereotype of a young person sitting alone at their computer instead of going out and socializing. That's changed enormously with myriad opportunities to connect socially through digital media. Most of the social media companies recognize that a hit of dopamine keeps people interacting and engaged and we can do the same in L&D by helping people connect socially online. I'm not going to list all the possible ways to do this but instead point you to some of the research on social connection and digital technology.

The latest *Towards Maturity* report, The Transformation Journey – 2019, emphasizes: 'Personal connection is vital for modern workplace learning with 91 per cent believing collaboration, 70 per cent mentoring and coaching and 81 per cent management support are either essential or very useful to learn how to do their job.' The report also concludes: '78 per cent of workers are excited to use technology to network and learn from each other'.

Digital learning designers – a side track into motivation

If you ask most people who deliver learning what they like about their jobs they'll say it's the chance to help someone at work or when they see the 'aha' moment. These are of course great rewards when you're working live with people whether it's in a face-to-face or virtual workshop or coaching.

But what happens to the e-learning designer who doesn't usually get that immediate feedback from the fruits of their efforts, particularly if they're an independent designer? Social connection is vital for everyone because loneliness is painful, so what can you do to get your fair share of the social connection if you're the designer?:

- Join a network like the e-learning network www.elearningnetwork.org (archived at perma.cc/BBZ6-E4S5).
- Collaborate and celebrate your successes with colleagues.
- Use social media yourself to connect with clients or colleagues rather than just sending e-mail.
- Work with a growth mindset and value all feedback.
- Learn to be open to the fact it won't always be exactly your vision – there are always compromises.
- Attend virtual learning sessions, webinars etc yourself.
- Many platforms have developers forums to support you – or for you to support others.
- Encourage your clients to celebrate successes with you – they are usually proud of what they've achieved too.

My colleague Sam Burrough of Transform ELearning tells me that, to be resilient, sometimes just connecting with others facing the same challenge is a great way to get things off your chest. 'There's lots of wingeing happens on Slack right now – just make sure you do it in the right channels.'

Virtual reality learning – how real is it?

Virtual reality is an experience that can transform people and has been used successfully in clinical applications to treat and retrain people with anxiety and stress disorders, eating disorders and pain management. One of the reasons may be because it gives people a much more lifelike opportunity to embody learning rather than it simply being a cognitive activity as it can be with other forms of digital or face-to-face learning.

One expert in cyber-psychology, Giuseppe Riva, suggests it's because virtual reality works a bit like our brains and he uses the experience of 'phantom limbs' to explain (Riva, 2017). Phantom limbs are not well under-stood but this research suggests your brain creates a 'virtual simulation' of your body and uses it to anticipate incoming signals using your stored memories to predict what might happen. However, without a limb there to generate real signals your brain uses only the stored memories and predicts incorrectly, causing pain in something that doesn't actually exist anymore. VR has been used to improve symptoms of pain for people with phantom limb syndrome by teaching the brain to predict differently.

This perceptual illusion called embodiment, or the body ownership illusion, can be created with a rubber hand. People have their left hand hidden out of sight. Experimenters then stroke the real hand and a lifelike rubber hand that the person can see. After a short time subjects begin to treat the rubber hand as if it's their own. fMRI scans show that if the rubber hand is 'threatened' with a sharp needle people show activity in the anterior cingulate cortex, which detects pain, and the pre-motor cortex which is for planning movement. Effectively the visual information overrides the information from your body as to whether the hand does or doesn't belong to you. VR works in a similar way to override what your senses are telling you. It creates a simulated world for you to explore and it tries to predict what you'll experience as a consequence of your actions. As a tool for learning it has many possibilities, but does it transfer well to reality?

In 1993 an experiment to see whether virtual reality training transferred well showed there was no difference in the transfer of learning from VR to real-world application compared to a group that had no training at all. Training in the real world showed significant transfer of learning. However, as you'll appreciate VR has come on in leaps and bounds since 1993 (Kozak *et al*, 2007).

In 2005 another study tested VR, real-life training and no training on building a Lego model of a forklift truck (Hamblin, 2005). This one showed that VR training did improve the complex model-building skills but not as much as real-world training. The researchers also concluded that VR learning required participants to have a higher level of general intelligence, more aptitude with computers and high spatial abilities to be effective. Perhaps VR may work for some but not for others seems to be the implication. But even since 2005 the technology has developed enormously and become much quicker and cheaper to develop.

A 2007 study showed that the skills acquired in VR training were transferrable to other VR training situations but not necessarily to the real world. These researchers concluded that VR itself needed to improve to make the transfer more effective (Kozak *et al*, 2007).

By 2017, however, things started to shift, particularly for training complex motor skills. Baseball players who'd been trained in a virtual environment performed later in the season better than others who had participated in normal training (Gray, 2017). One of the suggestions from the research was that the VR design included simulations that provided adaptive training which is difficult to create consistently in a live training environment, such as balls that defy the laws of gravity. The VR was designed to offer a 'high degree of variability to practice conditions and systematically adjusting the level of challenge based on the athlete's performance'. These are conditions that are known to be valuable for skills practice and potentially gave the players more varied opportunities to learn. And perhaps, similarly to the games players who are immersed in their game environment, it actually improves their ability to learn by providing a rapidly changing set of circumstances to which they need to adapt.

So VR is beginning to stack up well in the field of physical skills training; how is it doing with people skills? Empathy is certainly a skill that many people need at work and a study from October 2018 (*NeuroscienceNews*, 2018) shows that VR may offer a solution here too. Participants in two studies were given empathy training relating to homelessness, either VR training or face-to-face, or merely given information about it. The groups who had the training, whether it was in VR or face-to-face, both reported feeling more empathetic. However, the group who experienced homelessness through VR were more likely to sign a petition about homelessness than those who'd experienced a more traditional training approach. Studies with other social skills have also shown that VR can be a successful learning tool, such as a study from 2016 that helped young people with autism to improve their confidence in social situations. Tandra Allen, head of virtual training programmes at the Center for BrainHealth said, 'We saw a lot of growth in their ability to initiate and maintain a conversation, interpret emotions and judge the quality of a friendship' (*NeuroscienceNews*, 2016).

One of the biggest challenges for VR is still the cost of design despite the fact that cost of access may have come down. It's still usually a more expensive option.

Features of the digital world that don't help learning

Fear of technology

Fear of technology can put off some people from learning. However, with more and more exposure to technology in our everyday lives this will become less of a challenge. Already it appears that concerns about differences between the uptake of digital learning between younger learners and older ones are not coming to fruition. However, if people are being asked to use new, or rapidly changing technology, it makes sense to give them support to familiarize themselves with the technology before trying to use it for learning. A good example of this is that of a short optional webinar on how to use webinar technology before starting on a major virtual classroom programme. Andy Lancaster and I both recommend this in our easy to read *Webinars Pocketbook*.

Information overload

Overload of cognitive information is just as unhelpful in a digital world as it is in face-to-face learning. Many studies show that using both text and audio narration at the same time overloads the auditory channel and it's better to use audio and graphics without any text. In one study in 1999 a group with audio scored 64 per cent better on their task than a group with text and audio (Mayer and Clark, 2013).

Excessive choice

Too much choice creates overwhelm and can be confusing to learners – just because something can be included doesn't mean it needs to be and how choices are presented is vital. This is as true of digital learning as any other. Simon Howson-Baggott at LinkedIn told me, 'We saw four times more engagement on LinkedIn Learning vs Lynda.com because the layout was more accessible. The number of courses remained the same but they were easier to view and access.'

Lack of flexibility

Conversely, lack of flexibility leaves people frustrated because they are forced to follow a path where they may not be the relevant end-user or perhaps they are already familiar with the content. This doesn't mean they can actively recall the content (useful) or know how to use it but being re-presented with familiar material is no way to motivate and engage your audience.

Exposure vs learning

Exposure to information isn't learning. There is still plenty of compliance training that is poorly delivered as large amounts of complex information that people click through to confirm they've read it. These are little more than box-ticking exercises to prove someone has been exposed to the material but it isn't learning.

Lack of emotional connection

Whilst we're on the subject of technical or compliance training we need to consider the **lack of** emotional connection that is still apparent in some digital learning. You know that emotions make learning sticky and yet for some reason technical training often fails to deliver a strong emotional 'why' to the learner. Without a strong reason to connect with the content people are merely going through the process. Compliance or regulatory training is the stuff that keeps us safe, protects us from danger, prevents corruption, infection, accidents, cyber-crime and yet is often a prime candidate for boring e-learning. I've even seen vendors of compliance training who plainly state that the subject is boring but they can make the learning 'dazzle' with some gamification. This seems the wrong way to go about it. Perhaps a more credible approach would be to work to make the content vital, relevant and emotionally engaging rather than pop some bells and whistles on the top.

Reading difficulty

Some digital design makes reading more difficult. Literacy in a digital world is changing to be a far more complex skill than previously required as you need to interpret infographics, digital 3D images, hyperlinked text as well as simple text, whilst at the same time ignoring the distractions of unrequested pop-ups. However, reading is still a necessary requirement for digital learning because it's not all videos and VR, so in an ever more complex world it's necessary to make it easier and not more difficult to read text. If you put reading barriers in the way people are more likely to be distracted and less likely to focus on the learning. In the 'References and further reading' at the end of this chapter are two suggestions for writing guidelines from the British Dyslexia Association and European Blind Union with plentiful ideas to make reading easier for a wider range of people. These may occasionally conflict with design guidelines but designers are usually aiming for visual appeal not necessarily readability. I'm making a personal plea here to all digital designers: *Please don't use pale text on pale backgrounds because it's just annoying even if it's the most modern and up-to-date look*. It's not good for our eyes and strains our brains.

Try this little experiment. Write the words 'dog' and 'cat' in upper and lower case. Now draw a line around the words and look at the shapes. You'll see that the UPPER CASE WORDS have the same shape whereas the lower case words each have their own shape. When you read you're not only looking at the letters but your brain is also processing the shape of words to help you interpret. In upper case all words have the same shape which can slow down the reading process. In a world where we want people to learn more and faster there's no point adding additional cognitive effort for them; write in lower case.

More features of the digital world that help learning

Predictability

The predictability of digital learning can increase use because of its familiarity. Making the mobile version and the PC-based version of e-learning look the same reduces the threat response people can feel with technology. They can concentrate on the material rather than the medium.

Effective spaced learning

Digital learning is the perfect tool for creating really effective spaced learning because it can be accessed so much more readily and at precisely the right time to promote retention. Duolingo was used as an example to test out 'half-life regression' of words in digital language learning to predict how often users needed to be prompted with the same word to improve their retention and engagement. HLR was able to improve Duolingo daily student engagement by 12 per cent and reduce errors by 45 per cent (Settles and Meeder, 2016).

Effective use of AI

Effective use of AI and Bots can free up L&D from some of the previously laborious tasks of analysing data for learning needs analysis, sending appropriate follow-up information and answering queries, and can deliver user-relevant materials or messages at just the right time for maximum impact.

Availability

Availability is key because almost everyone has a device in their pocket or handbag. You can access learning where, when and how you want.

Create knowledge producers

To make digital learning work well we need to let learners become knowledge producers as well as consumers. It's easy now to ask learners to summarize their learning in short videos that they can, for instance, share with the next group of learners who will participate.

Create and solve problems

As with other forms of learning, letting learners create and solve problems is far more effective than straightforward information delivery. Delivery doesn't guarantee learning whereas active work, exploration, practice, feedback and reflection is more cognitively engaging and far more likely to deliver the required results.

Here's an example from one of our 'Other Voices' of a really interesting piece of digital design that takes into account the end-user's requirements, especially the social needs.

Other Voices

Emma Livingston-Jones, *Learning Specialist, Humanitarian Leadership Academy*

Early starts and the effects on learning

My organization provides learning that helps people all over the world respond to crises and disasters where they live. We aim to reach as many humanitarian workers and volunteers as possible. Most of these people live in places that are difficult to reach – like Yemen and Syria. So we focus on providing online learning through our platform Kaya (https://kayaconnect.org/ (archived at perma.cc/ZR2P-8NGM)).

The confession

I love my job but had a dark secret that I kept from my colleagues… I was no fan of e-learning. Even the word 'e-learning' made my heart sink. Before joining the organization, most of my e-learning encounters had been *click-click-boring*.

Trapped in e-learning prison

But there was no way out of it, my job was to make e-learning. So I started to dig deeper.

'Why exactly is e-learning often boring?' I asked myself.

I realized that bad e-learning makes me feel trapped, bored and passive; locking me into a frustrating, lonely experience without freedom to explore my ideas with anyone.

'But does it really have to be this way?' I wondered.

I had a learning project for humanitarian volunteers coming up. And I *really* did not want to subject anyone to e-learning prison (*clink-clink-boring!*). I needed inspiration.

Prison break-out

This took me to Brain Friendly Learning for Trainers. The course reinvigorated my thinking. It gave me ideas (my escape aides). Straight away I tried them on designing an immersive game 'The Flood' played via an app gamoteca (http://www.gamoteca.com/ (archived at perma.cc/9EDM-AUUQ)). The following table shows some things we did.

Brain friendly escape aide	What we did
Use your senses	Bring in more senses (than typical e-learning). The sound of torrential rain and crashing wind opens the game. A flickering light then darkness. We keep words to a minimum. It's up to the player to work out what's happening. During the game players write on paper, draw, take and upload a photograph, go and find someone. This brings in touch and movement.
Emotion	Use emotion, so messages pack a punch and are more memorable. We use story-telling. We show the effects of storms and floods on people. Affected people speak directly (and with emotion) to the player – who must respond.
Attention	Keep the player on his or her toes and out of passive mode. The player is challenged to make decisions (and sees the consequences). We keep it short: about 20 minutes. We break it up into three distinct chunks moving through a disaster response. The player must break gaze from the screen to do tasks.

Brain friendly escape aide	What we did
Social	Make it social. We encourage people to play the game together as a pair or group. During the game the player is prompted to find a friend to share perspectives and discuss solutions.

Future freedom

Next week we launch a test version of The Flood at an event in the Philippines with our partner CODE-NGO. This is a great opportunity for feedback. We have a forward plan of learning development with gamification, MOOCs and social learning: I'm excited about using brain friendly principles to innovate and keep people out of e-learning prison.

Top trumps for designing and delivering in a digital world

Digital learning is the technology that delivers the learning. What actually happens inside people's brains and bodies is the actual learning and that hasn't changed enormously, however much the technology advances. Most of the ideas you've already come across in the rest of the book can be applied to digital learning with a little creative thinking and imagination.

Recently I spoke to Lorna Matty of Toyota and Liz Brant from Pineapple Consulting who are working together to deliver powerful learning sessions through webinar technology. They have a strong belief that not only is this type of social digital learning saving money and delivering a return on investment but that there are distinct advantages for the learners too.

Lorna says:

For me, virtual classrooms give employees a voice they don't always feel they can express in a face-to-face environment and as a result they say more than they might do. If training is about being learner centred, then using virtual classrooms as a blend with other formats, helps us to do just that.

And Liz's view is:

Whatever we can do in a physical classroom we can do the same and better in a virtual classroom. Physical classrooms can seem very quiet and slow in comparison because in the virtual classroom people are continually interacting with each other. Virtual classrooms work best as part of a blend, but that is true of any learning event.

So with a view to designing fantastic digital learning based on understanding more about how people learn, here's a useful way of checking whether your digital designs are brain friendly or could be more so. Sharon Bowman, president of Bowperson Publishing & Training is a prolific writer and learning practitioner. In her book *Using Brain Science to Make Training Stick* (2011) Sharon has written about The Six Trumps™ for designing learning based on brain science.

These top trumps are just as relevant for digital learning as they are for any other sort of learning so here are Sharon's original six and then I've taken the liberty to add a few more with reference for digital design and delivery:

1 Movement trumps sitting.

2 Talking trumps listening.

3 Images trump words.

4 Writing trumps reading.

5 Shorter trumps longer.

6 Different trumps same.

Additionally for digital here are another six:

1 Interactive trumps passive.

2 Participant control trumps tutor control.

3 Social trumps solitary.

4 Recall trumps recognition.

5 Explore trumps click.

6 Guessing trumps being told.

Summary

Learning technology has been around since humans first drew pictures on cave walls and over the years many technologies have been criticized or accused of changing how we think and learn. Socrates worried about the impact of writing on how people learned and in one of his plays one character suggested that people would 'cease to exercise their memory and become forgetful'.

When the printing press was developed there were concerns that people would become intellectually lazy and that the power and value of the intellectuals and religious authority would be undermined.

Nobody would argue nowadays that reading, writing and books had damaged long-term learning but they did change how and what people learned. There was no study of psychology or neuroscience in those days to tell us exactly what had changed but with our brains being as plastic then as they are now there is no doubt there were changes. And so it will probably be with learning and digital technology, and whatever comes to replace it.

Learning is learning and always takes place in the context we find ourselves; so digital technology is just the latest tool that we're going to use because it's freely available and when it's good it's brilliant.

References and further reading

Bavelier, D (2010) You can train your brain with digital media, *Centre for Educational Neuroscience*, http://www.educationalneuroscience.org.uk/ resources/neuromyth-or-neurofact/you-can-train-your-brain-with-digital-media/ (archived at perma.cc/823D-V9X8)

Bowman, S L (2011) *Using Brain Science to Make Training Stick*, Bowperson Publishing, http://bowperson.com/wp-content/uploads/2014/11/ SixTrumpsArticle220101.pdf (archived at perma.cc/GB47-NK7C)

British Dyslexia Association (2018) Dyslexia Friendly Style Guide: Creating a dyslexia friendly workplace, https://www.bdadyslexia.org.uk/employer/ dyslexia-style-guide-2018-creating-dyslexia-friendly-content (archived at perma. cc/79DV-CVD8)

Carr, N (2008) Is Google making us stupid?, *The Atlantic*, https://www.theatlantic. com/magazine/archive/2008/07/is-google-making-us-stupid/306868/ (archived at perma.cc/N4LP-BNJG)

Collins, S and Lancaster, A (2015) *Webinars Pocketbook*, Management Pocketbooks, https://www.pocketbook.co.uk/product/webinars-pocketbook (archived at perma.cc/NNQ8-S42Z)

Cross, J (2006) *Informal Learning: Rediscovering the natural pathways that inspire innovation and performance*, John Wiley and Sons, Inc, CA

Davis, J (2011) Google effect: Changes to our brains, *International Business Times*, https://www.ibtimes.com/google-effect-changes-our-brains-299451 (archived at perma.cc/TS29-CGXY)

Digital Learning, https://en.wikipedia.org/wiki/Digital_learning (archived at perma.cc/KG5J-5G34)

Dirksen, J (2012) *Design for how people learn*, New Riders, Berkeley, CA

Erickson, K I, Boot, W R, Basak, C, Neider, M B, Prakash, R S, Voss, M W, Graybiel, A M, Simons, D J, Fabiani, M, Grattan, G and Kramer, A F (2010) Striatal volume predicts level of video game skill acquisition, *Cerebral Cortex*, **20** (11), pp 2522–30

European Blind Union (2017) *Making Information Accessible for All*, http://www.euroblind.org/publications-and-resources/making-information-accessible-all (archived at perma.cc/CG34-PV2Q)

Gray, R (2017) Transfer of training from virtual to real baseball batting, *Frontiers in Psychology*, https://doi.org/10.3389/fpsyg.2017.02183 (archived at perma.cc/754X-FYTU)

Green, C S, Pouget, A and Bavalier, D (2010) Improved probabilistic inference as a general learning mechanism with action video games, *Current Biology*, **20** (17), 1573–79, doi: 10.1016/j.cub.2010.07.040

Hamblin, C J (2005) Transfer of training from virtual reality environments, https://dl.acm.org/citation.cfm?id=1123949 (archived at perma.cc/LB3G-2J39)

Hart, J (2018) Top Tools for Learning 2018 [Online] https://www.toptools4learning.com/ (archived at perma.cc/FL99-85Q2)

Kozak, J J, Hancock, P A, Arthur, E J and Chrysler, S T (2007) Transfer of training from virtual reality, *Ergonomics*, **36** (7), pp 777–84, http://dx.doi.org/10.1080/00140139308967941 (archived at perma.cc/6Y3E-HFTF)

McCarthy-Jones, S (2017) Are social networking sites controlling your mind? *Scientific American*, https://www.scientificamerican.com/article/are-social-networking-sites-controlling-your-mind/ (archived at perma.cc/2TWR-YL4W)

Mayer, R and Clark, R (2013) 10 brilliant design rules for e-learning, https://donaldclarkplanb.blogspot.com/2013/01/mayer-clark-10-brilliant-design-rules.html (archived at perma.cc/NA4Y-LUNE)

NeuroscienceNews (2016) Virtual reality training improves social skills in people with autism, https://neurosciencenews.com/social-skills-autism-vr-5087/ (archived at perma.cc/82JQ-4BDL)

NeuroscienceNews (2018) Virtual reality may encourage empathetic behavior, https://neurosciencenews.com/virtual-reality-empathy-10039/ (archived at perma.cc/QWT2-CMMB) [accessed 17 December 2018]

Ophir, E, Nass, C and Wagner, A D (2009) Cognitive control in media multitaskers, Proceedings of the National Academy of Sciences USA, **106** (37), pp 15583–87, https://doi.org/10.1073/pnas.0903620106 (archived at perma.cc/WY4D-Q8B7)

Riva, G (2017) Virtual reality: Hacking our brain, https://www.linkedin.com/pulse/neuroscience-virtual-reality-riva-giuseppe/ (archived at perma.cc/7Z57-8UMF)

Settles, B and Meeder, B (2016) A trainable space repetition model for language learning, in *Proceedings of the Association for Computational Linguistics (ACL)*, pp 1848–58

Sparrow, B, Liu, J and Wegner, D M (2011) Google Effects on Memory: Cognitive consequences of having information at our fingertips, *Science*, **333** (6043) pp 776–78 [Online] https://science.sciencemag.org/content/333/6043/776.full (archived at perma.cc/NPW3-7NZH)

Taylor, D H (2017) *Learning Technologies in the Workplace*, https://www.kogan-page.com/product/learning-technologies-in-the-workplace-9780749476403 (archived at perma.cc/F4G7-D4VU)

Top Tools for Learning (nd) List produced each year by Jane Hart of the Centre for Learning and Performance Technologies [Online] https://www.toptools4learning.com/ (archived at perma.cc/FL99-85Q2)

Towards Maturity (2018) Challenging business assumptions about how workers learn, https://towardsmaturity.org/2018/12/06/challenging-business-assumptions-about-how-workers-learn/ (archived at perma.cc/24FF-5SJ8)

Towards Maturity (2019) The Transformation Journey – 2019, Annual Research Report [Online] https://towardsmaturity.org/2019/02/14/the-transformation-journey-2019-annual-research-report/ (archived at perma.cc/RG27-VP22)

Wolpert, S (2006) Don't talk to a friend while reading this, UCLA, http://news-room.ucla.edu/releases/Don-t-Talk-to-a-Friend-While-Reading-7212 (archived at perma.cc/N2W4-J5GX)

The future is   15
already with us

Mindfulness

How mindful are you? Mindfulness is still a hot topic and in an excellent blog about the research in the *BPS Research Digest 2015* Christian Jarrett says that 40 papers are published per month and 37 books had been written in one particular week alone (Jarrett, 2015). He rounds up numerous pieces of research putting the case both ways. Clearly many people value mindfulness. However, there is a lot of hype about the benefits and it may be that some potentially negative effects are being ignored or side-lined.

Studies have reported changes in attention and memory processes as well as emotional functions.

Subjects who were taught to meditate over a course of two months were seen to have permanent changes in the activity in their amygdala; ie the effects could be seen even when they were not being mindful but were doing normal everyday activities (Desborde *et al*, 2012).

One study showed that people engaging in mindful meditation, compared to subjects who merely mind wandered (the latest way to describe day dreaming), were more likely to generate false memories, which may have consequences for learning (Rosenstreich, 2016). However, a follow-up study was unable to replicate the results (Baranski and Was, 2017).

One mindfulness technique is to physically discard thoughts by, for example, writing a note and throwing it away. A study testing this found that subjects who put aside thoughts in this way were less likely to use the information later in decision making. Whether they were negative or positive thoughts that were discarded, they may have value in critical decisions and planning and effectively ignoring them could have a negative impact.

Additionally, retreating into mindfulness whilst enabling people to avoid negative emotions may also prevent them from critically approaching a challenge, preferring to escape a problem rather than thinking hard and solving it.

In terms of the science it's all rather interesting. Side effects are recognized as a by-product of any effective treatment; it's a scientific tenet 'every action has a reaction'. So, if mindfulness really has benefits for emotional and attentional control and memory, amongst other things, it is equally likely to impact on your mental process in some ways which may not always be entirely helpful. Overactive attention and memory systems can cause problems and we evolved emotional responses to help us learn and keep us safe. Now we know that real physical changes happen in our brains when we think and learn we need to be aware of the effects of any activity with the power to change the way our brains work.

Overview

You're nearing the end of this book so you're probably aware that there is a phenomenal amount of research on and interest in neuroscience at the moment and that the discoveries we're making about how our brains work in numerous areas are multiplying all the time. There are so many new things that it's impossible to give a comprehensive account of the hottest topics and this week's hot topic may well be superseded by next week's. So what you'll read here, visually described in the mindmap in Figure 15.1, is the briefest snapshot of three areas that may be relevant for people, like you, with an interest in the neuroscience of learning: the quantum brain, some aspects of technology and cognitive enhancement drugs. Other aspects of digital learning are now covered in their own chapter.

Figure 15.1　Ideas for the future

The quantum brain

When Professor Peter Higgs was asked to encapsulate the Higgs Boson in an interview he quite rightly explained that he'd spent most of his life studying quantum particles and there was no way he could explain it in a 30-minute interview. I think we can safely accept that neither you nor I are going to understand the quantum brain by the end of this book and that at a practical level it's probably not yet going to make much difference to the way you learn or help others learn.

You might not normally think of brain function in terms of physics but of course in a physical world everything does come down to physics in the end. Classical physics supposes that events are not random but caused by other events, whereas quantum physics is based on the probability that an event may or may not happen. This may allow us to start thinking about will, attention and consciousness in a different way because quantum theory could start to explain some of the puzzling differences between your brain and your 'mind'. Amy Brann in her book *Neuroscience for Coaches* (2015) does an excellent job of explaining the quantum brain for the layman and says 'we will continue to see more of the science that demonstrates the power of our mind to affect our brain'.

You can measure physical changes in your brain with fMRI scanners and EEG machines but that doesn't yet help to fully explain your thoughts and how those impact on your physical brain. We can, to a degree, describe psychological concepts such as consciousness, attention, intention and have an intuition that our thoughts have an impact on our physical brains and on our behaviour but there isn't a classical physics explanation for what that really means. Once you get into quantum physics and start talking about the possibilities of particles being in one place or another at the same time it becomes easier to start having a better scientific theory to explain your 'mind' rather than just your brain.

Elements of quantum theory are being used to try to explain some of the elements of fundamental brain function such as exactly how neurotransmitters really pass information across the synaptic gap. Neurotransmission relies on calcium ions being passed across the synaptic gap via minuscule ion channels but there is quantum uncertainty as to whether a particular ion will be absorbed or not. This leads to the possibility, at a simplified level, of you having one thought rather than another; it perhaps starts to provide an explanation of how you can choose your thoughts rather than them being determined.

Computational neuroscience

This second edition includes a chapter devoted to digital learning where you can find out more about how learning through technology may be shaping our brains. Here is an example of how the combination of neuroscience and technology can work together.

Computational neuroscience aims to explain human thinking through computer models and has passed through many phases of development such as artificial intelligence, Expert Systems thinking and now there are some fascinating developments in *cybernetics and robotics*. Kevin Warwick, a researcher in cybernetics at Reading University, is working on neural networks that control mini robots. He effectively takes rat neurons and connects them up to these robots and then analyses how the neural networks grow so that the robots 'learn' to run without bumping into the walls. This becomes a combination of the computational science that uses computers to model human learning and the neuroscience of living organisms.

Brain implants have successfully treated patients with deafness, epilepsy and Parkinson's disease amongst others but now there are experiments where a cognitive skill is being targeted.

In March 2018 one group of scientists effectively created a memory prosthesis by sending electrical information through two implanted wires into the brains of a small group of patients (Powell, 2018). Initially subjects had to do simple word recall memory tests and the areas of the brain associated with poor recall were noted. Later scientists found that disrupting those areas with an electrical pulse during the testing enabled other more successful memory areas to function and improved recall performance by up to 15 per cent.

In another study researchers recorded signals from the hippocampus as subjects got answers correct on short-term memory tests. They later delivered the same signals back into the brain and the test scores rose on average by 35 per cent. (This was also reported in *NBC News* by Powell, 2018).

The research is being funded initially to support military personnel with brain damage but researchers believe it will be available to patients with other memory problems such as Alzheimer's too. This type of research opens the doors to ideas such as enhancing your learning skills by adding cybernetic prostheses to your brain – and it's now nearer scientific fact than the wilder realms of science fiction.

Taking pills to make you smarter

Can taking drugs make you a better learner? Many drugs affect your brain and many of them have effects on your learning mechanisms but can you take drugs to specifically make you learn more effectively? Numerous magazine articles and scientific papers report significant numbers of healthy students taking drugs like Ritalin, usually prescribed for people with Attention Deficit Hyperactivity Disorder, or Modafinil, a prescription-only medication for narcolepsy, to help them get through exam time. A 2016 survey suggested 15 per cent of students at Oxford University resorted to drugs and this mirrored similar surveys in other UK universities. It seems that many of their lecturers and professors are also using similar drugs to help them think more effectively or concentrate better when they've got a paper to publish. With so many more psychoactive drugs being discovered and on the market to help with anything from ADHD to Alzheimer's it's inevitable that people will find they can take them to boost their normal brainpower. Some of these 'drugs' may be natural supplements and not controlled in the same way as prescription drugs. In a 2018 study, researchers (Weyandt *et al*) reported, contrary to popular belief and their expectations, that ADHD drugs didn't improve cognition in healthy college students and seemed to impair working memory.

There is a debate to be had over the moral and ethical consequences of taking these drugs in a similar way to which the sports world has had to address performance boosting drugs. A study from 2017 (*Science Daily*, 2017) reported that people performed better in a chess game with a computer after taking a drug called Modafinil. However, when you read the study it seems that though players thought more deeply and their cognitive skills appeared to be enhanced, they actually lost more games because games were timed to only 15 minutes and the deeper thinking took them longer to make decisions. So sometimes being smarter isn't the way to achieve what you need. Long-term use of this drug and others like Ritalin ultimately can reduce plasticity and damage memory in young brains. Scientists are certainly calling on governments and the rest of us to look at the reality of the situation and to think about what we want to do. Suffice it to say, regardless of what we as a society decide, people may have always taken drugs to help them think differently; it may even be something we have in common with our evolutionary ancestors. In 2015 there was a news report about chimps drinking naturally fermented palm wine (Hockings *et al*). Researchers don't know whether it's the rich source of sugar they like or whether they enjoy the feeling of inebriation; whatever the reason their brains are clearly affected and changed by the palm wine.

At the moment it's unlikely that we'll be seeing the big pharmaceutical companies with stands at Learning and Development conferences selling pills to help you learn, but it is worth being aware that the generations coming into and already working in your organization may be far more familiar with these drugs.

Summary

There are numerous new ideas from neuroscience that may have an impact on the practical aspects of learning, wherever it takes place. Here are four key ideas:

- The quantum brain – the application of quantum theory to neuroscience which is still in its infancy and probably has little immediate impact for your practice of Learning and Development.
- Mindfulness is still a popular idea amongst many as a way to improve focus and attention but it may also have some negative effects on memory and decision making.
- Cybernetics and brain prostheses are already being used in specific clinical areas of learning but may one day be available more widely.
- Cognitive enhancement drugs are a growing field which hasn't made much of an impact on the world of L&D at the moment but we need to be aware of them.

References and further reading

Baranski, M and Was, C A (2017) Mindfulness meditation may not increase false-memory and may instead protect from false-memory susceptibility, *Mindfulness*, 8 (6), pp 1569–79, https://link.springer.com/article/10.1007/s12671-017-0729-7 (archived at perma.cc/SK67-PSCL)

Brann, A (2015) *Neuroscience for Coaches*, Kogan Page, London

Desborde, G, Negi, L T, Pace, T W W, Wallace, B A, Raison, C L and Schwartz, E L (2012) Effects of mindful-attention and compassion meditation training on amygdala response to emotional stimuli in an ordinary, non-meditative state, *Frontiers in Human Neuroscience*, https://www.ncbi.nlm.nih.gov/pmc/articles/PMC3485650/ (archived at perma.cc/RY7H-SFK8)

Hockings, K, Bryson-Morrison, N, Carvalho, S, Fujisawa, M, Humle, T, McGrew, 0, Nakamura, M, Ohashi, G, Yamanashi, Y, Yamakoshi, G and Matsuzawa, T (2015) Tools to tipple: ethanol ingestion by wild chimpanzees using leaf-sponges, *Royal Society Open Science*, 2 (6), rsos150150

Jarrett, C (2015) [accessed 27 June 2015] The Psychology of Mindfulness, Digested [Online] http://digest.bps.org.uk/2015/06/the-psychology-of-mindfulness-digested.html (archived at perma.cc/7S9L-HRCX)

Kevinwarwick.com (archived at perma.cc/4JJ7-XN74) (2015) [accessed 2 July 2015] Kevin Warwick [Online] http://www.kevinwarwick.com/ (archived at perma.cc/USM4-D2ZZ)

Powell, C S (2018) Memory-boosting brain implants are in the works. Would you get one? *Mach*, https://www.nbcnews.com/mach/science/memory-boosting-brain-implants-are-works-would-you-get-one-ncna868476 (archived at perma.cc/47UH-APQZ)

Rosenstreich, E (2016) Mindfulness and false-memories: The impact of mindfulness practice on the DRM paradigm, *The Journal of Psychology: Interdisciplinary and Applied*, **150** (1), pp 58–71

Science Daily (2017) Cognitive enhancing drugs can improve chess play, scientists show https://www.sciencedaily.com/releases/2017/03/170306091726.htm (archived at perma.cc/NF5F-KBZE)

Singularity HUB (2010) [accessed 30 June 2015] Amazing Robot Controlled By Rat Brain Continues Progress [Online] http://singularityhub.com/2010/10/06/videos-of-robot-controlled-by-rat-brain-amazing-technology-still-moving-forward/ (archived at perma.cc/2EM8-TN2N)

Weyandt, L *et al* (2018) ADHD drugs do not improve cognition in healthy college students, *NeuroscienceNews*, 19 July 2018, http://neurosciencenews.com/adhd-drugs-cognition-9580/ (archived at perma.cc/SMT3-37JB) [accessed 12 December 2018]

The end of this journey and the start of more

Managing tube journeys

At an unconference in London in 2014 some of us were looking for a metaphor to explain our purpose in learning and development: something to represent us as being experts in the facilitation of learning rather than experts in knowledge itself. In case you've never attended an unconference it's a get-together of like-minded people but with the agenda decided by the participants rather than the organizers – a far more participative and engaging approach to conferences.

Was it something about having travelled into London on the Tube? Was it an unconscious sighting of a Tube map on the far wall (I only consciously spotted it later on)? Or was it something somebody said? I don't know what unconscious processes were operating but the metaphor that came to me was how L&D professionals in the 21st century are like the London Tube (or any other railway system really).

There is 'knowledge' kept at the stations that needs to be carried to other places and we can be conduits for that knowledge. The knowledge may be online, in the heads of experts, in documents (alight at Euston Square for the British Library) or in multiple other places. It could be factual, semantic knowledge or it could be intangible knowledge about how to perform a task or demonstrate a skill.

A colleague at the conference, Robert Weeks (@chutzpah84 if you're a Twitter user) tweeted my analogy: 'I think @stellacollins has just made me manager of a tube network… L&D connects networks and knowledge in organizations'. Robert suggested 'L&D need to connect up the stations and create more interchanges' and together we built the metaphor a bit more.

We can remove blockages, open train doors, help people move through the system with maps and timetables, suggest optimal routes, check their tickets for particular journeys, provide a kind word, help less able travellers, change routes if necessary, recognize times of stress on the system and passengers and adjust accordingly. Occasionally L&D need to build new stations or to redefine which station houses which type of 'knowledge'. Occasionally we might refurbish a station and change the décor but it will still be near the same landmarks.

One of the things I like about this metaphor is we all expect to travel on the Tube or any other railway network when we want and where we want and we don't expect someone to take us there. Passengers are generally self-reliant – they find information on the phone, on the Internet, on boards at stations, face to face, asking friends who travel regularly – isn't this how learners can become responsible for their own learning journeys? L&D can be seen as a system that helps people do their job and they may use us every day or they may only occasionally need us but either way our role is to take people from one place to another whilst they continue to do their key role. No analogy or metaphor is perfect but it feels like this one works as a starter. Perhaps you'll disagree, perhaps you'll find the place it breaks down or perhaps you'll build on it too. It doesn't really matter so long as we all keep thinking about our role in learning.

What you'll find in this final chapter

You'll review the role of neuroscience and psychology in Learning and Development and reflect briefly on the key ideas from each chapter (see Figure 16.1 for the chapter overview). You'll think about what it all means for you in your role of helping others to learn and you may hear a few thoughts about what makes me cross or excited. This chapter is really about the 'so what?' It's where you can start to put your learning into action. What can you do with the neuroscience of Learning and Development?

A race through a review

You galloped through some of the technical bits of brain structures and how science works. You explored the idea that neuroscience is a complex mix of disciplines: biological, psychological and even computational and have come across elements of most of them in this book. You read what happens to your brain when you're learning and you used the MASTER model to give structure to the process of learning. You thought about how to motivate learners, how information gets into their heads and how they pay attention. You considered different ways to explore information and to help people make sense of different types of learning before moving on to thinking about memory and what makes learning sticky. For effective learning, you need to test, experiment and practise, and you also thought about the role of habits. Reviewing turns out to be a key factor in learning and you considered different ways and times to review learning. You raced through some ideas about creativity, language, stories, music and the environment, you explored sleeping and digital learning before charging headlong into the future with thoughts about technology, quantum brains and smart drugs. And now you're here to think about what this all means for you: what you might do differently, some challenges we all face in L&D and some of the benefits to thinking about neuroscience.

Figure 16.1   End of the journey

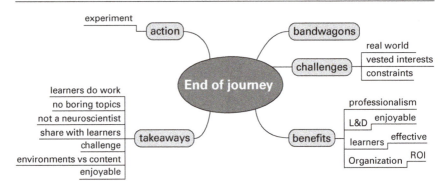

Some challenges of embracing neuroscience into your practice

The bandwagon of neuroscience

Over the past few years there's been an increase in popular interest about how our brains work. There are more programmes on the TV and a fountain of books, articles, websites and blogs. People are attending training to find out about the neuroscience of virtually everything from neuroeconomics to neuropolitics and you can buy neurotoys, neurodrinks and neuromusic. This is really exciting so long as it's not just a bandwagon fuelled by brain myths and a desire to have the latest fashion. The neuroscience of learning is hugely fascinating and what we don't know still eclipses what we do know, so there's plenty more to discover and learn. At least now you've got some useful questions (from Chapter 3) to ask when you hear 'research says...' or 'neuroscience shows...'.

Some of what neuroscience does is to provide data to 'prove' what is already obvious to the rest of the world. If an fMRI scanner can 'show' that mothers really do feel emotion when they look at babies it doesn't make that emotion any more or less real. Knowing that your working memory is located in your dorsolateral prefrontal cortex may be interesting but a) I can't ask you to 'fire up your dorsolateral prefrontal cortex' and b) it won't improve your ability to read this sentence.

But this data can help you in multiple ways. You may use it to influence other people who don't have the experience or background in practical training and learning that you have, and who are currently confusing learning with 'content'. You may be able to help them understand that you don't have a magic wand and that learning isn't a passive sponge-like absorption of information or skills. This is our opportunity to educate other people about L&D, and neuroscience and psychology give us some valuable ammunition to work with.

I started this book suggesting that you don't need to be a neuroscientist to be a great trainer, educator, coach, or learning facilitator. However, as you've seen, if you're a good trainer and people are learning you are fundamentally changing people's brains, so it is worth understanding enough about the hardware and software that you're working with to get the best results.

Real-world application

One of the biggest challenges to using the ideas from neuroscience is the application in your world. As you've read earlier, much of the research comes from laboratories full of WEIRD people, case studies of people who've suffered some kind of neural damage, or from developmental psychology and the education system. And the research is sometimes contradictory because the experiments are so specific that it can be hard to work out how they relate to learning at work. There's far less rigorous research done on learning in the workplace or with adult learners generally, so perhaps it's time to start changing that. Perhaps the next time you're asked to deliver a major training programme you can use it as an opportunity to do some research and measure, test and share the results of different practices. I know this throws up difficulties with operational issues and there may be complications in asking people to participate in research. After all, you don't want to spend two days learning customer service skills in a control group only to find it's not as effective as the new technique another group had. However, if, as learning professionals, we don't consider the possibilities of experimenting then we'll definitely never get there. With universities looking to collaborate more with business now there are more opportunities to do and share research from operational environments.

Vested interests

Whether you're an individual or an organization, vested interests may play a part when you're asked to change your practice. As an example, psychometric testing is an enormous industry. In a Freedom of Information document, the MOD alone revealed they spent over £245,000 on psychometric testing in 2013/14. A report in *Personnel Today* in 2007 suggested the world spend on psychometric tests was in excess of £1.5 billion. Some of those psychometric tests have been in use for many years. Myers–Briggs, one of the most famous psychometric instruments was invented by a mother-and-daughter team who developed their ideas from the work of Carl Jung and published their first Myers–Briggs Type Indicator (MBTI) tool back in 1943. The tool has been validated in the sense that many, many people have used it but it's based on old theories that have been largely superseded.

It may even be that personality testing itself is a flawed concept. In *Multiplicity: The new science of personality* (2008) Rita Carter questions the concept of having a unified personality and suggests we may all have multiple personalities, some of which we may be unaware of. Other research suggests that your environment has as much or more of an effect on you than your personality. In a famous 'Good Samaritan' study (Darley and Batson, 1973) it was found that even seminary students were more affected by how hurried they felt than by their own, presumably 'good' personality traits. When they were put into a hurried situation many of them were prepared to step over a slumped figure on the ground in order to get to a meeting to deliver a presentation about the Good Samaritan. More and more evidence suggests we are unconsciously influenced by environmental factors that can override our 'personality' and yet personality tests are big business.

My point is there are vested interests in keeping us using the same tools and techniques that have been around a long time even if new research seems to question them. Not only economic vested interests but you may also awaken some cognitive dissonance if you have to change your own or someone else's ideas about how 'training' happens. After all, if your organization has invested large amounts of money in a leadership development programme complete with complicated models and attractive resources it's not going to take kindly to the idea that there may be a different way to do this. Cognitive dissonance is the psychological struggle we feel when we hold two competing ideas and we tend to want to distance ourselves from anything that increases the dissonance.

Think about an L&D manager who's spent a lot of time and energy persuading the board that it would be really useful to do some psychometric testing to identify people's learning styles and then finally being successful and designing some training to meet those styles. Suddenly they find out there's some new research that debunks learning styles. Are they likely to go back to the board and say that 'everything I talked about for the past five years about learning styles may have been thrown into question and we have wasted some time and money'? This is likely to cause a significant threat response in all concerned, reducing good quality thinking and increasing the risk of 'fight or flight' behaviour to the new idea.

Fortunately, by embracing scientific principles you can navigate a way round this particular challenge. Instead of telling the rest of your organization that you're an expert on learning and know everything there is to know, you can tell them that you're a researcher into learning and that the sciences of psychology and neuroscience are adding to what you know. Explain that brain research is a growing discipline and we're learning more every day but there's more to discover than we currently know. As such, you will work with the best available evidence at any time but you reserve the right to change your methods if and when some better, more reliable evidence comes along. By setting yourself up as an investigator, a scientist, a learner yourself, you can more easily embrace new ideas and reduce the threat that experts feel when their expertise is challenged.

Neuroscience and psychology don't have all the answers and won't be able to fix everything for you but they do offer the opportunity for everyone to view L&D in a slightly different light.

Constraints

In an ideal world you'd have all the money and resources to invest in designing and delivering completely wonderful, Brain Friendly Learning environments based on all the best and most up-to-date science; but we all recognize the world doesn't work like that. There are constraints imposed for all sorts of reasons. For instance, this book doesn't embrace all the ideas from neuroscience that you could apply to sharing information; it's in black and white rather than colour, there's a limited number of pictures, there are few activities and you can't hear it or smell it or taste it. However, it does break information into chunks, includes multisensory language, metaphors and stories and uses as much direct, simple language as possible. Hopefully we both recognize the constraints of a book written in a particular format for a particular audience. Here are some ideas that will help you retain the general gist of the book even if you don't remember the details. Spend 10–15 minutes at the end reflecting on what you learned:

- Draw a picture or create a mindmap of the key elements.
- Rewrite the summaries in each chapter – either the mindmaps at the start or the bullet points at the end.
- Scan through the book and browse the headings – reread any areas that stand out for you.
- Go and tell someone else what you learned from reading it.
- Ask yourself questions about what you learned – if you can't quite remember then guess and immediately go back and check your answers.
- Summarize each chapter in a tweet.

In training you will also have constraints imposed because of timing, funding, operational elements, etc but what I'm suggesting is you challenge them when you can and when you know they will impact adversely on learning. And back up your challenges with research, studies or data. If the budget holder thinks it will save money because it's quicker just to tell people how to be compliant with the new food hygiene regulations you can counter with the amount of information they'll actually retain after 24 hours, the cost of being found non-compliant because they hadn't remembered the key facts, and how you can significantly increase their retention and compliance with some effective training. That will need more investment than a one-hour briefing by the compliance manager but the results will be better.

Having challenged as much as possible, use the neuroscience to work around the constraints and make up for what you can't change. If the training has to be webinar-based then what do you know from the neuroscience that will help you build rapport and increase participants' attention from a distance?

After Robert Weeks and I had reminded each other of the metaphor at the start of this chapter Robert added some more useful thoughts about how learners have different experiences of learning that may impact on how you work with them…

The other observation I'd make is that when you very infrequently use the Tube network (as I do) even though all the links are there, it can be very hard to navigate and find your way round.

'I know I want the green one and to head towards X' is what I keep repeating in my head as I walk amongst the crowds at rush hour trying not to stop at the map and cause half of the city to pile up behind me.

Compare that to a friend of mine who lived in London and frequently travelled on the Tube daily for work. She could play a game where she would tell you how to get from one random station to another in the shortest amount of time, and was experienced enough to vary her journey instantly if you said 'aha, but what if Embankment was closed for maintenance?'

If you use the network often, you can do this. If you don't, even if someone else has kept it well established, it can take a bit longer to find your way around... and we all love to travel effortlessly so it can be a bit off-putting.

Benefits of applying practical ideas from neuroscience

Your professionalism

Like all professions, in Learning and Development we need to continue to develop our practice and to learn, innovate and build. Sometimes we have a tendency to react to what the business demands of us and to want to provide what they ask rather than stopping to analyse what they need. By taking a step back and analysing what we know about how people think, how they behave and how they learn we can be more inclined to challenge and contribute to our organizations.

This is what good learning practitioners have always done but by embracing real scientific principles we can demonstrate that we are a profession that has rigour and guidelines rather than being seen as something 'pink and fluffy'.

We can also challenge ourselves to examine those woolly models, myths and ideas that have been lurking in the back of our professional cupboards and just see whether they stand up to the cold light of day. It's quite possible that some of them will dust off well and continue to be useful, but others could be retired in view of your current and growing levels of knowledge.

Perhaps it's time we renamed 'soft skills' – once you realize how much needs to go on inside your head to learn a new skill it becomes easier to see why so-called 'soft skills' are actually quite difficult. I'm not suggesting we call them 'hard skills' because that might be off-putting for learners. Whilst 'brain plasticity' is now a more common term, 'plastic skills' doesn't quite seem right. As these are the skills that can make the difference to whether someone is successful or not at work perhaps they can be called 'work skills'. And perhaps when they are measured more accurately and trained more precisely the name will matter less.

It's enjoyable for you, the trainer

Most people in Learning and Development love learning – that's often why they got into the profession. I've seen many people in the last few years incredibly enthused and excited about having this new area of neuroscience to study and apply, so, if nothing else, neuroscience gives you some great new learning opportunities, which may well flood your brain with curiosity-stimulated dopamine and other pleasure promoting hormones. It's certainly causing lots of new neuronal connections to fire and they'll wire together if you review and remember for the long term.

It's enjoyable and effective for learners

Applying the ideas from neuroscience, whether you call it Brain Friendly Learning or something else, makes learning so much easier, more enjoyable and more satisfying for learners. Watching people make connections, have light-bulb moments and enjoy the experience of learning is hugely rewarding. People regularly tell me it's the first time they've ever enjoyed learning something at work; sometimes since they were small children. Enjoying the learning is part of the battle but more importantly people remember what they learn long enough to apply it satisfactorily back at work.

The organization gets a better return on investment

Investment in learning happens in multiple ways. Usually organizations want to measure people's satisfaction with the learning experience, their retention of information and their changed behaviours at work. Understanding some of the neuroscience of learning and then designing and delivering training with that in mind could save time, heartache and money. It may take a little longer for someone to genuinely learn something than it takes to throw information at them wholesale but the benefits for their performance are obvious.

Top ideas to take away

Never do for the learner what they can do for themselves

When your work is about learning and you're committed and enthused it can become easy to start to take responsibility for what learners are learning, but you can't control what's going on in someone else's head. You certainly won't help learners learn by doing their learning for them. So, as often as you possibly can, let the learners do the work of learning.

If they ask you a question, ask them to guess the answer, see if someone else in the group can answer it or encourage them to go and find it somewhere (at least that way they know where to find the information a second time).

Let learners use equipment and experiment with it rather than picking it up and showing them again – this applies particularly if you're doing anything on a computer.

At the end of a training session, if you've really switched the responsibility for learning to the learners they are likely to feel energized and buzzing, but their heads will feel full, ready for them to go and get a good night's sleep to let the learning start sticking.

There's no such thing as a boring topic – only boring training

If you as the trainer are tempted to think a topic is boring then it's your responsibility to re-examine it and redesign it – there really are no boring topics in the world. If people are bored you've not found their motivation or you're presenting information poorly. Learners are not getting the experience of learning which in itself is inherently gratifying; all those neurotransmitters floating around and all those connections wiring. Some trainers think it's easier to motivate people to learn and to include multisensory resources, movement, engagement, challenge and discussion when it's soft skills training, but harder when there is something data or process driven. This isn't the case, of course – if it's vitally important that someone learns a process in a particular order then they need to be significantly motivated and attention, movement, Links, Emotion, Anchors, Repetition, Novelty and Stories become even more important. Learning isn't always easy but it should never be boring.

You don't have to be a neuroscientist

If you forget the names of parts of the brain or can't work out one neuro-transmitter from the next it's really not going to matter – unless possibly you're teaching neuroscience! You are a learning professional and you work with people in different ways, many of which have proved themselves to be reliable and effective ways of delivering learning. You may well have the practical experience that tells you something is effective even when there isn't currently any neuroscience to back it up – that doesn't mean it doesn't work. What neuroscience gives you is the opportunity to check what you're doing and measure it against what the research tells you but the ultimate test is whether someone learns effectively and can use their learning where it matters.

Share learning with learners – spread the word

There's no point in us as professionals having all this wonderful knowledge about how people's brains and minds work and keeping it to ourselves. Sharing what works with your learners helps them to be more effective and to learn better for themselves. Explaining to them that they need to review what they've learned, that sleeping on it will help, and giving them respon-sibility for learning will do more for your learners than any number of wonderfully prepared slides, detailed handouts or fantastic exercises.

Learning isn't all about 'fun'

This is more appropriate to the concept of Brain Friendly Learning rather than the pure application of neuroscience to learning but you may well hear that learning should be 'fun'. This is a very specific piece of 'advice' because I've worked with scientists, engineers and other people in technical roles who can be challenged by the concept of having 'fun' whilst learning. Not all of them, of course, but some people find the idea of 'fun' demotivating possibly because they've had training in the past where they've felt foolish because they were asked to do things they didn't enjoy but were labelled 'fun'. Use the principles of neuroscience to make learning 'enjoyable' rather than 'fun'. So long as the connections get made and retained it's not our place to decide what's 'fun', so I tend to avoid the label.

Challenge poor practice!

I think we have a duty as professionals to challenge what's not working. You would expect your doctor, accountant or lawyer to challenge poor practice where they see it and we should be equally confident in our ability to question what other less enlightened trainers might be doing. You may need to find a way to express your disquiet and to perhaps share with them what would be better practice, but we are responsible for ensuring that all L&D professionals take learning seriously. Recently I was at the receiving end of a poor piece of training and spent time writing some constructive feedback for the trainer before going up to discuss it face to face. My belief had been that he would receive this feedback in the spirit it was offered, of mutual support and development from a fellow trainer, so I was somewhat surprised when he took the 'evaluation form', barely glanced at it and said 'Oh, that's not for me – it's for the organization'. Fortunately this sort of response is rare but if we're to challenge poor practice we also have to be open to feedback ourselves.

Create learning environments rather than courses/ content

How can you create an environment where learning happens naturally rather than spending all your time creating content? The content most of us use at work has mostly already been produced; sometimes perfectly and sometimes imperfectly but it's probably available somewhere. It will continue to be produced but it's more likely to be produced by experts in digital design, hopefully in partnership with learning experts like you.

As learning professionals, we need to become better at curating the content that's available. We may do that through our own experience, or as seems increasingly likely in the future, using artificial intelligence and big data to do it. The right information at the right time needs to be easier for people to find and access, but we're not in charge of what people learn because we're not them, in their roles, doing their jobs.

Creating learning environments in which people find it easy to think, learn, experiment, challenge, fail, reflect and apply learning becomes a more important role. With self-directed learning becoming ever more common we also have a role in supporting people to learn effectively; busting erroneous myths and providing scaffolding, genuinely helpful models and practical tips for learning. We need to teach people how they learn and what the best methods are for them and then let them get on with their learning in context. I also believe we should teach well-educated learners to vote with their feet if something isn't helping them get the learning results they need; to demand more of us rather than passively accept poor e-learning design or boring classroom delivery.

Digital technology is playing a bigger part for all of us and we must embrace it and work with it without losing sight of our learners and their plastic brains. In an article about digital learning trends for 2019 amongst all the talk of bots, AI, microlearning and virtual reality, Kirstie Greeney of Elucidat (Greeney, 2018) pointed out that there was a 'strong call for a return to a people focus in learning'.

Your call to action

Whether you've read this book from cover to cover, dipped in and out or skipped straight to this last chapter, you will have changed something in your brain. What would be really valuable is that you change something in the outside world too so that you can demonstrate what you've learned.

> What top tips have you taken from this book and what will you change? How will you continue your learning?

The end of this particular journey

Only you know where you were on your journey into the neuroscience of Learning and Development as you started and only you know where you are now. I know in writing the book I've discovered new concepts, rethought my practice, reinforced some old learning and reminded myself of things I used to do and would like to do again. I shall continue my journey of discovery and invite you to continue yours too.

I hope you've got some new ideas to test and may have had your thinking challenged too. I trust you'll go and experiment with what you have learned to see what results you get. Behave like a scientist and learn from others, experiment yourself and adjust the variables; if the results aren't what you expect then analyse what it was that caused the variance. Perhaps you've started encouraging people to pay attention far more effectively but you're still not giving them opportunities to embed learning by reviewing because you're rushing at the end of a training programme. Perhaps you went for a quick win like thinking 'I'll get people moving' after an hour of PowerPoint, but is that really taking into account everything you've read about the neuroscience of learning? Perhaps you're thinking about neuroscience in the context of creating digital learning and you're not sure how or whether it applies. Perhaps you wonder whether culturally it will be different in other countries or societies.

Despite the fact every single brain is different because we've all been wired differently through our life experiences there are more similarities than differences in the way your brain and mine process information and learn. There's a similar pattern to the neuroscience of learning for all of us. The biggest thing we know currently is that there's far more we don't know than we do know so let's continue the journey because it's hugely exciting.

Thank you for accompanying me on this journey of exploration and enjoy learning for yourself and working with your learners. Let me know how you get on.

Summary

Here's what you covered in this final chapter:

- Speedily reviewed the content of the book.
- Thought about the challenges of using neuroscience in L&D.
- Bandwagon effect.
- Application in the real world.
- Vested interests.
- Constraints you'll face.
- Read about the benefits to:
  - you;
  - your learners;
  - the organization.
- Considered some top takeaways.
- Never do for the learner what they can do for themselves.
- There's no such thing as a boring topic.
- You don't have to be a neuroscientist.
- Share learning with learners.
- Learning isn't all about fun.
- Challenge poor practice.
- Create learning environments rather than content.

What actions will you take now?

References and further reading

Carter, R (2008) *Multiplicity: The New Science of Personality*, Little, Brown, London

Darley, J and Batson, C (1973) 'From Jerusalem to Jericho': a study of situational and dispositional variables in helping behaviour, *Journal of Personality and Social Psychology*, **27** (1), pp 100–08

Greeney, K (2018) https://www.elucidat.com/blog/digital-learning-trends/ (archived at perma.cc/33Q7-FDFL) [accessed 12 December 2018]

Ministry of Defence (2015) [accessed 28 June 2015] Psychometric Testing Letter [Online] https://www.gov.uk/government/uploads/system/uploads/attachment_data/file/418022/20150326_Psychometric_tests.pdf (archived at perma.cc/P8NQ-3MG3)

ANSWERS TO QUESTIONS IN CHAPTER 9

Q2. Hippocampus is the main area for memory processing.

Q3. Non-declarative memory is for things you can't describe easily, such as tying a shoe lace.

Q4. Semantic and episodic memories are declarative – you can talk about facts and events.

Q5. Procedural memories are non-declarative – they are often skills or habits.

Q6. Encoding, storage and retrieval.

Q8. Your memories are consolidated when you sleep.

Q11. LEARNS: Links, Emotion, Anchors, Repetition, Novelty, Stories.

INDEX

Note: Numbers are filed as spelt out, with the exception of entries for stages of NREM sleep, which are listed chronologically. Acronyms and 'Mc' are filed as presented. Page locators in *italics* denote information contained within a figure or table.